Christ's Ambassadors

Christ's Ambassadors

WALKING WITH JESUS
VOLUME EIGHT

*An Expository Commentary
based upon Paul's Letter to the Ephesians*

(CHAPTER SIX VERSES 10–24)

ROBERT B. CALLAHAN SR.

RESOURCE *Publications* • Eugene, Oregon

CHRIST'S AMBASSADORS
An Expository Commentary based upon Paul's Letter to the Ephesians
(Chapter Six Verses 10–24)

Copyright © 2013 Robert B. Callahan Sr. All rights reserved. Except for brief quotations in critical publications or reviews, no part of this book may be reproduced in any manner without prior written permission from the publisher. Write: Permissions, Wipf and Stock Publishers, 199 W. 8th Ave., Suite 3, Eugene, OR 97401.

Resource Publications
An Imprint of Wipf and Stock Publishers
199 W. 8th Ave., Suite 3
Eugene, OR 97401
www.wipfandstock.com

ISBN 13: 978-1-60899-652-0

Manufactured in the U.S.A.

All scripture quotations, unless otherwise indicated, are taken from the Holy Bible, The King James Study Bible, Copyright ©1983, 1988. (Previously published as the Liberty Annotated Study Bible and as The Annotated Study Bible, King James Version) Copyright © 1988 by Liberty University. Thomas Nelson Publishers

For my wife, Ginger,
whose encouragement, faith,
love, and objectivity contributed
significantly to Walking with Jesus

Topical Categories in Walking with Jesus
(An Expository Commentary)

Volume One	Volume Two	Volume Three	Volume Four
The Triune God Speaks to the Saints	*Sin and Redemption*	*Christ's Prisoner*	*Walking As Mature Christians*
To the Faithful in Christ Jesus	Sin and God's Wrath	For This Cause—God's Glory	Living in Harmony With Christ
God's Will—Spiritual Blessings	God, Rich in Mercy and Grace	Revealing God's Hidden Truths	Unity in the Triune God The Holy Spirit
Trusting in Him	A Right Relationship With God	Praying to the Father	The Lord Jesus Christ
Praying for Christians	Reconciliation	Believing God's Power	God, the Father
	Praying Through the Holy Spirit		Grace According to Christ's Gifts
	God's Foundation (Apostles and Prophets)		Maturing in Christ

Topical Categories in Walking with Jesus
(An Expository Commentary)

Volume Five	Volume Six	Volume Seven	Volume Eight
Following Christ	*Walking Wisely*	*Satan and God's Armor*	*Christ's Ambassadors*
Alienated from God	Christ-Like Conduct	Family Relationships	A Call to Discipleship
Ye Have Not So Learned Christ	No Inheritance in the Kingdom of God and Christ	Life's Basic Relationship	Wearing God's Armor
Christ-Like Conduct	Walking in the Light	The Whole Armor of God	Christ's Ambassadors
	Walking Circumspectly	Satan and His Evil Forces	
	The Marriage Relationship		
	Christ and His Church		

Ephesians "brings one into an atmosphere of unbounded spiritual affluence that creates within one's heart deepest peace and assurance. It is impossible to live habitually in Ephesians and be depressed."

RUTH PAXSON

Contents

Volume Eight: Topical Categories xi
Foreword xiii
Preface xv
Acknowledgments xvii
The Question of Authorship xix
Introduction xxi

1	Assurance, Change and Opposition	1
2	Believing and Rejoicing in Assurance	9
3	Quench Not the Spirit	17
4	Whence Knowest Thou Me?	25
5	Self	32
6	Things Appointed	41
7	The Battle Call	48
8	A Divine Visit	56
9	Discipline: What God Requires	64
10	Responding in Faith	71
11	Gird Your Loins	79
12	The Girdle of Truth	87
13	The Righteousness of God	96
14	Christ's Righteousness	105
15	Stand and Go Forth	113
16	Choices, Decisions, Priorities	121

17	Shield of Faith	128
18	The Helmet of Salvation	135
19	The Sword of the Spirit	143
20	Stand Therefore—Praying Always	150
21	Hearing, Obeying, Persevering	159
22	Ambassadors of Christ	167

Outline Questions   177
Bibliography   223
Scripture Index   225

Volume Eight: Topical Categories

Category	Scripture	Chapters
A Call to Discipleship	Eph. 6:10–12	1–110
Wearing God's Armor	Eph. 6:13–17	11–20
Christ's Ambassadors	Eph. 6:16–24	21–22

Foreword

Robert Callahan's multi-volume work of Paul's Letter to the Ephesians is both a welcomed and long-overdue guide for Christian living today. The Apostle's sense of the eternity and greatness of God, his emphasis on the living reality and exaltation of Christ, his devotion to God's grace as an unearned gift of enduring love, and his call to an ardent and faithful discipleship all witness to an urgency and renewal critically needed in our time. Callahan's heart and style rise to meet this challenge and to convey God's message of hope and promise, of presence and courage, to Christian souls of any and every contemporary Christian tradition.

Callahan's format allows for both a devotional and studious usage. One can permit one's soul to savor every spiritual nuance the author uncovers, verse by verse, mark the passage, and return later for further nourishment. Or one can linger from text to text, gleaning with the author both theological and spiritual insight for enhancing personal discipleship, equally applicable in the arena of church and society.

The author draws on an array of insightful theological and spiritual wisdom, garnered from scholars and saints alike, theologians and missionaries. Calvin's Institutes guide Callahan's expositions, as well as the work of Markus Barth—known for his commentary on Ephesians and his delineation of Pauline theology. The author cites frequent and astute observations from Barth's exegesis of this nature. In addition, Callahan makes wise usage of Martyn Lloyd-Jones' emphasis on "experiencing the living Christ." For Lloyd-Jones, as well as the author, mere intellectual knowledge of the Christ fails to undergird one's faith or discipleship, when life's journey truly becomes sore bestead. Callahan also draws from the great 17th century theologian William Gurnall's delightful work: The Christian in Complete Armour. Perhaps students of Church history remember how both John Newton and Charles Spurgeon prized Gurnall's approach and piety and preferred it to many perspicacious studies available in their time. Gurnall's Complete Armour is known for its pithy, fervent, and wise counsel that confronts human vagaries with the truth about the self. In that respect, so too does Robert Callahan's gentle but firm counsel enrich the Christian heart and inspire one to a higher level of discipleship. No one can fail to sense this in Walking with Jesus. Whether encouraged to venture this methodology owing to his own years as a Presbyterian elder, or as an avid member and participant of the bi-annual Calvin's Colloquiums for the past 30 years, or as a fond reader of Ruth Paxson's The Wealth, Walk and Warfare of the Christian, the result is the same: a powerful, inspirational, and theologically heart-warming guide to discipleship today.

Ministers, Christian educators, seminary students, laypersons, and lovers of Jesus' life will find Callahan's work immensely valuable. His volumes deserve our grateful and sincere attention, as we too seek to walk with Jesus.

Benjamin W. Farley
Younts Professor Emeritus of Bible, Religion, and Philosophy
Erskine College, Due West, South Carolina

Preface

Paul's Epistle to the Ephesians shows us the joy and challenge of being united to Christ in his death and resurrection. It takes us from being seated with Him in the heavenlies (chapter 2), down to the battles we must wage, in His armor, with powers of evil (Eph. 6). In a balanced and judicious manner, longtime Presbyterian elder, Bob Callahan, exercises remarkable insight in opening to believers the vital truths of Ephesians; truths that once taken in, transform the attitude towards life, and often set the soul singing!

As a professor of theology, I have carefully worked through one of his multivolumed series, and found it to be theologically sound: evangelical and scholarly at the same time. It has spiritual depth and is extremely practical; it is accessible in good, clear English. It is neither a commentary, nor a series of sermons. In some ways it reminds me of some of the ancient Patristic engagements with a series of texts of Holy Scripture. It brings the reader into the presence of the Most High, and—if considered thoughtfully and prayerfully, is likely to cause him to sit down under the canopy of God's love.

The journey of Christians in today's world is very demanding indeed, and Bob's work is intended to be a guide to help every pilgrim 'Walking with Jesus.' It will be a rich resource for Sunday Schools, Bible studies, as well as for individual devotions.

Douglas F. Kelly
Reformed Theological Seminary
Charlotte, NC

Acknowledgments

The crafting of Walking with Jesus was not a "one man show" but numerous people working together to present a formidable work. Three guiding lights have been paramount in the minds of those making significant contributions: one, presenting the theology in accord with the tenets of the Reformed Faith; two, employing language that presents the Gospel in a meaningful and understandable light; and, three, expounding upon Scripture in a clear, concise, and forthright manner.

It has been God's blessing that the following ministers and theologians have enthusiastically and willingly provided their time and talents to enhance this work. They are:

- Dr. Frank Barker, Founder and Pastor Emeritus of the Briarwood Presbyterian Church, Birmingham, AL

- Dr. Benjamin W. Farley, Younts Professor Emeritus, Bible, Religion, and Philosophy, Erskine College, Due West, SC

- Dr. James C. Goodloe, IV, Executive Director, Foundation for Reformed Theology, Richmond, VA

- Dr. Todd Jones, Senior Minister, First Presbyterian Church, Nashville, TN

- Dr. Douglas Kelly, Richard Jordan, Professor of Theology, Reformed Theological Seminary, Charlotte, NC

- Dr. Norman McCrummen, Senior Pastor, Spring Hill Presbyterian Church, Mobile, AL

- Dr. Mark Mueller, Senior Pastor, First Presbyterian Church, Huntsville, AL

- Dr. Richard Ray, Former Managing Director of John Knox Press, Montreat, NC

Without the knowledge, wisdom, and encouragement of these individuals this work would neither have become a reality nor available to individuals seeking a better understanding of the teachings of the Scripture and the joy of walking daily with the Lord Jesus.

Several others have labored diligently to create this work, and to produce the finished product. Our daughter, Karen Callahan Myrick, made significant contributions during the drafting process through her knowledge of grammar. Ms. Lynn Sledge, as the copy editor, judiciously reviewed the manuscript and made valuable contributions for improving it. Four ladies, Helen Marshall, D'Anne Dendy, Kelly Comferford, and Elizabeth Annan, worked tirelessly, with dedication, to prepare draft after draft and to make positive contributions to the project. In addition, Wick Skinner made invaluable contributions through his attention to details, grammar, and vocabulary.

It is not possible to thank them sufficiently for their dedication to making this volume a desirable repository of Christian truths, and in so doing to cheerfully work on draft after draft, to recommend enhancements, and to make appropriate changes in the text. Their unselfish contributions are too many to enumerate. May God bless them.

The Question of Authorship

Recent scholars have questioned the authorship of the letter to the Ephesians and have been less convinced that it was the Apostle Paul. However, for the sake of simplicity of expression we will abide by the traditional view and refer to Paul as its author.

Introduction

The creation of this work was the result of unusual developments which some would attribute to happenstance and others to God's providence. You may be the judge after considering the following.

During May 2000 a friend invited my wife and me to visit the Spring Hill Presbyterian Church in Mobile and hear their new minister, Norman McCrummen. We accepted his invitation.

The following March, Dr. McCrummen was preaching on anything but Ephesians when he interrupted his sermon, paused long enough to slowly scan the congregation twice, and said, "I want everyone to read the first and second chapters of Ephesians by next Sunday" and promptly returned to his sermon. The next day I called him and said, "I can't do it" a few times. Finally, his light went on and he said, "What can't you do?" I said, "I can't read the first and second chapters of Ephesians by next Sunday." He asked, "Why can't you? It will only take ten to fifteen minutes." I responded, "I have fifty-eight to sixty expository messages on the first two chapters of Ephesians that took thirty to thirty-five minutes to present." His response was, "I want to read all those and everything else you have on Ephesians." Thus began the long, arduous, and heart-warming journey of converting handwritten notes along with printed ones into the written word. It has been a joyful, though demanding experience.

Paul's Letter to the Ephesians has been described as "The holiest of the holies." My love affair with it began in the 1980's when I read a book containing great sermons of the twentieth century. The most impressive one was written by Martyn Lloyd-Jones. As a result, I read other works of his including his exposition of Ephesians. Thereafter, unexpectedly, I was asked to teach an adult Bible Study Group. They said they would provide the material, but I demurred and said, "I would gather my own material." This set in motion the process of acquiring knowledge through the best expository works available at the time on Ephesians including Martyn

Lloyd-Jones, William Gurnall, Ruth Paxson, Markus Barth, John Calvin, Otto Weber, and others.

The objective was to present the essence of Paul's letter as it was presented to him by the Lord Jesus and the Holy Spirit. Further, to mine the gold available in the fruitful works of those fertile minds that God had cultivated and enabled to expound upon the truths that His only begotten Son had revealed to His apostles and disciples. Therefore, it was a paramount obligation to express God's truths in a simple, straightforward manner according to the dictates of the Holy Spirit so that the reader may grasp it and interpret it according to the will of our Lord and Saviour Jesus Christ.

The need for the truths of the Gospel is as great today as it was in the first century. The conditions are similar and the challenges facing our culture reveal the need for knowing the living God and His Son. Today, the people of faith require the same spiritual nourishment as those brave souls of the early days after the Resurrection, who would rather face death than deny their Lord and Saviour.

There are people in responsible positions in Christ's church who deny Him by: their passivity; seeking secular acceptance; and failing to honor Him in public. These apostasies negatively impact members of organized Christian churches as well as non-believers.

They create an environment in which unrighteousness flourishes. This results in irreverence as aptly described by R.W. Dale, "Where there is irreverence for the divine law the vision of God becomes fainter; as the vision of God becomes fainter the restraints of the Divine Righteousness are lessened and at last the vision of God is lost altogether." May God enlighten us regarding His infallible Word so that we will hunger and thirst for righteousness, and for the vision of God to shine brighter and brighter as we serve Him with courage, wisdom, justice, and self-control.

This expository commentary is designed to bring individuals, whether they are spiritually children, adolescents or adults into a closer, more mature relationship with the Lord Jesus Christ. It begins with the Triune God; presents the doctrines of the Christian faith; reminds us "that we henceforth be no more children, tossed to and fro . . . but speaking the truth in love, may grow up into Him in all things, . . . even Christ." It continues by emphasizing the importance of being renewed in the spirit of your mind; putting on the new man, which after God is created in righteousness and true holiness; using the whole armor of God to thwart the manifold attacks of Satan; and concluding with the admonition to conduct ourselves as Christ's ambassadors.

The spiritual food contained ranges from milk and honey to tough meat. The flavor of this exposition encompasses all varieties—sweet, sour, pleasant, bitter, tart, tasteless, dry, burned, and succulent. Do not reject the nourishment because of its texture or flavor, but seek to understand it despite your preferences, since it provides food for good health and strength for joyful living. May God's truths flourish in your heart and mind, and enable you to withstand the tests, trials, and tribulations that come your way as you are "Walking with Jesus."

In presenting this work, I realize everyone has different challenges. The fascinating part of God's Word is that it meets us where we are. The question is, will we meet Him there, hear what He has to say, and accept the nourishment He offers?

The words of William Gurnall are appropriate and enlightening in contemplating God's Word. He said prior to expounding upon Ephesians, "The fare that I shall be serving during the coming weeks will be from God's own table. If perchance it does not go down well or should not have the flavor that you desire, please do not despise the provider of the food, but blame the cook who has prepared it and is serving it." To that I say, Amen!

The courses being served by this cook are described herein. May they provide the taste and nourishment you are seeking.

Robert B. Callahan, Sr.

1

Assurance, Change and Opposition

> *Finally, my brethren, be strong in the Lord, and in the power of his might.*
> *Put on the whole armor of God, that ye may be able to stand against the wiles* (schemes) *of the devil.*
> *For we wrestle not against flesh and blood, but against principalities, against powers, against the rulers of the darkness of this world* (age), *against spiritual* (hosts of) *wickedness in high places* [Eph. 6:10–12].

The facts and events in the life of Christ have an impact upon the people hearing about them, just as they did on the people witnessing them. An individual's perception or interpretation of the Master's teachings, activities, and practices is affected by many factors, including mindset, receptivity, peer pressure, and knowledge. This is true whether or not there is complete acceptance, complete rejection, or something in-between, or because there is real faith and trust or the absence of it, or various combinations of the different factors.

When Christ is ignored or merely acknowledged as having lived, He still has an effect on people, upon individuals. When people come to hear about Him or to learn more about Him, He has an effect. When individuals come to know Him, He has a significant, positive impact upon their lives. When He dominates a person's life, His Word grows within them producing fruit, much fruit.

This impact can produce several things in people. It can bring about assurance, change, or opposition. These elements can be seen in the Apostle John's description of the developments occurring immediately after Jesus raised Lazarus from the dead. Scripture reveals, *he hath been dead four days*, when Jesus arrived.

What happened after Lazarus came forth? What would you expect to happen? Scripture contains two different responses. First, *many of the Jews* who were there and saw what happened *believed on Him*. However, there were others who apparently did not, or they were afraid, or they had some vested interest, because they left and went to the Pharisees.

Christ performed this great miracle, but not all who witnessed it believed. The word *believe* in this instance means "to trust" and "to have confidence." "Miracles may produce vastly different results. They can prepare a person for faith, or they can confirm it," as Calvin notes.

On the other hand, there are those who reject the evidence with hearts as hard as stone. Ungodliness infects and corrupts the works of God. Consequently, the hearts of some who were present when Lazarus came forth from the grave turned against Christ and went to the Pharisees. Changes were brought about among the witnesses, the leaders, and observers. Many believed; some did not.

It is difficult to imagine people being present when Jesus performed this miracle and not believing in Him, not accepting Him, not admiring and praising Him. However, there are those who reject or ignore what Christ has done, who are opposed to His practices. "Unbelief is always proud and a despiser of God; but, it does not always breakout into open conflict with God," according to John Calvin's insightfulness regarding those who reject the Triune God.

It is interesting concerning the people who went to the Pharisees. They told them what Jesus had done; they did not deny it, but affirmed it. Yet they knew that the Pharisees were opposed to Christ and wanted to kill Him. Why did they want to stir up more opposition and hatred? Possibly to ingratiate themselves with the authorities or to receive favors from the clergy of that day. Or, they did not want people following Christ.

Remember what happened after Jesus fed the five thousand. They followed Him to Capernaum. Why? Jesus provides the answer saying, *Not because ye saw the miracles* (signs), *but because ye did eat of the loaves and were filled* [John 6:26]. Then Jesus proceeded to tell them what they must do: they must partake of what He has to offer, namely Himself, His teachings, and His obedience to the Father. What happened to the large group that followed him to Capernaum? *From that time many of his disciples went back* (away), *and walked no more with him* [John 6:66]. Why? There may have been many reasons, but basically they were interested in themselves, what they were doing, and their relationships to other people or groups; they wanted to continue to see miracles and to receive material blessings and tangible rewards; they did not accept Him as the Messiah, the Son of God; and something kept coming between themselves and God, namely self.

When the Pharisees heard how Jesus raised Lazarus from the dead and the reports of many other witnesses, what did they do? They concerned themselves with how they could oppose Him, how they could take additional action against Him, and how they might get rid of Him!

They thought if they opposed Him they could block His path, prevent people from following Him, send Him into oblivion, and not hear of Him anymore, and then He would never bother them again. People through the ages have done the same thing. They tell the authorities what He is doing and that they oppose Him. The same thing is happening in the twenty-first century, but it does not work.

What concerned the Pharisees and the high priests was that Jesus would continue doing miracles. Further, if they left Him alone, others would believe on Him and follow Him. As a result, the Romans would come and destroy the temple and the nation. If these things happened, the Pharisees' status quo would be upset, and conditions would change. Therefore, Caiaphas made both a judgment and a prophesy at one and the same time. He did not intend to do so, but he did because of the Holy Spirit.

Caiaphas thought it would be expedient to get rid of Jesus. Therefore, he uttered these prophetic words, *Ye know nothing at all, Nor consider that it is expedient for us, that one man should die for the people, and that the whole nation perish not* [John 11:45–50].

Further, Caiaphas *prophesied that Jesus should die for that nation; And not for that nation only, but that also he should gather together in one the children of God that were scattered abroad* [John 11:51–52]. Caiaphas did not intend to prophesy. He wanted to render a judgment. He wanted to preserve the position of the scribes and Pharisees. He wanted to eliminate any opposition.

However, God used Caiaphas. These verses show that our salvation is accomplished by bringing the scattered sheep together into one flock. The people of God are gathered together into the body of Christ.

God foreordained that one man will die for those people, that they shall not perish. It is through that one person that the sinners, the alienated, dispersed, and scattered are brought together and made one as members of Christ's body. This prophesy of Caiaphas's should remind us *That in the dispensation of the fullness of times he might gather together in one all things in Christ, both which are in heaven, and which are on earth; even in him* [Eph. 1:10]. Then, as Scripture says, . . . *all the chief priests and elders of the people took counsel against Jesus to put him to death* [Matt. 27:1].

We see in John's Gospel assurance, change, and opposition. Yet, we should see something having a greater impact and effect: the hand of God working, and God using both followers and opponents to achieve His purposes. Yes, we love to hear about what Jesus did during His earthly ministry. Yes, we want to believe. We are like the father who brought the child with the dumb spirit to Jesus [Mark 9:17–26]. The father said to Jesus with tears, *Lord, I believe; help thou mine unbelief* [Mark 9:24].

But there is something more that we seek, and it is important. We seek assurance, but do we really want it? These words and this thought are important. Do we really want assurance? Consider the question, do we want the assurance that the Lord Jesus is the Son of God and that through Him we receive salvation and life eternal [2 Pet. 1:1–11]? Remember, the same Word that offers us pardon calls us to repentance and obedience.

It is well to ask, what happens when we receive assurance? There will be a change. We will seek to learn and to know the truth as it is revealed in the Lord Jesus. We will seek to stop, look, listen, and obey His commandments. We will seek to worship and to serve Him.

Then there is the matter of opposition. People will be opposed to what we do or do not do. There will be opposition to the teachings of the Master and to expounding upon them. Further, we will encounter opposition within ourselves. We will want to do things that we did not do in the past, and we will refrain from doing things we used to do.

Assurance is a two-edged sword. Therefore, ponder it carefully before accepting it, believing it, and committing oneself to it. Consider other portions of Scripture,

> *For our gospel came not unto you in word only, but also in power, and in the Holy Ghost, and in much assurance* [2 Thess. 1:5].

> *Because he hath appointed a day, in the which he will judge the world in righteousness by that man whom he hath ordained; whereof he hath given assurance unto all men, in that he hath raised him from the dead* [Acts 17:31].
>
> *These things have I written unto you that believe on the name of the Son of God; that ye may know that ye have eternal life, and that ye may believe on the name of the Son of God* [1 John 5:13].
>
> *Let us draw near with a true heart in full assurance of faith, having our hearts sprinkled from an evil conscience, and our bodies washed with pure water* [Heb. 10:22].

The writers of the Epistles had assurance. They wanted to pass it on to the saints and faithful. Yes, justification is by faith, but assurance, confidence, and trust come from worshipping, acquiring knowledge, and practicing the commandments. *Lord, I believe; help thou mine unbelief* [Mark 9:24]. Assurance enables us to enjoy the fruits of our salvation, to rejoice in the Lord always, and to witness on both the good and not so good days. No wonder *the wiles of the devil* are opposed to assurance.

Thomas Brooks, a great Puritan, confidently wrote: "Such is Satan's enmity and envy against a Christian's joy and comfort, that he cannot but act to the utmost of his life to keep poor souls in doubt and darkness. Satan knows that assurance is a pearl of that price that will make the soul happy forever; he knows that assurance makes a Christian's wilderness to be a paradise; he knows that assurance begets in Christians that most noble and generous spirits; he knows that assurance is that which will make men strong to do exploits, to shake his tottering kingdom about his ears; and therefore he is very studious and industrious to keep souls off from assurance, as he was to cast Adam out of Paradise."

How does Satan use his wiles with respect to assurance? By offering counterfeits, things which masquerade as peace, joy, rest, and assurance. By offering a false sense of security. The Lord Jesus told the Apostle John to write the following:

> *And unto the angel* (messenger) *of the church of the Laodiceans write;* ...
> *I know thy works, that thou art neither cold nor hot:* ...
> *So then because thou art lukewarm, and neither cold nor hot, I will spew* (spit) *thee out of my mouth.*

> *Because thou sayest, I am rich, and increased* (have become wealthy) *with goods, and have need of nothing; and knowest not that thou art wretched, miserable, and poor, and blind, and naked:*
> *As many as I love, I rebuke and chasten: be zealous therefore, and repent* [Rev. 3:14–17, 19].

The members of the church at Laodicea appeared to be in good condition on the surface, but in reality they were not. They were self-satisfied and everything was going their way, but not God's. However, God still loved them despite their self-centered ways. Therefore, He called them to repent and be zealous in so doing.

Paul tells the Corinthians, *Examine yourselves, whether ye be in the faith; prove your own selves. Know ye not your own selves, how that Jesus Christ is in you, except* (unless you do not stand the test) *ye be reprobates* [2 Cor. 13:5]? He wants them to examine themselves in the light of the Gospel, not by their own standards. They should know that there is one Christ and that He dwells in all the members of His body: the ministry, the teachers, and the members. All of them are to act accordingly. Therefore, if they examine themselves in the light of Christ, they will change their ways.

Paul's words to the Corinthians tell them what to do. They are to have assurance, and they are to strengthen their belief. Paul declares that those who doubt their place as members of Christ's body are nothing but reprobates. We are to grab hold of God's grace with, "firm and steadfast assurance," nothing less, as Calvin says. When we do this we are to *put on the new man, which after God is created in righteousness and true holiness* [Eph. 4:24].

What is the difference between true and false assurance? True assurance is based upon the teachings of the Master as revealed and supported in Scripture. We are to examine ourselves according to Christ's standards, not ours. May we reach the point where we can say with Paul, *I am crucified with Christ: nevertheless I live; yet not I, but Christ liveth in me: and the life which I now live in the flesh I live by the faith of* (by faith in) *the Son of God, who loved me, and gave himself for me* [Gal. 2:20]. This verse does not mean we are to dedicate our lives to God, or to act, at times, as if He were watching us, but, as Calvin says, "to live the life of God" as Christ exhibited so obediently and with much assurance.

Are we able to examine ourselves each and every day, to go forth with assurance, and to change those thoughts and practices that do not conform to the accepted standard, Christ Himself? This requires effort, objectivity, and supreme honesty. Remember, Paul told the Corinthians *Examine yourselves*, but in a certain way. The wiles of Satan do not want us to do that. They want us to stop at justification by faith. The devil wants us to proceed with euphoria, whereas the New Testament writers were cognizant of the daily struggles that people encountered. However, some people wish to proceed as if there are no problems, no difficulties, no doubts.

What is the condition of the person who has assurance and who has been changed by the life of Christ? First, there is "A sense of wonder, amazement, and surprise. In other words, the true Christian does not say, 'Of course I am saved.' He says, it is an amazing thing that I should be saved at all. How did the almighty God ever bring Himself to look upon me?" as sagaciously described by Martyn Lloyd-Jones in awe and wonder. The Apostle Paul cannot get over this. Neither can we, nor should we!

Charles Wesley wrote, "And can it be, that I should gain an interest in the Saviour's blood? Died He for me, who caused His Pain? For me, who Him to death pursued? Amazing love! How can it be, that thou, my God, should die for me?"

Isaac Watts describes it in that beautiful hymn, entitled with its first line,

> When I survey the wondrous cross,
> On which the Prince of glory died,
> My richest gain I count but loss,
> And pour contempt on all my pride.

Second, assurance from God produces humility, whereas man's assurance in himself produces pride. The New Testament writers possessed humility. The true saints and faithful throughout the ages possessed humility. They did not boast in themselves, or have confidence in themselves, or exhibit glibness. No, their boasting, confidence, and foundation were in Christ Himself.

Third, God's assurance produces a hunger and thirst for righteousness and for knowledge of the Master. Certainly, it does not produce self-satisfaction, complacency, indifference, or apostasy.

The more assurance one receives, the hungrier and thirstier he or she becomes. The more a person receives, the more he or she realizes that there is more available for the asking and seeking. Think of the Apostle Paul writing to the Philippians after all he had received, experienced, and shared, *Brethren, I count not myself to have apprehended: but this one thing I do, forgetting those things which are behind, and reaching forth unto those things which are before. I press toward the mark for the prize of the high calling of God in Christ Jesus* [Phil. 3:13–14]. Paul thanked God for what he had received, but also was grateful for what lay ahead.

What assurance did Paul want? He provides the answer. saying, . . . *not having mine own righteousness, which is of the law, but that which is through the faith of Christ, the righteousness which is of God by faith: That I may know Him, and the power of His resurrection, and the fellowship of His sufferings* [Phil. 3:9–10].

Paul knew there were deficiencies and obstacles in living. The other New Testament writers knew the realities of life and of living in the world. But what did they receive, what did they possess? They had the assurance that Christ was the Son of the living God and that He was able to work within them, to strengthen them, and to support them.

This assurance produced a change in their lives as they witnessed to Him and for Him. It also brought opposition. *The wiles of the devil* wish to keep us from receiving and exhibiting assurance.

Pray God that we can say with Peter,

> *That the trial* (genuineness) *of your faith, being much more precious than of gold that perisheth, though it be tried* (tested) *with fire, might be found unto praise and honor and glory at the appearing* (revelation) *of Jesus Christ:*
>
> *Whom having not seen, ye love; in whom, though now ye see him not, yet believing, ye rejoice with joy unspeakable and full of glory* [1 Pet. 1:7–8].

May we be like the early disciples: hearing, believing, and conducting ourselves with much assurance.

Amen!

2

Believing and Rejoicing in Assurance

> THEREFORE *being justified by faith, we have peace with God through our Lord Jesus Christ:*
> *By whom also we have access by faith into this grace wherein we stand, and rejoice in hope of the glory of God* [Rom. 5:1-2].

Have you ever had certain thoughts keep surfacing in your mind? What about the following? John the Baptist said, *He must increase, but I must decrease* [John 3:30]. The man blind from birth receiving his sight from the Lord Jesus and seeing the light was queried by the authorities, and finally he said to them *One thing I know, that, whereas I was blind, now I see* [John 9:25]. The Lord Jesus said, *I am the way, the truth, and the life, . . .* [John 14:6] and that we are to obey His commandments. Many people were more interested in seeing or hearing about the miracles than in knowing and following the One performing them. *Lord, I believe; help thou mine unbelief* [Mark 9:24].

These thoughts and others should capture our minds as we continue examining the various facets of *the wiles of the devil*. Further, we can accept with assurance that the Lord Jesus is the only begotten (unique) Son of God the Father and that His presence gives us wisdom and inner strength. These thoughts lead to others.

Yes, justification is by faith. Therefore, if we accept Jesus Christ as our Lord and Saviour, why do we have doubts? Why are we concerned about our relationship to Him and to God? Why are we dissatisfied with ourselves? Why are we unhappy and disgruntled? Why do we lack assurance? There is not a single, simple statement to answer these questions and satisfy our longing for a blissful life.

Certain factors contribute to our uneasiness and our unrest: *the wiles of the devil*; the lack of knowledge and understanding; and the importance of self, our desires, and our perceptions. These components plus additional ones make us question the reality of obtaining assurance, having a right relationship with God, and recognizing that our deficiencies and sins serve as an impediment to our relationship with God, not God's relationship with us.

Consequently, people claim, "I am unworthy to be a child of God." Or, "What works must I perform, or what effort must I exert, in order to receive God's favor?" Some people think it is preposterous to claim salvation. Yet others think that everyone will obtain salvation and, as the saying goes, "go to heaven." Others state, if you were really a Christian you would never suffer any setbacks, injuries, or losses.

What does Scripture say? *These things have I written unto you that believe on the name of the Son of God; that ye may know that ye have eternal life, and that ye may believe on the name of the Son of God* [1 John 5:13]. The Apostle seems to repeat himself but he does so for emphasis. John writes to those who are believers to remove doubts and to affirm that they may know they have eternal life. They are to accept it, not question it.

These words were written to believers, whether they were new in the faith or had exhibited growth and maturity. The members of Christ's body to whom the Apostle was writing were to grow in faith and know the assurance of eternal life. They were to acquire knowledge of Christ, continue to learn about Him, and know Him the rest of their lives. Their pockets of unbelief, plus weaknesses in faith, were addressed by Paul.

When the Apostle John says, *that ye may believe*, what does he mean? That you are to remain steadfast in believing, trusting, and placing confidence in the Son of God. It is to be a continuous process accompanied by increased knowledge through learning and revelation. It is not a one-time occurrence.

Strange as it may seem, we are to progress in believing. We are not to be static, nor are we to think that we will achieve some lofty pinnacle upon which we can rest. We are to continue proceeding until that day when the gates of heaven will open to receive us. Paul writes to the Philippians, *Rejoice in the Lord always: and again I say, Rejoice* [Phil. 4:4]. He does not say rejoice in things, people, or conditions. But he does say, *Rejoice in the Lord always*. We are prone to look inward, to look at our feelings, and to look at our situations. However, we are told to focus on the Lord *always*.

This exhortation is directed toward people who have dissensions, difficulties, problems, persecutions, ambitions, pleasures, and doubts, and who have been exposed to false teachings and prophets. They are people like you and me. They have questions. They are searching and seeking. They believe, but they are seeking strength and assurance.

The Apostle tells them to *Rejoice in the Lord always* and in Him alone. By his repetition, Paul is saying, your joy is to be continuous. It is not for a moment only or for a brief interval. It is to go on and on, and it is to increase and increase. This cannot happen unless you focus on the Lord Jesus Christ.

This raises a question. Are you going to accept the teachings of God and apply them, or are you going to go with the teachings of the world? The source of our learning is very important.

When confronted by obstacles, negatives, and hostilities, it is very difficult to rejoice and to be joyful. Yet our joy is to be in the Lord. We must realize that the Lord sends the rain and the cold weather. He also sends tests and trials. It is by these that we grow and increase in strength or become enmeshed in self-pity or defeatism, thereby forfeiting the joy of knowing the Lord, and rejoicing in Him always.

There are other ways by which the devil makes us question the assurance that is available. First, what if I should claim to be a member of Christ's body and then do something wrong? So what? We are going to stumble, but we are to seek, trust, and obey Him. Second, there is a teaching that you cannot really be a Christian if you do not have the assurance of salvation. Therefore, how can you be assured?

Consider Martin Luther. While a monk he was unhappy. He thought he was not good enough to be accepted by God, that he needed to be perfected. Then what happened as he wrestled with his plight? His mind became riveted on the fifth chapter of Romans, *being justified by faith* and *the just shall live by faith*. Luther's heart and mind were opened, and "He saw that this righteousness of God is given through faith and that it is something which can be received immediately," as Martyn Lloyd-Jones acknowledged.

You may receive God's righteousness, but you may not have its assurance in your mind and heart. That is why we consider what John wrote in his First Epistle, *that ye may know that ye have eternal life*. The

Apostle John wrote to believers who were not confident of the reality of their relationship to God in Christ. The author of the Letter to the Hebrews makes the same point. We are to be assured of our relationship and to rejoice in it. Yes, you can be in a right relationship to God without having assurance. However, we are meant to have assurance, and we are to rejoice in it.

The devil makes us question our assurance in both direct and subtle ways by: (i) reminding us of things we should not have done; (ii) asking questions that cause consternation, distress, and remorse; (iii) insinuating that our motives and conduct are self-serving; and (iv) mocking the futility of our efforts to know Christ, accept Him, hear Him, and follow Him as His disciples. These and other negative thoughts are contained in the poisonous darts that Satan hurls at us in an effort to keep us from obtaining and maintaining the assurance of faith in the Lord Jesus and rejoicing *in the Lord always.*

How are we to handle these attacks, these torments? Realize you cannot undo the past and that the Lord looks upon the heart. Recognize that it is the present and future that matters. You have been justified by faith through the blood of the Lamb of God on the Cross. Realize that to be downcast and unhappy in the present means that you cannot function properly, nor can you witness effectively. Realize, *for the joy of the Lord is our strength* [Neh. 8:10]. Remember the devil is a liar and the father of lies. Recall what Christ has said, and claim His promises. Remember, the devil will try to play tricks upon your heart and mind, causing grief and despair. Keep in mind the Lord our God said, *I will not fail thee, nor forsake thee* [Josh. 1:5].

Yes, there can be grievous thoughts and actions within each of us. But we are assured that God has forgiven and cleansed us. Therefore, Satan is to get behind thee. This is a hard lesson to learn and even more difficult to put into practice. It does not matter what you have said or done in the past. What matters is how you look upon the Son of God now and what you are trying to do. Recall the admonition:

> *But ye have not so learned Christ;*
> *If so be that ye have heard him, and have been taught by him, as the truth is in Jesus:*
> *That ye put off concerning the former conversation* (conduct) *the old man, which is corrupt according to the deceitful lusts;*
> *And be renewed in the spirit of your mind;*

And that ye put on the new man, which after God is created in righteousness and true holiness [Eph. 4:20–24].

There are people who place great emphasis upon their feelings and moods and believe that they should always be "floating in the clouds." Further, they think that they should never experience "any rain on their parade" throughout life. They believe they should never encounter any difficulties and should always feel good or be on the heights. Have you ever realized that when you focus attention on your moods, feelings, and condition that you cannot devote the proper emphasis to your relationship with the Lord Jesus Christ? The Apostles James and John, who were brothers, came to Jesus and said,

> *. . . Master* (Teacher), *we would that thou shouldest do for us whatsoever we shall desire.*
> *And he said unto them, what would ye that I should do for you?*
> *They said unto him, Grant unto us that we may sit, one on thy right hand, and the other on thy left hand, in thy glory.*
> *But Jesus said unto them, Ye know not what ye ask: . . .*
> *But to sit on my right hand and on my left hand is not mine to give; but it shall be given to them for whom it is prepared.*
> *. . . whosoever will* (desires to) *be great among you, shall be your minister* (servant)*:*
> *And whosoever of you will* (desires to be first) *be the chiefest, shall be servant of all.*
> *For even the Son of man came not to be ministered* (served) *unto, but to minister* (serve), *and to give his life a ransom for many* [Mark 10:35–38, 40, 43–45].

Of course, the other apostles who were with them were not happy when they heard what James and John had asked Jesus. When Jesus saw this He gathered the twelve together and described for them what their responsibilities would be when He left. He told them that in order to be great they had to minister to others, and whoever desires to be first among them *shall be the servant of all*. Jesus was saying to the disciples that it was the relationship that mattered, not the position they occupied. He reminded them that He came to minister and to serve.

Did you notice what James and John asked? *We would that thou shouldest do for us whatsoever we shall desire* [Mark 10:35]. James and John wanted a position whereby they would feel important. Instead they were told that they were to minister unto others, to be a servant of all, and to give their lives as a ransom for many. The Lord Jesus pointed out that it was their relationship to Him that mattered, not how they felt or the position they occupied or wanted to occupy.

There is an anecdote told by an unknown author about the Scottish evangelist John McNeil that may help us to understand this point. He traveled quite a bit and would be gone for extensive periods of time proclaiming the Gospel. One time, when he came home tired and weary, he said to his wife, "Who are all these children?" He had seven or eight. She responded, "Well, John they are your children." He was tired and exhausted, so he said to his wife, "You know, Mary, I do not know what it is, but I somehow do not realize, I do not feel that they are my children." Patiently and lovingly she replied, "It does not matter whether you feel it or not, John, you are their father!"

That is something to which we can all relate. It is not just how we feel that counts. It is the actual relationship that matters. We have a relationship with the Lord Jesus Christ. But there are times when we question it, when we say, what difference does it make if we do so and so, or such and such? *The wiles of the devil* bring these thoughts to mind and affect our believing, rejoicing, and assurance.

Then there are times when we stumble or fall, when we do not act as Christ would have us act, or when we do not say what Christ would have us say. Therefore, we turn inward, or we turn against someone else. We forget about our relationship to Christ. Though James and John expressed their desires, the Master did not cast them out. He told them and the other disciples what they must do.

Our actions and our thoughts do not change the relationship, though they may have an effect on it as far as we are concerned. The best-known example is the prodigal son. He wanted to come back and be a hired servant though he had been demanding, and in so doing he squandered his inheritance, dishonored the family name, and turned his back on the family. What happened? The father rejoiced, welcomed him home, and assured him of their relationship.

One night, at the close of a long day, I went to another room to turn off the television. There was a stand-up comedian performing and talking about families. He was funny and his humor was enjoyable. Then he said something that was intended to be humorous but contained a great truth. He said, "One thing about the family is that whenever you go home, no matter what you have done, they have got to take you in." Whenever, wherever, and under whatever circumstances when we go to the Father and the Son they will take us in because we are part of the family. Our sins and our failures do not alter the relationship that has been established with the Father and the Son. However, our obeying, believing, and rejoicing may have to be strengthened. *Lord, I believe; help thou mine unbelief* [Mark 9:24].

These teachings apply to the members of Christ's body, the called out, the set apart, the true church. They do not apply to those who attend church for a while, who occasionally participate in various activities, or who serve in different capacities for a period of time. They may appear to be members of Christ's body, but they are not.

The Apostle John addresses this point, saying, *They went out from us, but they were not of us; for if they had been of us, they would no doubt have continued with us: but they went out, that they might be made manifest that they* (none of them) *were not all of us* [1 John 2:19]. "Just as the chaff mixed with wheat on the same threshing floor cannot be called wheat," according to John Calvin. As Calvin further noted, those who profess the Gospel fall into three categories: "Those who feign godliness," those who "keep up a pretence before men, but even dazzle their own eyes, so that they seem . . . to be worshipping God aright," and those who "have the living root of faith and carry a testimony of their adoption firmly fixed in their hearts." It is to the third group that Scripture is speaking about believing, rejoicing, and practicing.

At times, we are all troubled by our lack of faith, lack of understanding, and lack of love. We say, *Lord, I believe; help thou mine unbelief* [Mark 9:24]. When we say that from the heart, we are turning from ourselves to Him. That is a strong statement.

In closing, may I share with you these beautiful words and thoughts expressed in a poem by John Shairp?

> *'Twixt gleams of joy and clouds of doubt*
> *Our feelings come and go;*
> *Our best estate is tossed about*
> *In ceaseless ebb and flow:*
>
> *No mood of feeling, form of thought,*
> *Is constant for a day;*
> *But thou, O Lord, thou changest not,*
> *The same thou art always.*

> *I grasp thy strength, make it mine own,*
> *My heart with peace is blest;*
> *I lose my hold, and then comes down*
> *Darkness and cold unrest.*
>
> *Let me no more my comfort drown*
> *From my frail hold of thee;*
> *In this alone rejoice with awe,*
> *Thy mighty grasp of me.*

May we believe and rejoice, and be assured of our relationship with Him and His mighty grasp on us.
   Amen!

3

Quench Not the Spirit

Pray without ceasing.
In everything give thanks: for this is the will of God in Christ Jesus concerning you.
Quench not the Spirit [1 Thess. 5:17–19].

What do you do with a gift? Use it? Return it? Hide it? Become familiar with it?

The Lord Jesus Christ was specific about the gift He was going to provide the apostles and His followers from that time forward and forever more. The gift was and is the person, the Holy Ghost. Christ and God the Father knew that we needed the Comforter to be available for our instruction; prepare us for service in Christ's kingdom; strengthen us to withstand the pressures of the world; and teach us all things revealed by God the Father, and the Lord Jesus Christ, His Son.

Jesus made it clear that He was sending... *the Comforter* (Paraclete), *which is the Holy Ghost, whom the Father will send in my name, he shall teach you all things, and bring all things to your remembrance* [John 14:26]. He made it very plain that He was going to provide the Holy Spirit unto His followers when He said, *But when the Comforter* (Helper) *is come, whom I will send unto you from the Father, even the Spirit of truth, which proceedeth from the Father, he shall testify of me* [John 15:26]. Jesus promises to send the Comforter to the saints and faithful, saying, *Nevertheless I tell you the truth; It is expedient* (advantageous) *for you that I go away: for if I go not away, the Comforter* (Helper) *will not come unto you; but if I depart, I will send him unto you.* [John 16:7].

When Jesus speaks of the Comforter He is speaking of the Holy Spirit. It is important to know the full meaning of the Greek word for Comforter used in this instance. It is *paraklētos*. It means "to call to one's side," "to call to one's aid." It suggests the capability of giving aid to someone.

The Lord Jesus is explicit as to what the Comforter, the Holy Spirit, will do. He will convict the world of three things: sin, righteousness, and judgment. Please recall the setting when the Lord Jesus speaks often and emphatically of the Holy Spirit. He is talking to the disciples about things of the utmost importance. They are part and parcel of His last words.

It is interesting to examine these three things that Jesus says the Comforter will do. First, He will convict us of sin. Otto Weber defines it thusly, "Sin is hostility toward the grace of God." Is that not beautiful? "We fail to recognize God in that we are not willing to accept that he is good to us. We fail to recognize ourselves in that we are not willing to accept (the truth) that we should submit ourselves to him," as insightfully stated by Otto Weber. When Christ talks about sin, He ties it deliberately to the statement, *Of sin, because they believe not on me* [John 16:9]. Sin and the lack of belief go hand in hand.

In these verses from John's Gospel, the Master speaks about the gift of the Spirit, or "the power of the Spirit, which appears in the outward teaching of the gospel and the voice of men," as accurately described by John Calvin. How do men's voices reach into the hearts and minds of people and change them so that they become members of Christ's body? It is by the power of the Holy Spirit!

It is important to recognize that Jesus was imparting this knowledge to the disciples during His last night, because it was necessary for them to know "the importance of the gift being bestowed upon them—the Comforter." The disciples needed to know that His gift was available for them, that it was a most unique gift, a gift that was not to be ignored. They were to become familiar with the gift, the Comforter, the Holy Spirit, to know Him and to call upon Him.

Second, the Lord Jesus says that the gift will convict us *Of righteousness, because I go to my Father, and ye see me no more* [John 16:10]. Note the sequence of the teaching: first sin, then righteousness. People will not hunger and thirst after righteousness until they realize their sinful condition and the need to be in a right relationship with God. "Believers particularly . . . cannot progress in the Gospel until first they have been humbled, and this cannot happen until they are aware of their sins," as Calvin had learned.

The Greek word for *righteousness* is *dikaiosunē*. It means several things: "whatever conforms to the revealed will of God [Matt. 5:6, 10, 20]"; "whatever has been appointed by God to be acknowledged and obeyed by man [Matt. 3:15, 21:32]"; "the sum total of God's requirements [Matt. 6:33]"; and "the duties of each member of Christ's body [John 16:1-18]."

Christ tells His disciples what will happen in just a few hours, and He tells us what happened. He has risen! He has ascended to the Father. He sits on the right hand of God the Father. He has all authority. He sheds His grace on whom He will. He has paid the debt. Therefore, the Gospel is proclaimed by and through the power of the Holy Spirit, and we become convicted of righteousness.

Third, the Lord Jesus says, *Of judgment, because the prince* (ruler) *of this world is judged* [John 16:11]. What does this mean? The Greek word translated into *judgment* is *krisis*. It denotes "a separation," "a decision," and finally, "divine judgment." Recall the sequence. The Comforter, the Holy Spirit, will come. He will convict us of sin, righteousness, and judgment.

Why will there be judgment? *Because the prince* (ruler) *of this world is judged* [John 16:11]. Christ has triumphed over Satan. The Holy Spirit convinces us of *the wiles* (schemes) *of the devil* and of the evil emanating from Satan. He enables us to stand and to understand the teachings of the Master. Therefore, the Lord Jesus brings these three things to our attention: sin, righteousness, and judgment. He does so to stress the importance of: His teachings; the Holy Spirit interpreting them aright in our hearts and minds; and adopting and practicing these truths.

Then what does the Master do? Does he leave them? Does he go off on a tangent or in a different direction? No! He does not! He further enlightens and assures them that they will be comforted and strengthened. Note the confident manner in which the Lord Jesus says,

> *I have yet many things to say unto you, but ye cannot bear them now.*
> *Howbeit when he, the Spirit of truth, is come, he will guide you into all truth: for he shall not speak of himself* (on his own authority); *but whatsoever he shall hear, that shall he speak: and he will show you things to come.*
> *He shall glorify me: for he shall receive of mine* (what is mine), *and shall show* (declare) *it unto you* [John 16:12-14].

The Lord Jesus makes a clear and direct statement that the Holy Spirit will guide us in all truth. He will testify of the Lord Jesus. He will show us things, and He will glorify Christ.

One of the best examples of this Scripture is the first four chapters of Ephesians. Paul, under the influence of the Holy Spirit, "explains the treasures of this hidden wisdom which even the angels in heaven learn with amazement through the Church," as Calvin wisely discerned.

What happened to the disciples after that last night when the Lord Jesus taught them so much? Acts reveals what Jesus told the disciples after His resurrection. . . . *ye shall be baptized with the Holy Ghost not many days hence* [Acts 1:5], and *Ye shall receive power, after that* (when) *the Holy Ghost is come upon you* [Acts 1:8], and Luke tells us that *they were all filled with the Holy Ghost* [Acts 2:4].

Many people place emphasis on speaking in tongues when the important point is *being filled with the Holy Ghost*. Paul puts it in the proper perspective saying,

> *He that speaketh in an unknown tongue edifieth himself; but he that prophesieth* (expound) *edifieth the church.*
>
> *I would that ye all spake with tongues, but rather* (even more) *that ye prophesied; for greater is he that prophesieth than he that speaketh with tongues, except he interpret, that the church may receive edifying* (building up).
>
> *Now, brethren, if I come unto you speaking with tongues, what shall I profit you, except I shall speak to you either by revelation, or by knowledge, or by prophesying, or by doctrine* (teaching) [1 Cor. 14:4–6]?

Paul believed the emphasis should be placed on interpreting Scripture, obtaining knowledge, expounding the Word, and presenting the truths contained in Christ's teachings. Then he explicitly states where the emphasis should be placed, saying, *I thank my God, I speak with tongues more than ye all: Yet in the church I had rather speak five words with my understanding, that by my voice I might teach others also, than ten thousand words in an unknown tongue* [1 Cor. 14:18–19]. Paul's concern was upbuilding the other members of Christ's body. Apparently, Paul was multilingual, but he did not boast about it. He wanted to proclaim the Gospel and wanted it interpreted correctly.

Throughout the New Testament there is heavy emphasis on the Holy Spirit. The early saints and faithful were cognizant of the Holy Spirit and realized that He exercised great influence over the early church and its members. This is definitely noticeable in the Acts of the Apostles and the various Epistles. The Holy Spirit was known to the early church. He was accepted by the members, and they rejoiced in the fact that, "He convicts us, quickens us, enables us to believe, and gives us faith, produces the new nature, the rebirth in us, leads us and guides us in the process of sanctification and in many other ways," as aptly described by Martyn Lloyd-Jones.

Yes, this was true. Pray God it will be true today! Then, may I ask, why did Paul, in writing to the Thessalonians, say *Quench not the Spirit* [1 Thess. 5:19]? Remember, we are to be filled with the Spirit. We are to receive power; we are to rejoice; we are to pray without ceasing; and we are to give thanks. But we do not always do this. We succumb to *the wiles* (schemes) *of the devil*. We do not always stand. Therefore, the Apostle reminds us of the power and nature of the Spirit. It is the Spirit that enlightens our hearts and minds, and provides the light to receive and to enjoy the grace of God.

When you quench the Spirit you are preventing the Word from enlightening your heart and mind. How do we quench the Spirit? By laziness, by not wanting to read and hear the Word every day, by not wanting to understand what Scripture is saying in the original text, by not being grateful for the Word and for receiving the proper interpretation of Scripture, and by not giving thanks for the gifts God has bestowed upon us.

It is our responsibility to *Quench not the Spirit*. We are to continually ask God to enlighten us, refresh us, strengthen us, and preserve us. How is this done? By the written Word, "Sola Scriptura."

There are people and groups today who ignore the written Word and say the Spirit is working in them. They prefer the knowledge they have acquired from their experiences; they deny that there is anything special about the apostles, prophets, and Scripture; and they do not think that a right relationship with God can have a dramatic impact upon a their lives.

Consequently, these people depend upon the knowledge they have acquired in the world from their impulses, feelings, and impressions or from uninformed sources. They do not realize what Scripture says regarding false spirits, examining Scripture, and being aware of false prophets. Christ said, *When he, the Spirit of truth, is come, he will guide you into all truth: for he shall not speak of himself* (on his own authority); *but whatsoever he shall hear, that shall he speak: and he shall show you things to come* [John 16:13]. It is difficult, but we must learn to listen to what Christ says and to what Scripture is saying. One of *the wiles* (schemes) *of the devil* is to quench the Spirit and to hinder Him from working with believers and from reaching nonbelievers.

What is meant by *Quench not the Spirit*? It is not referring to excitement or ebullience. It is concerned with allowing the Holy Spirit to work within you, recognizing that the Holy Spirit was sent by the Lord Jesus, and knowing that the power of the Holy Spirit can have a positive impact upon you and others.

Read about and recall the impact of the Holy Spirit upon the early church, the Reformers, the Waldensians, the Moravians, the Puritans, and the early Methodists. They did not quench the Spirit. They thanked God for Him. They respected Him. They listened to Him. They knew that the Holy Spirit was part of the Holy Trinity and had been sent by the Lord Jesus. They knew the teachings of the Master concerning the Spirit. But what is more important: they appropriated that teaching; they believed it; and they exhibited it.

We need to be looking and listening for the Spirit. We need to claim the promises and teachings of the Lord Jesus. The Master says, *If a man love me, he will keep my words: and my Father will love him, and we will come unto him, and make our abode* (home) *with him* [John 14:23]. Listen to what Paul says to the Corinthians,

> *What? know ye not that your body is the temple of the Holy Ghost which is in you, which ye have of God, and ye are not your own?*
>
> *For ye are bought with a price: therefore glorify God in your body, and in your spirit, which are God's* [1 Cor. 6:19–20].

We are to remember Paul saying to the Ephesians,

> *Ye are no more strangers and foreigners, but fellow citizens with the saints, and of the household of God;* . . .
>
> *In whom ye also are builded* (being built) *together for a habitation* (dwelling place) *of God through the Spirit* [Eph. 2:19, 22].

That is what we are to realize! That is what we are to be! We are to remind ourselves of these truths. We are to provide for the Spirit working within us.

We are not to quench the Spirit. We are to fan the fire within us, not dampen it. When John the Baptist was asked if he were the Christ he responded by saying,

> I indeed baptize you with water; but one mightier than I cometh, the latchet (strap) of whose shoes (sandals) I am not worthy to unloose: he shall baptize you with the Holy Ghost and with fire:
> Whose (winnowing) fan is in his hand, and he will thoroughly purge (clean out) his (threshing) floor, and will gather the wheat into his garner (barn); but the chaff he will burn with fire unquenchable [Luke 3:16–17].

We are not to quench the Spirit, but as Paul says, we are to *be filled with the Spirit* [Eph. 5:18]. Every day we are to be filled with the Spirit, guided by the Spirit, and listen to the Spirit. We have a responsibility to exercise and a witness to perform.

John the Baptist said the Lord Jesus will baptize us with the Holy Ghost and fire. What qualities are evident when the fire is fanned, not quenched? First, it gives light and understanding. The Spirit working within enables us to understand the mysteries of the faith and to grab hold of them.

Second, the fire provided with the Holy Ghost gives warmth. Cold ashes give no warmth. The flame within each of us is to be fanned so that the fire will glow and provide warmth to others. A cold person professing to be a Christian does irreparable harm to the body of Christ.

Third, the fire provided by the Holy Ghost gives assurance that our sins are forgiven and that we are members of Christ's body.

Fourth, the person in whom the fire glows knows that God the Father and Christ the Son love him or her. But the person also loves the Lord Jesus and God the Father. He or she loves them and wants to please them. As a result, that person wants to show gratitude by praising God and obeying Christ.

The Lord Jesus, has given us a most remarkable gift. The more we rejoice in it, the more we are to *Quench not the Spirit*, but to *be filled with the Spirit*.

In closing, recall those beautiful words of the glorious hymn "Spirit of God, Descend Upon My Heart," which is attributed to George Croly.

Spirit of God, descend upon my heart;
Wean it from earth; through all its pulses move;
Stoop to my weakness, mighty as Thou art,
And make me love Thee as I ought to love.

Teach me to love Thee as Thine angels love,
One holy passion filling all my frame;
The baptism of the heaven descended Dove,
My heart an altar, and Thy love the flame.

Amen!

4

Whence Knowest Thou Me?

> *And Nathanael said unto him, Can there any good thing come out of Nazareth? Philip saith unto him, Come and see.*
> *Jesus saw Nathanael coming to him, and saith of him, Behold an Israelite indeed, in whom is no guile* (deceit)*!*
> *Nathanael saith unto him, Whence* (How) *knowest thou me? Jesus answered and said unto him, Before that Philip called thee, when thou wast under the fig tree, I saw thee* [John 1:46–48].

Characteristics displayed by the true believers in Christ are evident in all types of people: the simple and complex, joyful and sad, happy and glum, laughing and crying, confident and doubting, good and bad, physical and spiritual, trusting and doubting. The list could go on. It is interesting, amusing, and yes, sad that we accept some things at their face value, yet others we reject, and still others we ignore.

Scripture is explicit about the Lord Jesus Christ, His birth, life, death, and resurrection; the Holy Spirit, His power, strength, and availability; and witnessing to the Lord's ministry and His resurrection. Yet, we question the reality and the presence of both the Lord Jesus Christ and the Holy Spirit. We may not question the reality and presence of either one all the time, but we do part of the time. Also, we restrict or select where and when either one may be present and working. Is it not interesting that we do not question a human voice or electricity?

You cannot really see, touch, or feel a human voice. It originates within the body, is formed within the throat and mouth, is projected out through the lips, and covers a distance where it is heard by other human ears. Yet nothing can be seen or touched. Electricity is very similar. You cannot see it or touch it, but you can flip a switch, and a light comes on, or an appliance begins to operate.

Our Scripture for this message reveals Philip found Nathanael under the fig tree and brought him to Jesus. How did this happen? By and through the Lord Jesus Christ. Jesus found Philip and said unto him, *follow me*. After his initial encounter with Jesus, Philip went to find Nathanael, to tell him about it and to bring him to Jesus. We are to have fellowship with Jesus, to hear Him say, *follow me*, and to tell others what Moses, the prophets, and apostles have to say about Him.

Pray God that each time we have a need the Holy Spirit will throw a switch whereby we can hear not only what Christ has to say, learn not only what Christ did and would have us do, but also that we *quench not the Spirit*. We are to become filled with the Spirit and allow Him to mold us, form us, and direct us. The challenge is to relinquish ourselves to the Spirit, to allow Him to strengthen us, and to walk with Him.

Apparently, Nathanael's first reaction was to resent and/or reject Philip's invitation, yet he came. By coming he demonstrated that he was willing to see Him and to learn. When we come to hear the Word we should be teachable regarding the truths of God and of Christ, but knowledgeable enough to withstand *the wiles* (schemes) *of the devil*. We are to stand on God's truths, not succumb to false teachings and then fall.

Remember when inviting someone to come hear the Word or to know the Master that they will have questions, doubts, and other priorities. Yet we are to keep asking, until they completely accept or reject the invitation.

Why did Jesus say to Nathanael, *Behold an Israelite indeed, in whom is no guile* (deceit) [John 1:47]? Because He wanted to distinguish between the true believers and the nominal ones. Or as Gil Green said, "There are heart Christians and there are nominal Christians. The heart Christians know the Lord Jesus Christ."

During Jesus' earthly ministry, there were many who called themselves believers because they were of the lineage of Abraham, not because they obeyed the teachings of God as revealed through Moses, the patriarchs, and the prophets. They gloried in their ancestry, their phylacteries, their rules, and their do's and don'ts. Christ says there is no guile in the true Israelite. This also applies to the members of Christ's body. Christ "gives a timely warning that there are only a few true Israelites among those who claim the name of Israelite," as noted by John Calvin.

When Nathanael meets Jesus for the first time he asks a question that has been asked many, many times since, *Whence* (How) *knowest thou me*? Nathanael was a sincere and quiet person. You may ask, was it a coincidence that he was sitting under a fig tree when Philip came to him? No, it was not. That was the custom of many Jews of that day when they wished to be quiet, to pray, and to meditate. Also, Jesus said to Nathanael, *Before that Philip called thee, when thou wast under the fig tree, I saw thee* [John 1:48].

It is believed by some scholars that Nathanael was wrestling with his faith, his doubts, and the teachings of the patriarchs and the prophets. Probably, he prided himself on being sincere in his faith and wanting to do the will of God. However, he was able to ask the question openly, honestly, and sincerely. *Whence* (How) *knowest thou me* [John 1:48]?

The key point is not Nathanael's question, nor that Christ had seen him under the fig tree when Christ Himself was not there, but that Jesus is able to look into the heart and mind of a person, to know his or her thoughts and desires, and to meet them. Jesus met Nathanael's need! So often Satan distracts us or wants us to focus on the insignificant points instead of concentrating on the primary ones.

In addition to meeting Nathanael's needs, what else did Jesus do? He was able to know and understand what was in Nathanael's heart and mind and to know the condition of Nathanael's heart, that it was sincere, because there was no guile in it. It was pure! Pray God the Lord Jesus may find our hearts to be like Nathanael's.

There are other important points to consider. We are observed by Christ, even when we are not thinking of Him. If He was able to observe Nathanael from afar during His earthly ministry, how much more can He observe us now that He has ascended to the Father? He is able to bring us to Himself when we are afar off or when, as Calvin says, "we have withdrawn from Him."

When Nathanael was confronted by the Lord Jesus, what did He do? He confessed that Jesus was the Son of God and the King of Israel. When confronted by Christ, we are to follow Nathanael's lead. We are to hear the Word, we are to know who He is, and we are to allow our faith to respond to Him. We are not to quench the Spirit!

Jesus tells Nathanael that he shall see greater things than what he has already seen. He wants him to focus on the kingdom of God and the things of God. We are to see the glory of God, His reality, and the presence of the Lord Jesus. He is to be as real to us as He was to Nathanael.

Nathanael could have succumbed to *the wiles* (schemes) *of the devil*. He could have quenched the Spirit. But neither of these things happened. Instead, he was filled with the Spirit. Note that with Nathanael there was doubt, there was a question, but he came to hear, to see. Who? The Son of God, the King of Israel.

What happens when a person is led by the Spirit and does not quench it? The Spirit moves him and provides him with energy and the power to witness. We all have the ability to witness when the Holy Spirit works within us.

Think of this. In John's Gospel, Simon Peter says he is going fishing. This is after the resurrection, after the episode with doubting Thomas, but before Pentecost. However, after the Spirit took hold of him and Peter yielded himself, he no longer went fishing for fish. The Spirit enabled Peter to witness and to proclaim the Gospel. The Spirit enables us to witness and to proclaim the Gospel according to the capabilities given unto us.

There are certain things to remember concerning Nathanael: Jesus' call; responding in faith; meeting his needs; witnessing; being filled with the Spirit; and *standing against the wiles* (schemes) *of the devil*. The teachings of the New Testament are meant for us, as much as they were directed to the first century followers. Peter says, *For the promise is unto you, and to your children, and to all that are afar off* [Acts 2:39]. The promise is to the Jews and their children, and also to the Gentiles.

The Holy Spirit works in and through all the members of Christ's body. There is no such thing as a priesthood and a laity. We are all members of His body. We are all saints and the faithful. We may have different callings, but we are members of His body.

There is not a text in the New Testament which says that this blessing of the power and of the fire of the Spirit is to be confined only to certain people, to exceptional saints, to preachers, or to someone God wants to use in a special manner. No, it *is unto you, and your children, and . . . to all that are afar off*. We are to respond to the Spirit. We are not to be as the bride in the Song of Solomon. When her beloved knocked she did not answer. She had excuses. She waited, then she went to the door. But her beloved was gone.

When the Spirit comes we are to respond. We are not to resist Him. We are not to make excuses. We are not to delay. Though we may have questions, doubts, or concerns we are to go see Him and hear what He has to say.

What keeps us from responding to the call to *come and see* Jesus? What are additional *wiles* (schemes) *of the devil*? First, there is discouragement. We may feel or believe that we live in difficult and discouraging times, or under less than desirable circumstances. Therefore, we allow our temperament, attitude, and outlook to be affected. "We focus our eyeballs inwardly" instead of outwardly, as Chuck Swindoll said in order to focus our attention.

When we become discouraged and focus on the negatives we are not able to stand against *the wiles* (schemes) *of the devil*. When we are discouraged, or focusing inwardly, we have difficulty helping one another and witnessing to others. Suppose Philip had been discouraged; he might not have gone to Nathanael and told him to *come and see*. We are not to become depressed. We are to remind ourselves of what Christ has done for us and that the Holy Spirit will work within us when we let Him.

Second, we are not to focus on the negatives. Nor are we to think that we are not growing in the Lord, not increasing in knowledge, not increasing in strength, not serving the Lord, and not maturing in the faith. Those thoughts are *the wiles* (schemes) *of the devil*! It is easy to succumb to these wiles, but we must look to Scripture and to Christ. When people realize they are growing, increasing, and serving then they experience more growth, more knowledge, and more service.

It is like building a house. A brick, nail, 2x4, or piece of sheet rock are rather insignificant when seen by themselves. But by fitting them together properly, they can grow into a house, they can increase in strength, they can withstand the storms of life, and they can serve the family as a beautiful, loving home. Paul says to the Corinthians,

> *But now are they many members, yet but one body.*
> *Nay, much more those members of the body, which seem to be more feeble* (weak), *are necessary:*
> *And those members of the body, which we think to be less honorable, upon these we bestow more abundant honor; and our uncomely* (unpresentable) *parts have more abundant comeliness* (modesty).
> *For our comely* (presentable) *parts have no need: but God hath tempered* (composed) *the body together, having given more abundant honor to that part which lacked:*
> *That there should be no schism* (division) *in the body; but that the members should have the same care one for another* [1 Cor. 12:20, 22–25].

There is no such thing as an unimportant member of Christ's body. There may be different talents and personalities, but they are all important and they all perform a service.

Third, recall what Paul says to the Galatians, *And let us not be weary in well doing: for in due season we shall reap, if we faint not* (do not lose heart) [Gal. 6:9]. There are times when we want to refrain from doing good, but we are not to do so. We are to be like the little nail, one brick, 2x4, or sheet rock that is never seen when the house is finished. Each one does its part in making the house, strengthening it, and serving those who enter its doors.

Fourth, there are two common maladies that afflict all of us sooner or later. They are called worry and anxiety. Our Lord at the close of His earthly ministry says to His disciples,

> *Take heed to yourselves, lest at any time your hearts be overcharged* (weighed down) *with surfeiting* (carousing), *and drunkenness, and cares of this life, . . .*
> *Watch ye therefore, and pray always, that ye may be accounted worthy to escape all these things that shall come to pass, and to stand before the Son of man* [Luke 21:34, 36].

When Jesus was visiting Martha and Mary he said to Martha, *Martha, Martha, thou art careful* (worried) *and troubled about many things: But one thing is needful; and Mary hath chosen that good part, which shall not be taken away from her* [Luke 10:41–42]. Mary was spending time with Jesus, while Martha was hustling and bustling about in a dither, preparing a meal.

The devil wants us in a state of anxiety, because when we are we cannot concentrate on the things of the Spirit, and the Spirit cannot work within us. Everyone receives discouraging or alarming news from time to time. Sometimes it comes in bunches. When it does, pray God we can remember the words of Paul to Timothy. Paul had received discouraging reports from Timothy, who apparently was upset, or complaining, or beset with anxiety, so he reported his concerns to Paul. Where is Paul when he receives these reports? In prison, confined, and unable to minister as he would like. Yet he writes to Timothy saying, *For the which cause I also suffer these things: nevertheless I am not ashamed* (suffering, in a dither, upset): *for I know whom I have believed, and am persuaded that he is able to keep that which I have committed unto him against* (until) *that day* [2 Tim. 1:12]. We are to be concerned about things, but in the proper perspective. This is easier said than done. Scripture tells us that our focal point is to be the Lord Jesus Christ. He is to be the center of our attention. We are to confess that He is the Son of God.

Probably Paul's most meaningful exhortation about anxiety is in Philippians,

> *Be careful* (anxious) *for nothing; but in everything by prayer and supplication with thanksgiving let your requests be made known unto God.*
> *And the peace of God, which passeth all understanding shall keep* (guard) *your hearts and minds through Christ Jesus* [Phil. 4:6–7].

Oh, that we may do that! We should take heart by the fact that John Calvin was beset with anxiety. William Bouwsma describes Calvin's struggles with anxiety in his biography of Calvin, "He was also aware of the anxiety at the center of his life's work; he recognized in himself a terrible self-concern hardly consistent with the security he attributed to faith. 'The thought repeatedly recurs to me' he once confessed, . . . that I am in danger of being unjust to God's mercy by laboring with so much anxiety to assess it [God's mercy] as if it were doubtful or obscure."

In closing, it is well to remember what Paul said about worry in his letter to Timothy: *For God hath not given us the spirit of fear; but of power, and of love, and of a sound mind* [2 Tim. 1:7]. The *sound mind* means "self-control," "discipline," and "orderliness." Paul reminds Timothy (and us) that we receive these things from above, that the Holy Spirit provides for our needs. As Philip said to Nathanael, *Come and See.* As Jesus said to Nathanael, *Believest thou? Thou shalt see greater things than these* [John 1:50]. And he did!

Pray God that we may respond to the Master and that we will hear Him speak to us. May the Holy Spirit bring us closer to Jesus and strengthen us with His power to repel *the wiles* (schemes) *of the devil.*
Amen!

5

Self

> *Finally, my brethren, be strong in the Lord, and in the power of his might.*
>
> *Put on the whole armor of God, that ye may be able to stand against the wiles* (schemes) *of the devil.*
>
> *For we wrestle not against flesh and blood, but against principalities, against powers, against the rulers of the darkness of this world* (age), *against spiritual* (hosts of) *wickedness in high places* [Eph. 6:10–12].

We are called to be members of Christ's body, to be separated unto God, to be part of the world, but to be apart from the world. God speaks today just as He spoke to Moses, saying, *Speak unto all the congregation of the children of Israel, and say unto them, Ye shall be holy: for I the Lord your God am holy* [Lev. 19:2]. These words are as true today as then. God the Father is the same yesterday, today, and tomorrow. His commandments do not change.

The command to *be holy* was spoken to all the children of the congregation of Israel. Note the wisdom of God in that exhortation. He did not say speak to the adults, speak to the men or the women. No, He said to all the children. This denotes the future generations, of which we are part.

The calling of God sounds so nice and simple. It is so attractive and alluring. We can be part of that group, we can be members of a respectable church organization, part of the team. We can come and go as we please since we have joined the fellowship. Further, we can bring all our toys, our pet ideas, our books, and our practices with us and say, "Here I am, Lord, all of me, just as I am."

The tendency is to say, "I'm here Lord." I'm going to work, I'm going to teach, I'm going to sit in the pew, I'm going to contribute, I'm going to sing." Have you either served in the armed forces or been in the hospital, at least over night? What happens? You go in with all your things, including your mindset as to what you are going to do and when you are going to do it. Then once you are in, someone says, maybe not in a friendly tone, "Put your things over there, and take off your clothes," and there you are! Not as self-confident, nor as self-assured. Then someone says, "Put on this uniform," or "Put on this hospital gown." A change begins to come over you, some slowly, some more rapidly.

Then someone says, "Here is what you are going to do." "Here is the schedule." "This is a list of the do's and don'ts." As a result more change occurs in the individual. How many times have you heard someone say about another person after they have returned from boot camp or a stay in the hospital, "My, how they have changed"?

It is safe to say that each of us loves the hymn, "Just as I Am, Without One Plea," by Charlotte Elliott. Too often, the emphasis is placed upon the words, *Just as I Am*, whereas, in reality the emphasis should be placed upon three things. The first is Christ:

> *Thy blood was shed for me;*
> *Thou biddest me to come to Thee.*

The second is the individual's condition:

> *Though tossed about*
> *With many a conflict, many a doubt*
> *Fightings and fears within, without,*

Third, is the acknowledgment of what Christ can do:

> *Rid my soul of one dark blot:*
> *Whose blood can cleanse each spot,*
> *Wilt welcome, pardon, cleanse, relieve;*
> *Because Thy promise, I believe.*

We come to Christ because He first called us. We can come one of two ways: first, as an inductee or as an occupant; second, as a visitor or an observer.

The former puts on new clothes and becomes a new person, while the latter observes but does not participate, views the proceedings but does not partake of the food, the wine, the commands, the body, the

Spirit, or the true fellowship. When we come to Christ we not only become members of His body, but we become one of His co-workers. Our relationship to the Lord Jesus Christ is unique.

We are members of His body; we are His servants and co-workers. Please note, it says co-worker. Paul describes our relationship with God, saying to the Corinthians,

> Who then is Paul, and who is Apollos, but ministers by whom ye believed, even as the Lord gave to every man? I have planted, Apollos watered; but God gave the increase.
> So then neither is he that planteth any thing, neither he that watereth; but God that giveth the increase.
> For we are laborers (God's fellow workers) together with God: ye are God's husbandry (field), ye are God's building [1 Cor. 3:5–7, 9].

When we become members of Christ's body we are involved in His work, His labor, His concerns, and His objectives. We are to be used willingly by Him since we have accepted His call, and in so doing we agree to become knowledgeable and obedient.

God takes us and uses us to accomplish His tasks, transmit His word, and be His instruments, even though we are insignificant and incapable. It is His power that provides the ability to become and to perform what He would have us do. "Paul does not teach here what men are capable of by their natural powers, but what the Lord does through them by His grace. He, by Himself, acts through them in such a way that they, in turn, work with Him for a common end," as John Calvin communicates this truth to us.

When we labor for God, the primary requirements are to know what He wants, do what He would have us do, and concentrate on Him. If you are in the armed forces or in the hospital you usually know what they want, you do what they tell you to do, and you had better concentrate on what they are telling you. Remember, we may plant, we may water, but it is *God that giveth the increase*. Our obedience is to be unto God, and we are to concentrate on Him. If we do not, then we will become distracted and focus our attention on the pleasures of the world or ourselves, and we will become subject to *the wiles* (schemes) *of the devil*.

What happens when we concentrate on God? Oswald Chambers states it in a penetrating manner, "When once the concentration is on God, all the margins of life are free and under the dominance of God alone. There is no responsibility on you for the work; the only responsibility you have is to keep in living, constant touch with God, and to see that you allow nothing to hinder your cooperation with Him. But, be careful to remember one thing only. To be absolutely devoted to your co-worker." What a beautiful, insightful statement!

Further, it is well to remember that God engineers everything; wherever He puts us, our one great aim is to pour out a wholehearted devotion to Him in that particular work. *Whatsoever thy hand findeth to do, do it with thy might* [Eccl. 9:10]. What keeps us from concentrating on God? What makes us fall instead of being *able to stand against the wiles* (schemes) *of the devil*?

During the past few chapters we have considered a number of different topics and tactics used by the devil to tempt us, thwart us, and distract us. Now we are considering the primary impediment to concentrating on God, being obedient to Him, and acquiring knowledge not about Him, but of Him. What is that impediment? *Self!* What caused the original Fall? *Self*-pride in self. It is the stumbling block! "Throughout the Bible it is clear that *self* is the outstanding problem in human life, . . . as you read the Old Testament and the New there is no problem that raises its head more frequently than this horrible, terrible problem of self, whether seen in individuals, groups, or nations. What havoc this whole problem of self has caused in the long history of the human race," as Martyn Lloyd-Jones informs us.

Oh, that we would listen to the Master when he says, *Verily I say unto you, Except ye be converted, and become as little children, ye shall not enter into the kingdom of heaven* [Matt. 18:3]. The child wants to know, and the child wants to please. But more importantly, children have a simplicity about them, and "they are ignorant of degrees of honor and provocations to pride, [therefore] Christ deservedly and rightly puts them forward as examples," as observed by John Calvin and thoughtfully expressed.

Adults are different. They covet honors, and they take pride in their person, possessions, position, talents, and gifts. What did James and John want after they had been with Jesus for three years? To sit on his right hand and his left! What did Jesus look for? The person who humbled himself and ignored or was unaware that he possessed anything in which he should take pride.

Calvin provides us with a brief, beautiful description of humility. "He is truly humble who neither claims anything for himself over against God, nor proudly despises his brethren, affecting superiority, but regards it sufficient to be reckoned as one of the members of Christ and desires nothing but that the Head [Christ] alone have the pre-eminence." Oh, how that hits home. Each of us can wear that uniform or gown.

You can be sure of one thing: the devil knows human nature. He knows how self thinks and acts. He knows how a person takes pride in the gifts he or she has received such as intellect, perception, understanding, knowledge, physical attractiveness, and capabilities such as preaching or singing. As Paul points out to the Corinthians,

> *For to one is given by the Spirit the word of wisdom; to another the word of knowledge by the same Spirit;*
> *To another faith by the same Spirit; to another the gifts of healing by the same Spirit;*
> *To another the working of miracles; to another prophecy; to another discerning of spirits; to another divers kinds of tongues; to another the interpretation of tongues:*
> *But all these worketh that one and the selfsame Spirit, dividing* (distributing) *to every man severally* (individually) *as he will* [1 Cor. 12:8–11].

It is the Spirit that divides these gifts among the members of Christ's body. Oh, how I fool myself when I think or believe that I created one of the gifts that have been given to me. The last verse of Paul's first letter to the Corinthians says, *But covet* (desire) *earnestly the best gifts: and yet show I unto you a more excellent way* [1 Cor. 12:31]. What does the Apostle mean? He means that the Corinthians should desire and seek those gifts, that are the most effective for upbuilding the followers as members of Christ's body, as witnesses to His calling, and as His co-workers. The Corinthians were coveting things for themselves and ignoring the teachings of Christ. They were focusing on self.

What was Paul stressing? That they should build up each other and concentrate on the things of God, not on themselves. How else does *self* get in the way and keep us from concentrating on God? By focusing upon our experiences. Some people boast regarding how they came to know the Lord in the works they have performed and in what they have done or are doing, when in reality it is the Lord's doing. "There is nothing about us that the devil cannot take hold of. It is because it has happened to us, because it is ours, because it is we who have done it. And, he will take even the most glorious gift and will twist it in this subtle manner. He will so bring self into it that the whole thing will be ruined," as Martyn Lloyd-Jones causes us to consider two important truths: Satan and self.

How else does *self* intercede? John, in his third letter, talks about Diotrephes saying, *but Diotrephes, who loveth to have the pre-eminence among them, receiveth us not* [3 John 1:9]. Here was a person who was a member of the church, the called out, but he wanted to have pre-eminence.

There are those who succumb to temptations and become guilty of self-satisfaction. This happens to individuals, to groups, and to congregations. Recall those piercing words the Lord Jesus Christ spoke to the members of the church in Laodicea,

> *Because thou sayest, I am rich, and increased with goods* (have become wealthy), *and have need of nothing; and knowest not that thou art wretched, and miserable, and poor, and blind, and naked:*
> *To him that overcometh will I grant to sit with me in* (on) *my throne, even as I also overcame, and am set down with my Father in* (on) *his throne.*
> *He that hath an ear, let him hear what the Spirit saith unto the churches* [Rev. 3:17, 21–22].

They were self-satisfied, they were basking in their own glory, they were extolling their own virtues and they were congratulating themselves. They were measuring themselves by their own standards. Then the Lord pointed out their weaknesses, ineptness, deficiencies, and shortcomings. He wanted them (and us) to face reality, hear His voice, open the door, and let Him come in and sup with them. *He that hath an ear, let him hear what the Spirit saith unto the churches* [Rev. 3:22].

There are those who have an extreme case of self-confidence in their own capabilities. They believe that they can only do good and will always stand regardless of what they do. Paul admonished the Corinthians, with whom *God was not well pleased*. They were self-satisfied. They were defiant toward God, self-centered, and self-confident, and they believed they were not accountable to anyone but themselves. Paul, after describing the error of their ways, says to them, *Wherefore let him that thinketh he standeth take heed lest he fall* [1 Cor. 10:12].

Paul points out that we are not to pride ourselves on what we were, what we are, and what we are becoming. We are not to boast about our accomplishments. But we are to recognize "that there are two kinds of assurance: The first rests on the promises of God, so that the believer is convinced in his heart that God will never leave him, and relying on this unconquerable conviction he stands up to Satan and sin, as one who is cheerful and undaunted. At the same time, however, remembering his own weakness, he falls back on God in fear and humility, and in his anxiety willingly commits himself to Him. This kind of assurance is a holy thing, and cannot be separated from faith," as John Calvin wisely counsels us.

What other types of assurance are expressed by *self*? Nonchalance, pride in what has been received and self-satisfaction with what one possesses, as if it were all one's own doing. Paul wants us to depend upon God, not upon men and not upon *self*. Paul wants us to be known for *The steadfastness of your faith in Christ* and to be *Rooted, and built up in him, and stablished in the faith, as ye have been taught, abounding therein with thanksgiving* [Col. 2:5, 7].

What other defects are exhibited by *self*? What about selfishness and self-centeredness? These maladies breed diseases causing untold trouble and many, many problems. Think of the offspring produced by these defects: jealousy, envy, malice, and hatred, and sensitivity to insults, slights, and being shunned. *Self* covets many things and as a result makes excessive demands. It becomes irritated and hurt when things do not go as planned or desired. It also produces quarrels, divisions, and unhappiness. These facts need to be faced, as well as the self-generated demands placed on one's self.

When enumerating the impediments generated by *self*, it should be accompanied by questions such as: why do these things happen to members of Christ's body? When accepting Christ and professing faith in Him, there should be a change in our lives, our attitude, our priorities, and our conversation (tenor of life). That is true, but we are still subject to *the wiles* (schemes) *of the devil*, to being tempted, and to denying our Lord. We need to recognize this and know the demands that self places on us. Therefore, we are to pray to God for the strength and power to concentrate on Him and to serve the Lord Jesus Christ.

What does Scripture say about *self*?

> *And these things, brethren, I have in a figure* (figuratively) *transferred to myself and to Apollos for your sakes; that ye might learn in us not to think of men above that which is written, that no one of you be puffed up* (proud) *for one against another.*

> *For who maketh thee* (distinguishes you) *to differ from another? and what hast thou that thou didst not receive? now if thou didst receive it, why dost thou glory, as if thou hadst not received it* [1 Cor. 4:6–7]?

Paul writes to the called out, the members of Christ's body. He wants them to work together and to realize that any gifts they possess were received from God.

St. Augustine provides an excellent exposition of this passage that each of us should earnestly contemplate, saying, "It is not nature nor heredity that implants any excellence in us, nor is it our own free will that enables us to procure any great talents, but it is God's mercy that bestows the gifts upon us." Therefore, how can we boast of the gifts we have received? Paul, under the influence of the Holy Spirit, states it concisely to the Corinthians,

> *And last of all he was seen of me also, as of one born out of due time.*
> *For I am the least of the apostles, that am not meet* (worthy) *to be called an apostle, because I persecuted the church of God.*
> *But by the grace of God I am what I am: and his grace which was bestowed upon me was not in vain; but I labored more abundantly than they all: yet not I, but the grace of God which was with me* [1 Cor. 15:8–10].

Paul attributes whatever contribution he was able to provide or make during his ministry to the grace of God working within him. Recall the change in Paul from one who had *self* in the forefront of his being to one who depended fully on the grace of God. After serving the Lord for many years, Paul wrote to the Corinthians,

> *LET a man so account* (consider) *of us, as of the ministers* (servants) *of Christ, and stewards of the mysteries* (hidden truths) *of God.*
> *Moreover it is required in stewards, that a man be found faithful.*
> *But with me it is a very small thing that I should be judged of you, or of man's judgment* (day): *yea, I judge not mine own self.*
> *For I know nothing by* (against) *myself; yet am I not hereby justified: but he that judgeth me is the Lord* [1 Cor. 4:1–4].

We are stewards, and we are to carry out our duties faithfully. Of course, the prime example of denying *self* and not allowing *self* to come between us and God comes from Scripture. Paul provides a beautiful description of denying self and serving God to the Philippians,

> *Let this mind be in you, which was also in Christ Jesus:*
> *Who, being in the form of God, thought it not robbery to be equal with God:*
> *But made himself of no reputation, and took upon him the form of a servant, and was made* (coming) *in the likeness of men:*
> *And being found in fashion* (appearance) *as a man, he humbled himself, and became obedient unto death, even the death of the cross* [Phil. 2:5–8].

Christ was called from His heavenly abode. He was with the Father, He was in the beginning, and through Him all things were made. Yet, He was called out. He received a new uniform and new instructions. He was obedient, faithful, and knowledgeable. He did the Father's will, He did not boast, He did not have pride, He did not desire pre-eminence. Why? Because, He came to serve His Father, no matter the cost.

With the Lord Jesus, *self* never came between Himself and the Father. He was and is God's co-worker. He is the epitome of the exhortation *whatsoever thy hand findeth to do, do it with thy might* [Eccl. 9:10].

Pray God that we follow in His footsteps as His co-workers.
Amen!

6

Things Appointed

And I answered, Who art thou, Lord? And he said unto me, I am Jesus of Nazareth, whom thou persecutest.
And they that were with me saw indeed the light, and were afraid; but they heard not the voice of him that spake to me.
And I said, What shall I do, Lord? And the Lord said unto me, Arise, and go into Damascus; and there it shall be told thee of all things which are appointed for thee to do [Acts 22:8–10].

Many things can be said about the Apostle Paul, but there were two things he focused upon after his conversion on the road to Damascus. First, he grabbed hold of the Lord Jesus Christ and would not let go. The Lord Jesus became his guiding light and his constant companion. With the other hand, he grabbed hold of life, of people living with their problems, their fears, their desires, their lack of faith, their weaknesses, their mindsets, and their self-centeredness. Paul never lost sight of these two guiding lights. He was the Lord's servant, and became a servant of the people with whom he came into contact.

How did Paul bring together these two factors? By proclaiming the Word and applying it to his daily living; by preaching, teaching, and pastoring to people from all walks of life with diverse gifts and capabilities; and by continually being aware of who he was and what he was called to do. Therefore, a question to ponder is, "Are you constantly aware of who you are and what you are to do?"

Each of us knows our given names and our family names. Have you ever realized that both Paul and Peter received their given names from the Lord? Therefore, day in and day out they were aware, or should have been, regarding who called them and named them.

What difference would it make if we were constantly reminded that we are members of God's family and Christ's body? If we were living in constant touch with our Father and the Head of the body, would it have an impact upon our thoughts, words, actions, and conduct? Would we realize that the Bible stresses a right relationship to God, not a moral code? Would we be more concerned about what we said and how we acted if we realized as we walk or drive that it is just the same as walking along the road to Emmaus and that the same Lord goes with us who went with those two men?

Recall that Jesus said to Peter, *Follow me*. What does this mean? It does not mean just to tag along or to be like the dog following his master on a walk. The Greek word means to be a follower who develops a union, a likeness, and a way about him or her that is the same as that which is found in the One they are going to follow. When Jesus called Peter, He began preparing him for the violent death he would endure at a later time. As Calvin points out, Christ said "that Peter may obey God more willingly when He calls him to the cross [since] Christ offers Himself as the leader."

It is highly improbable that any of us will be crucified as was Peter, but we are called to follow Christ, to become like Him, to have union with Him, and to accept His ways. We are to obey His commandments, no matter what conditions or opposition we may encounter. We are not to be politically correct, but we are to be Christ-correct.

Why? Because He first called us, He first loved us, and He gave Himself for us. When we love Him in response, we willingly obey His commands as we come to know them.

John Leith says something very meaningful, revealing, and truthful about love, "Whenever a person falls in love—that is, if he or she loves very deeply—there is always something in the life of the person loved that reaches out and elicits love. You simply do not fall in love by making up your mind that you are going to fall in love. There is always something about the person loved that calls forth love. And yet love is called forth in such a way as to do violence to our own will. We live freely. In fact, we are never so free as when we do the will of the person whom we love. But love can never be explained in terms of our own will." Pray God that we may love Him as He wants us to love Him.

We should remember what transpired on the road to Damascus. We should learn from it, because those truths apply to each and every one of us. Remember what Paul said after the Lord had spoken to him. He asked, *Lord, what wilt thou have me to do* [Acts 9:6]? Oh, that we would ask the same question, then listen and seek an answer. And if only when people first hear the call to come to church, they would ask the same question. Paul makes the appropriate start by inquiring as to what the Lord wants him to do.

The Lord Jesus tells him three things, and they apply to each of us. First, *Arise*. Therefore, we are to get up and to go in faith. Next, *Go into Damascus*. There are places for us to go, but they should be designated by the Lord Himself. Third, *And there it shall be told thee of all things which are appointed for thee to do* [Acts 22:10]. Scripture tells us the things we are to do. However, we are to listen and then go do them. We are neither to ignore them, nor to reject them.

You have to appreciate the circumstances surrounding this event on the road to Damascus and the instructions given to Paul. Here is this man who only hours before was . . . *breathing out threatenings and slaughter* (murder) *against the disciples of the Lord*, . . . [Acts 9:1] who was overly confident in his mind, his capabilities, and his achievements, who possessed tremendous gifts, but misused them, and who was self-centered with a definite mindset, and what happens? He is told to find out what has been appointed for him. That boggles one's mind!

What may we learn from this encounter? When we come to Christ, sooner or later we must ask the personal question, *Lord, what wilt thou have me to do* [Acts 9:6]? Note all the words. They are to be asked openly and willingly of the Lord Jesus.

I doubt Paul would have listened to Ananias before he left Jerusalem. After receiving the command from the Lord Jesus, he was willing to hear the Word and to receive instructions from a devout man who realized the presence and claims of God. "We are not to be unwilling to hear Him [Christ] speaking by the tongue of men," as John Calvin admonishes us.

Third, and this is most enlightening, Paul was blind until he submitted himself as a beginner in the faith, as one needing to learn.

When we first come to Christ we have some of Saul in us and some of Peter the fisherman in us. We are to become individuals who *put off . . . the old man, . . . and put on the new man, which after God is created in righteousness and true holiness* [Eph. 4:22, 24].

God has appointed things for us to know and to do. Pray God that we may be blessed with some of the humility bestowed on Paul and

Peter, so that we may learn what has been appointed for us. It is important to know the will of God, not what we think about God or what other people think about Him, but what is God's will as revealed in His Son, Christ Jesus. What are we to learn and to do? *That ye may be able to stand against the wiles* (schemes) *of the devil* [Eph. 6:11] as you proceed along your daily path and perform your allotted tasks.

This means that our conduct and behavior are to reflect the fact that God is our Father and Christ is the Head of our body. We are to remember, as James says, *Faith without works is dead* [Jas. 2:26]. "Faith is not merely an intellectual assent; it involves the whole personality. It not only involves the mind, but the heart, the will and therefore every aspect of practice and behavior," as revealed through the wisdom of Martyn Lloyd-Jones by the grace of God. The whole person is involved in faith, not just the intellect. *Show me thy faith without thy works, and I will show thee my faith by my works* [Jas. 2:18].

God's children, of all ages, are to acquire knowledge from the Word of God, and apply it to their daily living. This is the initial phase in increasing and strengthening one's faith. However the ultimate challenge is to obey unambiguously the commands contained in both the Old and New Testaments. Obedience is the hallmark of Christ's followers.

> *But be ye doers of the word, and not hearers only, deceiving your own selves.*
> *For if any be a hearer of the word, and not a doer, he is like unto a man beholding* (observing) *his natural face in a glass* (mirror):
> *For he beholdeth himself, and goeth his way, and straitway forgetteth what manner of man he was* [Jas. 1:22–24].

We are to be like Peter and Andrew when the Lord Jesus said, *Follow me, and I will make you fishers of men* [Matt. 4:19]. And like Paul after the Lord Jesus said, *It shall be told thee of all things which are appointed for thee to do* [Acts 22:10].

We are to obey the truths revealed by the Lord Jesus as well as those contained in the entire Word of God. It all emanated from our heavenly Father. When hearing the Word of God in a sermon or lesson, we are to put it into practice, not ignore it. We are to remember it is the Word of God, and it is to be obeyed. It is not merely an intellectual faith to observe or acknowledge. Our faith is to be exhibited seven days a week in the home, the shop, the market, the playing fields, and wherever we are called to be.

Of course, this means disciplining ourselves. Even though we are under grace we cannot do as we please. We should remember that we belong to Christ's body. Therefore, we have a responsibility to learn and to practice Christ's teachings as revealed in the New Testament. How can we do this? By the power of the Holy Spirit!

How do we grow in grace? By knowing the Word of God and the will of the Father, obeying His commandments, spending time in prayer, and abiding by the Master's teachings. We are to do those things appointed for us. Peter states it very well, saying,

> *. . . because Christ also suffered for us, leaving us an example, that ye should follow his steps:*
> WHO DID NO SIN, NEITHER WAS GUILE (DECEIT) FOUND IN HIS MOUTH:
> *Who, when he was reviled, reviled not again* (in return); *when he suffered, he threatened not; but committed himself to him that judgeth righteously* [1 Pet. 2:21-23].

Christ committed himself to doing the will of His Father. Peter amplifies upon this, saying,

> *Dearly beloved, I beseech you as strangers and pilgrims, abstain from fleshly lusts, which war against the soul;*
> *Having your conversation* (conduct) *honest* (honorable) *among the Gentiles: that, whereas they speak against you as evildoers, they may by your good works, which they shall behold, glorify God in the day of visitation* [1 Pet. 2:11-12].

We are to realize that the world is judging God Himself by what they see in us, just as people judge a mother or father by what they see in a daughter or son. Admonitions are given not just for the times we are assembled together in a class or in worship, or for the times we are alone. They are given for the times spent in the market place, the business world, social activities, and wherever we go. Consider the following:

> *Take heed to yourselves, lest . . . your hearts be overcharged* (weighed down) *with* (the) *cares of this life* [Luke 21:34].

> *Be ye not unequally yoked together with unbelievers: for what fellowship* (in common) *hath righteousness with unrighteousness* (lawlessness)?
> *What part hath he that believeth with an infidel?;*
> BE YE SEPARATE, *saith the Lord,* AND TOUCH NOT THE UNCLEAN THING; AND I WILL RECEIVE YOU [2 Cor. 6:14-15, 17].

These are specific commands to follow and to practice.

Christ and the New Testament writers were cognizant that although the saints and faithful had responsibilities outside their immediate fellowship, that they were also subject to peer pressures and temptations. That is why the Lord Jesus said to Peter, *Watch and pray, that ye enter not into temptation: the spirit indeed is willing, but the flesh is weak* [Matt. 26:41]. There are other everyday occurrences that contribute to following Christ and doing the appointed things, or rejecting them. Paul describes some of these things in writing to Timothy,

> *For the love of money is the root of all* (kinds of) *evil: . . . they have erred from the faith, and pierced themselves through with many sorrows.*
> *But thou, O man of God, flee these things; and follow after righteousness, godliness, faith, love, patience, meekness.*
> *Fight the good fight of faith, lay hold on eternal life, . . .*
> [1 Tim. 6:10–12].

Scripture says do not lust for money. Why? Because coveting it causes some to err from the faith. "From avarice there can come the greatest evil of all—apostasy from the faith," as Calvin stated with heartfelt kindness. Paul exhorts us to establish the proper priorities, stating unequivocally *follow after righteousness, godliness, faith, love, patience, meekness*. Note the order. First, a right relationship with God, then putting on His faithfulness, His truthfulness, and fulfilling His nature and His promises. Righteousness means knowing and obeying God's commands, and conforming to His revealed will. Then follows: *godliness, faith, love, patience, meekness*.

These attributes strengthen us in the times of adversity and enable us to repel the attacks of Satan by doing the things appointed by the Master. Therefore, we are to rejoice in our relationship with Him, knowing that His strength enables us to do His will. Paul realized the difficulties besetting Timothy (and surrounding us). Therefore, he exhorts us to *Fight the good fight of faith* and *lay hold on eternal life*. "By telling them to lay hold upon it, he forbids them to give up or to grow weary in midcourse . . . Nothing has been achieved until we have obtained the future life to which God invites us," according to John Calvin in words that should compel us to forge forward in our life with Christ, despite any obstacles, until we meet Him face-to-face on that glorious day.

How can we follow Him and do the appointed things? First, lay hold of the Word and the truths contained in it. Peter says, *Dearly beloved, I beseech you as strangers and pilgrims, abstain from fleshly lusts, which war against the soul* [1 Pet. 2:11]. Paul says, *For our conversation* (citizenship) *is in heaven, from whence also we look for the Saviour, the Lord Jesus Christ* [Phil. 3:20].

Second, realize Christ's body is not divided. There is not a religious elect, elite, privileged group, or a laity. We are all saints and the faithful. John says, *Beloved, now are we the sons* (children) *of God, and it doth not yet appear what we shall be: but we know that, when he shall appear, we shall be like him; for we shall see him as he is* [1 John 3:2].

Third, temptations come in different ways and attack us where we are most vulnerable. It is also profitable to remember, *Wherefore let him that thinketh he standeth take heed lest he fall* [1 Cor. 10:12]. *Walk in the Spirit, and ye shall not fulfill the lust of the flesh* [Gal. 5:16]. Then there are John's powerful words, *If we say we have fellowship with him, and walk in darkness, we lie, and do not* (practice) *the truth* [1 John 1:6]. Those are strong words, they tell it like it is, they give us the message loud and clear.

Also, bear in mind these other words by John. *If we confess our sins, he is faithful and just to forgive us our sins, and to cleanse us from all unrighteousness* [1 John 1:9]. *Ye are of God, little children, and have overcome them: because greater is he that is in you, than he that is in the world* [1 John 4:4].

"The Holy Spirit is in you. God takes up His abode in you . . . We are not left to ourselves," as beautifully described by Martyn Lloyd-Jones.

Therefore, we are to continuously thank God for His mercy and grace and for the Holy Spirit who strengthens us, so that we may do *all things which are appointed for thee to do* so that we *may be able to stand against the wiles* (schemes) *of the devil*.

Amen!

7

The Battle Call

> *Wherefore take (up) unto you the whole armor of God, that ye may be able to withstand in the evil day, and having done all, to stand* [Eph. 6:13].

The Apostle Paul, that great servant of the Lord Jesus Christ, was interested in presenting the Gospel to anyone who would listen. He is noted for his usage of *contrasts* in presenting the Word of God.

First, there is a contrast in his life, conduct, and attitude before beginning that fateful journey to Damascus compared to his disposition and demeanor after hearing from Ananias as to what was appointed for him to do.

Second, there was a contrast in his service. He had previously served the Sanhedrin, the high priest, the Pharisaic Law, and the customs prevalent in that day. After the Damascus Road encounter, he served the Lord Jesus Christ and God the Father, studied the teachings of the Master and was obedient to them.

Third, there was a contrast in his writings. Nowhere is this more evident than in Ephesians. He begins this letter in a manner we all love to hear, calling us the saints and faithful in Christ Jesus and saying grace and peace be unto you *from God our Father, and from the Lord Jesus Christ.* Then, he adds those beautiful and comforting words, *who hath blessed us with all spiritual blessings in heavenly places in Christ* [Eph. 1:2–3]. What meaningful words and thoughts! How comforting, and how true!

What more could we ask than to be one of the saints and faithful, to receive grace and peace, and to be blessed with all spiritual blessings? You cannot argue with those things. It sounds so easy, delightful, and enjoyable. What more could we ask? It has been done for us.

Then comes the contrast in the final verses of this Epistle. Listen, you saints and faithful. You've got to stand *strong in the Lord, and in the power of his might* [Eph. 6:10].

Who me? Wait a minute, that is not the tune you were playing earlier. You have to *put on the whole armor of God.*

You have a continuing battle to fight. You have to choose sides. You have to be prepared to contend against adversaries. That is not what I expected. I thought if I was blessed, had received peace and grace, and was a faithful saint according to my standards that I would not have to contend against powers and principalities, darkness, and spiritual wickedness, but that I could do my own thing. Now you are telling me that I have to work, to fight, to train, to discipline myself, and to prepare for battle.

In addition, there are things you have to do to stand on God's side. For example, you are going to have to learn to use God's armor rather than yours. You may have thought your armor was sufficient, and maybe it has been, but remember, Paul thought the same thing prior to starting down the road to Damascus. There comes a time when we, like Paul, must ask, *Lord, what wilt thou have me to do?*

So what do you have to learn? You are to girt your loins about with the truth, not just any truth, but the truth of God as revealed in Christ Jesus.

Then put on that breastplate of righteousness. You are to keep it shiny and in good repair. Most importantly, you are to confidently depend upon it to keep you from harm, and you are to use it to serve the Lord.

Next, you are to have *your feet shod with the preparation of the gospel of peace* [Eph. 6:15]. Why put this on your feet? Because they carry you wherever you go in your daily activities.

Also, you are to *take the helmet of salvation, and the sword of the Spirit, which is the word of God* [Eph. 6:17]. A natural question is, "How am I going to do that?" You are going to do it by learning, studying, praying, and practicing. By knowing God's way.

When putting on and using God's armor you have other things to do. You are to pray in the Spirit. This requires knowledge and practice. In addition to praying, you are to be watching, you are to be alert, and you are to be aware. You have responsibilities to discharge.

God provides the armor, but we have to put it on and use it. It is not done for us. Therefore, we are to learn more about the whole armor of God, and we are to practice using it. Yes, we are the saints and the faithful, and yes, we receive grace and peace and spiritual blessings, but also we receive a call to battle. We need to resurrect "Onward, Christian Soldiers" by Sabine Baring-Gould because there is a dangerous foe seeking to devour us. Listen to how that magnificent hymn speaks to us who are Christ's soldiers.

Onward, Christian soldiers, Marching as to war,
With the cross of Jesus, Going on before:
Christ the Royal Master Leads against the foe;
Forward into battle, see, His banners go.

Refrain: Onward, Christian soldiers, Marching as to war,
With the cross of Jesus, Going on before.

Like a mighty army Moves the Church of God;
Brothers we are treading Where the saints have trod;
We are not divided, All one body we,
One in hope and doctrine, One in charity.

Refrain

Crowns and thrones may perish, Kingdoms rise and wane,
But the Church of Jesus Constant will remain;
Gates of hell can never 'Gainst that Church prevail;
We have Christ's own promise, And that cannot fail.

Refrain

Onward, then, ye people, Join our happy throng,
Blend with ours your voices In the triumph song;
Glory, laud, and honor Unto Christ the King;
This through countless ages Men and angels sing.

Refrain

What does all this have to do with us? Those claiming to be members of Christ's body are to grasp and to understand the teachings contained in this Epistle and other books in both the Old and New Testaments. Remember to whom these letters were written. They were sent to the saints and the faithful. They have been preserved for us. They were not written to those outside the body of Christ who do not understand the teachings contained therein, nor written to those who do not believe in a spiritual realm, nor to those who do not believe in God, the Lord Jesus Christ, and the Holy Spirit.

Why do we go to class and church, and read Scripture? To learn, to worship, to be in a right relationship with Christ. May I suggest another reason for so doing? Because we need help. We realize the difficulty of living the Christian life, of serving the Master, and at the same time participating in everyday events and tasks. The New Testament believers had to deal with nonbelievers. They had to make choices. They had to withstand pressures. They had to associate with people for whom they did not care.

Paul identifies the blessings we have received, yet at the same time forewarns and forearms us. He wants to prepare us for the opposition we will encounter. He wants us to know that following Christ is not easy, that all the problems of life will not disappear. The New Testament Epistles were written not to tell us how to live a life of ease, but how to withstand the pressures, subtleties, disappointments, defeats, and failures of life and to be *more than conquerors* in Christ.

What does the Apostle tell us to do? Two things, and they go together like ham and eggs or peanut butter and jelly. First, *be strong in the Lord and in the power of his might* and second, *Put on the whole armor of God*. Note what comes first, the Lord and His power, and second, *Put on the whole armor of God*.

We must be aware of the relationship between these two exhortations and make sure they are considered together. Some people say, "All you have to do is hand it over to the Lord, and rely on His strength." Others say, "We can put on this armor when we will and handle the situation." The former do not concern themselves with the whole armor of God, while the latter are not dependent upon being *strong in the Lord, and in the power of his might*.

Why did the Holy Spirit guide Paul to write these enlightening words? Paul mixed and mingled with people. He listened to them and their concerns. He was not only a preacher and teacher, he was a pastor, and he visited from house to house. He had challenges, conflicts, rejections, temptations, and confrontations with *the wiles* (schemes) *of the devil*. However, most importantly, he knew the Lord Jesus Christ. Therefore, when beginning to draw this great letter to a conclusion he says, *Be strong in the Lord, and in the power of his might* [Eph. 6:10].

This is not a verse to be repeated every day as a form of psychology or as an urging to be better and better every day in every way. It is not something by which we are to pump ourselves up and persuade ourselves that everything is coming up roses. We need to realize that God and the Lord Jesus Christ never try to fool us, they never try to get us to think that things are different from what they really are, and they do not want us built up to a high for one day or one event. They are interested in the long haul.

We are not to abuse Scripture, or sing hymns lightheartedly, or feel better temporarily. We are to know Scripture and understand it. We are to apply it to our everyday living, to the temptations, confrontations, and disappointments that come our way, and we are to realize the power of the forces arrayed against us. Peter stresses to the first century Christians and to us, *Your adversary the devil, as a roaring lion, walketh about, seeking whom he may devour* [1 Pet. 5:8]. Scripture is to become part of our being and everyday living.

What other reasons are there for standing and withstanding in the evil day? It is neither because of international issues or developments that occur in other places and to other people, nor is it because confusion exists among the church at large or among the leadership of the different denominations. We need *the power of his might* in our daily lives and in the events we encounter each and every day. We need it in the so-called little things of life, which also exhibit our witness to Him and for Him.

We need to *be strong in the Lord* so that we will not fail in life or in responding to His call to live as members of His body. Yes, we may stumble and fall or make mistakes, but we are not to become miserable and unhappy members of Christ's body. We are members of God's family, and we are to be strong members. We are to discharge our duties and responsibilities accordingly. They are to be performed in *the power of his might* and in obedience to His commands. They are to be done for the Lord. When we pour out our life's energy for Him, He fills us with *the power of his might*. You can never tell what impact it will have on others when He does. However, it enables us to stand and to withstand.

One reason for coming to the Lord Jesus Christ is that we have weaknesses and need *the power of his might*. It is wonderful when we can admit that we do not have the resources or strength to carry the day and can go to God in weakness and faith. What poignant words Paul addressed to the Corinthians regarding personal difficulties and weaknesses when he confessed to them,

> *And lest I should be exalted above measure through the abundance of the revelations, there was given to me a thorn in the flesh, the messenger of Satan to buffet* (beat) *me, lest I should be exalted above measure.*
>
> *For this thing I besought* (pleaded with) *the Lord thrice, that it might depart from me.*
>
> *And he said unto me, My grace is sufficient for thee: for my strength* (power) *is made perfect in weakness. Most gladly therefore will I rather glory in my infirmities* (weaknesses), *that the power of Christ may rest upon me.*
>
> *Therefore, I take pleasure in infirmities, in reproaches, in necessities, in persecutions, in distresses for Christ's sake: for when I am weak, then am I strong* [2 Cor. 12:7–10].

The Apostle Paul faced much opposition. He had a thorn in the flesh and believed that Satan sent a messenger to buffet him. There is much speculation as to what the thorn may have been. Was it temptations from Satan or the opposition that continually plagued Paul as he continued on his missionary trips? Was it a bodily ailment that kept recurring or a problem with his vision? The exact cause of the thorn is not known and will not be known in this life. However, what is known is that Paul upon hearing from the Lord Jesus was able to deal with the problem effectively.

Paul recognized that when he was tempted or attacked it was Satan's doing. "Thus at every touch of temptation we should rouse ourselves and quickly put on our armor to drive back Satan's attacks," as Calvin wisely admonishes the true believers. The Apostle realized two things as to why we learn slowly. First, the Word of God comes through people like Ananias, who told Paul what was appointed for him to do, and second, Satan sends messengers to the members of Christ's body through people.

When Paul says he was buffeted, he means that he suffered a severe indignity. Though he had been beaten or was suffering from an infirmity and was ashamed, he learned humility. Paul was subject to many indignities. Many of us have experienced embarrassments or have been ashamed of some word expressed or deed committed. Undoubtedly Paul was concerned about this and had sought an answer from God. Augustine helps illuminate this matter, saying, "For this should be borne in mind . . . , for if they have defects mixed with their virtues, if they are persecuted out of hatred, if they are attacked with curses, these are not merely the rods of their heavenly instructor, but the buffetings which are designed to restrain all haughtiness and fill them with modesty. Therefore, let all godly men take note. What a dreadful poison pride is, so that the only antidote to it is another poison." These words of Augustine are to be taken to heart and to become fixed in our minds.

Augustine also provides additional understanding and asks a pertinent question with the following words: "The Apostle Paul had the thorn in the flesh, he was opposed, rejected and buffeted. He besought the Lord three times in prayer. What answer did he receive?" The Lord Jesus said, *My grace is sufficient for thee: for my strength* (power) *is made perfect in weakness* [2 Cor. 12:9]. Was that the answer Paul wanted? I doubt it. What did Paul say? *Most gladly therefore will I rather glory in my infirmities* (weaknesses), *that the power of Christ may rest upon me* [2 Cor. 12:9].

A person's pride may keep him or her from seeking or receiving His grace, peace, and spiritual blessings. "We make room for Christ's grace when with a resigned mind we feel and confess our own weakness," as wisely stated by John Calvin. Therefore, Paul says he will most gladly glory in his infirmities because through them he will receive the grace of the Lord Jesus Christ. Please note, he does not boast about them, but glories in them.

We cannot overlook the last verse of this section where Paul says, *Therefore, I take pleasure in infirmities, in necessities, in persecutions, in distresses for Christ's sake* [2 Cor. 12:10]. "When a person truly desires to be strong, he must not also refuse to be weak," as properly expressed in the wisdom of John Calvin. When a person recognizes that he or she is weak in their own right then they may become *strong in the Lord, and in the power of his might*.

This is in contrast to many teachings of the last century. However, we should remember that "The greatest saints have always testified to the fierceness of the battle, to their own weakness, to their own inability," as affirmed and declared by Martyn Lloyd-Jones. Certainly each of us can say along with Paul, *For the good that I would* (want to do) *I do not: but the evil which I would not, that I do* [Rom. 7:19].

When people accept Christ, they become new creatures. They may say they are going to change and conform to the teachings contained in Scripture and that they are going to do it under their own power. It cannot be done! No, it cannot be done! It can be done only through God's power. Think. The Apostle Paul has described in some detail how we are to live from Ephesians 4:1 through Ephesians 6:9. Then he says very appropriately, *Finally, my brethren, be strong in the Lord, and in the power of his might* [Eph. 6:10].

He knew that the first priority was to live as Christ would have him to live. Can we know less? It requires knowing Him, studying about Him, placing our confidence in Him, meditating about Him, reading about Him, opening our hearts and minds to His way, and recognizing our weaknesses.

Much has been given to us, as is noted in the opening verses of Paul's letter to the Ephesians. However, much is required of us, as is identified in the closing verses of this letter. We are not called to a life of ease, but to one of service and righteousness. We are to be in a right relationship with God, the Lord Jesus Christ, the Holy Spirit, our neighbors, and ourselves.

May we remember the contrast that the Lord Jesus said to the Apostle Paul, *My grace is sufficient for thee: for my strength* (power) *is made perfect in weakness*. May we apply it, and may it help us understand to *be strong in the Lord, and in the power of his might* [Eph. 6:10].

Amen!

8

A Divine Visit

> *Jesus saith unto her, Mary. She turned herself, and saith unto him, Rabboni; which is to say, Master.*
> *Jesus saith unto her, Touch* (Do not cling to me) *me not; for I am not yet ascended to my Father: but go to my brethren, and say unto them, I ascend unto my Father, and your Father; and to my God, and your God.*
> *Mary Magdalene came and told the disciples that she had seen the Lord, and that he had spoken these things unto her*
> [John 20:16–18].

Paul appropriately begins the closing section of this letter with the exhortation, *Finally, my brethren, be strong in the Lord, and in the power of his might*. There is one prayer that I have that the Lord Jesus Christ will reveal Himself to each and every one of us, and that by the power of the Holy Spirit we may come to know Him in a most intimate, confident, understanding, trusting, loving, serving, and obedient way. We are to seek, yet we are to be open to hear, to see, to ask, and to listen.

Think of two events. First, Mary Magdalene went to the sepulcher and saw that *The stone was taken away*. She ran to tell Peter and John. The three of them returned to the sepulcher. Peter and John looked and left. What about Mary? She stayed, she waited, she wanted to know where the Lord was, and she wanted to be with Him. Her focus was on the Lord Jesus, not herself. What happened? He revealed Himself to her. Note, she did not find Him, He found her.

Second, consider the two men on the road to Emmaus. What were they doing as they walked toward their home? They were talking about the Lord Jesus. They had gone to the sepulcher. They were returning home. Then what happened? Jesus visited them and they listened to Him as He expounded the scriptures. They invited Him in, they did not want Him to leave, and they did not rush to other things. What happened? Their eyes were opened. Note what they said after Jesus left, *Did not our heart burn within us, while he talked with us by the way, and while he opened to us the scriptures* [Luke 24:32]? Then according to Scripture, after Jesus left they returned to Jerusalem during the same hour in order to tell the eleven disciples who were gathered together.

What did Mary and the two men receive? *A divine visit.* The Lord revealed Himself to them. They became aware not only of the presence of the Master, but of the power and authority of God. If we want the Lord to visit us, if we want to walk with Him and to be aware of His presence, then there are things we must do and things we must not do. We are to provide time for the Word, for it is through the Word that God reveals Himself.

What is revealed to us? *A divine visit.* The Holy Spirit will visit us. But He comes according to God's plan and pleasure, not in response to our demands or our timetable. John Leith states it forcefully and simply, "The Holy Spirit is God personally at work in the world . . . The Holy Spirit is God personally at work to inspire, to make alive, to convince, to enable Christians to speak and act as Christians.

"The Holy Spirit unites Jesus Christ with His work and our salvation. It is not enough to know Him as an objective historical person and to know what He has done for us unless we also know that He is in us, not substantially, but in a personal union." The Lord Jesus commanded the disciples after His resurrection . . . *that they should not depart from Jerusalem, but wait for the promise of the Father, which . . . ye have heard of me* [Acts 1:4]. Then He added, *But ye shall receive power, after that* (when) *the Holy Ghost is come upon you: and ye shall be witnesses unto me . . . unto the uttermost part of the earth* [Acts 1:8]. May we have the capacity to wait and to receive *a divine visit.* May we realize the Lord Jesus wants to unite with us, but it is on His terms, not ours.

These portions of Scripture should help us understand Paul's exhortation *To be strong in the Lord, and in the power of his might* [Eph. 6:10]. Paul urges us to do this after saying,

- *Walk worthy of the vocation wherewith ye are called;*
- *Keep the unity of the Spirit;*
- *Come in the unity of the faith and of the knowledge of the Son of God;*

- *Put on the new man;*
- *Be ye followers of God;*
- *Be filled with the Spirit; and*
- *Submitting yourselves one to another in the fear of God.*

[Selections from Ephesians Chapters 4 and 5]

Paul knew that the saints and the faithful were in Christ, but that they also labored in the world and were susceptible to its pressures.

Why should we *be strong in the Lord, and in the power of his might* [Eph. 6:10]? Probably the best explanation is provided by Calvin who said, "If the Lord aids us by His extraordinary power, we have no reason to be irresolute in battle." Further, Calvin encourages, enlightens, and counsels them with the following strong words, "He exhorts them (the faithful) to courage, but then reminds them to ask from God a supply of what in themselves they lack; and at the same time promise that, if they ask for it, the power of God will be displayed."

May we ask for what we lack? Think what that means. We have to acknowledge our weaknesses, our insufficiencies, our needs. That can be very difficult. However, we are to be confident that God will provide His power. Remember those comforting words, *My grace is sufficient for thee; for my strength* (power) *is made perfect in weakness* [2 Cor. 12:9].

Some questions need to be asked. Why is there this call to battle, to put on the whole armor of God, to be strong in the Lord? Why is there this emphasis on power and might? Why the emphasis on peace and love? What are we required to do? If we are going to obey the Lord's commands, then we need His strength, His power, and His might. The author of Hebrews tells us that Christ is *the captain* (author) *of their salvation* [Heb. 2:10]. A captain is a leader in the armed forces. He is the one to follow and to obey.

One fact to realize is that salvation is God's plan, not ours. If we are participating in it then we should follow the commands of the Captain. He is the one who decides what is to be done. We not only receive our orders from Him, but He prepares and guides us. And, He provides the necessary strength.

There is something else to realize about the struggles we face as we journey through life. The renowned pastor/preacher, Martyn Lloyd-Jones, clarifies this issue in his own inimitable fashion, by casting a positive light on it and enabling us to understand from "whence cometh our help," and that "This is God's battle, we are given the privilege of being in it and of fighting as individual soldiers, but God's honor is involved in it all . . . His glory, and His honor are involved at every point! Be strong in the Lord, remember that He is there and it is His battle." Further, "the whole movement of salvation is for God's glory; not simply for our deliverance, but for God's glory primarily."

How does God strengthen us and provide the power and might for His faithful soldiers? The psalmist provides insight to answering this question, saying, *The angel of the Lord encampeth round about them that fear him, and delivereth them* [Ps. 34:7]. We may think we are by ourselves, or on our own, but the angel of the Lord is *round about*. Again the psalmist says, *HE that dwelleth in the secret place of the Most High shall abide under the shadow of the Almighty* [Ps. 91:1]. Jesus says, *No man is able to pluck* (snatch) *them out of my Father's hand* [John 10:29]. This is true of the members of Christ's body. The Lord is strong. He is almighty, and He keeps His own. Paul states it clearly and concisely,

> *For I am persuaded, that neither death, nor life, nor angels, nor principalities, nor powers, nor things present, nor things to come,*
> *Nor height, nor depth, nor any other creature, shall be able to separate us from the love of God, which is in Christ Jesus our Lord* [Rom. 8:38–39].

Why is this true? Because if there were something that could separate us, then God would not be the God of the universe, nor God omnipotent! It would mean that God could be defeated, and that is not true! Peter says that the members of Christ's body are those *Who are kept by the power of God through faith unto salvation ready to be revealed in the last time* [1 Pet. 1:5]. Of course, we cannot overlook the Apostle Paul saying, *But God, who is rich in mercy, for His great love wherewith he loved us, Even when we were dead in sins, hath quickened us* (made us alive) *together with Christ* [Eph. 2:4–5].

Think about that! God quickens us by His power. After He does that, He continues to abide with us and to watch over us. That is a great, heartwarming truth. Paul prays that, *The eyes of your understanding being enlightened; that ye may know what is the hope of his calling, and what* (are) *the riches of the glory of his inheritance in the saints, And what is the exceeding greatness of his power to us-ward who believe, according to the working of his mighty power* [Eph. 1:18–19].

Paul also says, *Whereunto I also labor, striving according to his working, which worketh in me mightily* [Col. 1:29]. Calvin interprets this statement as an acknowledgement by Paul "that the power of God shines forth in His ministry" and makes possible the works that He is performing.

An illuminating verse is, *For our gospel came not unto you in word only, but also in power, and in the Holy Ghost, and in much assurance* [1 Thess. 1:5]. The power in this verse refers to the *spiritual power of doctrine*. It is God who makes it possible. These verses and others reveal that the power and might of the Lord as well as His strength are important ingredients in our relationship with the Lord Jesus Christ. Then there are those wonderful words of Jesus, *And I will pray the Father, and he shall give you another Comforter* (Paraclete), *that He may abide with you forever; . . . for he dwelleth with you, and shall be in you* [John 14:16-17].

Throughout the scriptures, the Word of God keeps telling us that He is round about us and that His strength, power, and might are available. Further, He will support us and help us. It does not say that He will do it all, nor that we can do it all on our own power and strength. These words need to be taken to heart.

Why bring these things to your attention? Since the latter part of the nineteenth century there has been a teaching that says, "Hand it over to the Lord," and then there was Norman Vincent Peale's book "Let Go and Let God." Yes, there are things that only God can do. But I cannot find any place where Scripture says, "Hand it over, let go, let God, let Him do it, do not struggle, it is simple, it is easy, retire, you do not have to do anything." Or, "The Lord will do it, go your own way, or as others say surrender yourself to the Lord and He will do it, or abide in the Lord, and be baggage that He carries along." God the Father and the Lord Jesus provide us with numerous commands we are to obey, but not one of them says we can retire, take it easy, or do nothing.

As we have just seen, the Master said simply yet meaningfully, *That he may abide with you forever . . . for he dwelleth with you and shall be in you* [John 14:16–17]. These teachings need to be addressed according to what Scripture says. Therefore, let us take a brief journey through the New Testament. James says, *Resist the devil, and he will flee from you* [Jas. 4:7]. Please note that you are to resist. James does not say, "hand it over," or "look to the Lord and He will resist the devil for you." He says, "you are to resist." You are to do it.

Peter says, *Be sober* (watchful), *be vigilant; because your adversary the devil, as a roaring lion, walketh about, seeking whom he may devour: Whom resist steadfast in the faith* [1 Pet. 5:8-9]. We are exhorted to watch, to be vigilant, and to resist, steadfast in the faith. We are not to turn it over to the Lord or to let go and let God. *For if ye live after the flesh, ye shall die: but if ye through the Spirit do mortify* (put to death) *the deeds of the body, ye shall live* [Rom. 8:13]. What does that mean? You have to do it *through the Spirit*. You do not let go and let God do it. Paul says to the Philippians, *Work out your own salvation with fear and trembling* [Phil. 2:12]. We have to work it out ourselves. It is not done for us. Pray God that this Word may reach those who go along their merry little way and think it does not make any difference what they do or do not do.

Paul says to Timothy, *. . . be strong in the grace that is in Christ Jesus* [2 Tim. 2:1]. Also, *. . . follow after righteousness, godliness, faith, love, patience, meekness. Fight the good fight of faith, lay hold on eternal life* [1 Tim. 6:11-12]. The Apostle tells Timothy what he must do. He does not say "Hand it over," or "Lay back, it will be done for you." No, he tells him what he must do. We are to remember what Scripture tells us to do and then do it.

Paul says to the Ephesians (and us), *Take unto you* (take up) *the whole armor of God, that ye may be able to withstand in the evil day, and having done all, to stand* [Eph. 6:13]. Again, note what we have to do. *Watch ye, stand fast in the faith, quit you* (be brave) *like men, be strong* [1 Cor. 16:13]. *I therefore so run, not as uncertainly; so fight I, not as one that beateth the air: But I keep under* (discipline) *my body, and bring it into subjection* [1 Cor. 9:26-27]. Paul tells them that they are not spectators when they are members of Christ's body. They are participants. They run, and they fight, because they are in a constant battle with Satan, the evil one.

Paul further counsels us with these meaningful words,

> *That I may know him, and the power of his resurrection, and the fellowship of his sufferings, being made conformable unto his death;*
>
> *If by any means I might attain* (arrive at) *unto the resurrection of the dead.*
>
> *Not as though I had already attained, either were already perfect: but I follow after, if that I may apprehend that for which also I am apprehended of Christ Jesus.*

> Brethren, I count not myself to have apprehended: but this one thing I do, forgetting those things which are behind, and reaching forth unto those things which are before,
>
> I press toward the mark for the prize of the high calling of God in Christ Jesus [Phil. 3:10–14].

The Apostle says in these few poignant verses that we are to:

- *Mortify the deeds of the body;*
- *Work out our own salvation;*
- *Be strong . . . in Christ Jesus;*
- *Fight the good fight of faith;*
- *Take unto you the whole armor of God;*
- *Withstand in the evil day;*
- *Stand fast in the faith;*
- *That I may know . . . the power of His resurrection and the fellowship of His sufferings;* and
- *I press toward the mark . . . of the high calling of God in Christ Jesus.*

What powerful statements! What requirements for Christ's followers! What demands they place on those claiming to be Christians!

These are examples of what we must do. We must exert the effort, but the strength, power, and might come from the Lord. This is different from what some modern teachings would have us believe. However, Lloyd-Jones sets the record straight with his enlightening words, "The Bible is full of exhortations, and appeals and arguments and demonstrations and reasonings . . .These New Testament teachings would never have been necessary at all if those other teachings were correct. All the Apostles would have had to say . . . Now then, you have been converted, you have been saved, you have been justified." That is step number one.

So much for the teaching to hand it all over to the Lord, and He will keep you and do everything you need. So much for the advice to not do anything, do not strive or struggle, hand it over to the Lord, let go and let God. Because that is not what the New Testament says. There is no short-cut to the life in Christ. As someone once told me, "The only place that a short-cut leads to is disaster."

The teachings that we hear are to be tested in one way and in one way only, according to Scripture. Some teachings may sound nice, simple, and easy, but are they according to Scripture? What does Scripture say? Not that we are to be happy or to have a life of ease, but *to be holy*, to obey His commandments, to rejoice in the Lord always, to be strong in the Lord, and in the power of His might, to fight the good fight, to keep the faith, to listen, to wait, to be open.

May I leave you with these words from that beautiful hymn, "Spirit of God, Descend upon my Heart," attributed to George Croly?

> *Spirit of God, descend upon my heart;*
> *Wean it from earth; through all its pulses move;*
> *Stoop to my weakness, mighty as Thou art,*
> *And make me love Thee as I ought to love.*
>
> *I ask no dream, no prophet ecstasies,*
> *No sudden rending of the veil of clay,*
> *No angel visitant, no opening skies;*
> *But take the dimness of my soul away.*
>
> *Hast Thou not bid us love Thee, God and King?*
> *All, all Then own, soul, heart, and strength, and mind.*
> *I see Thy cross; there teach my heart to cling:*
> *O let me seek Thee, and O let me find!*
>
> *Teach me to feel that Thou art always nigh;*
> *Teach me the struggles of the soul to bear,*
> *To check the rising doubt, the rebel sigh;*
> *Teach me the patience of unanswered prayer.*
>
> *Teach me to love Thee as Thine angels love,*
> *One holy passion filling all my frame;*
> *The baptism of the heaven descended Dove,*
> *My heart an altar, and Thy love the flame.*

Amen!

9

Discipline: What God Requires

Finally, my brethren, be strong in the Lord, and in the power of his might [Eph. 6:10].

The Lord Jesus used everyday occurrences, situations, and events to teach His disciples and followers. He wanted the hearers to relate to what He was telling them and to apply it to their own circumstances and needs.

The Scripture being considered contains a question that has been in the minds of all of us at one time or another. What shall we do, that we might work the works of God? Jesus responds, *This is the work of God, that ye believe on him whom he hath sent* [John 6:29].

Oh, the Gospel is so simple, yet it is so demanding and complex. Have you ever thought of it in this way? We are simple, we like simple, basic things, yet we like demands placed upon us. Yes, and we like to learn how to use recipes, to do puzzles, to learn things, to solve problems.

In the sixth chapter of John's Gospel, a great multitude was looking for Jesus. Why? The day before, He had fed the five thousand, and there was food left over. So what did the people do? They went looking for Jesus for one reason. To get more food! Not for any other reason. So what did Jesus tell them? He said, *Ye seek me, not because ye saw the miracles* (signs), *but because ye did eat of the loaves, and were filled* [John 6:26]. Can you imagine Him saying that? Then what does He say after He has stopped them cold in their tracks? He gets them to change the focus of their attention from themselves to God by saying, *Labor not for the meat* (food) *which perisheth, but for that meat* (food) *which endureth unto everlasting life, which the Son of man shall give unto you: for him hath God the Father sealed* [John 6:27]. Yes, we are to labor for food and shelter, but that can be done even when a person's priority is serving the Lord Jesus Christ. The Lord Jesus wants our eyes focused physically and spiritually on serving food and on eternal life.

Our stomachs and bodies are fed by the food we ingest. Some is good for us; some is not. Our hearts, minds, and souls are fed by the teachings we ingest. Some is good; some is not. Therefore, we have to be selective and choose that which is good. "Our souls are fed by the teaching of the Gospel, when it is efficacious by the power of the Spirit. Therefore, as faith is the life of the soul, all that nourishes and advances faith is compared to food," as simply and effectively expressed by Calvin.

We need the food that is available from Christ, especially if we want to do the works of God. We want to be filled. Just like the people who were filled with the loaves and fishes one day and came seeking the Lord Jesus the next day. The question is, what is going to fill us? If we want to do the work of God then we should be willing to follow directions, to know what is required, and to act accordingly.

We are not to wander aimlessly, ignore God's grace, or be guided by our own self-interests. We are to understand God's commandments and strive to obey them. How can this be done? By effort, thought, and preparation. By selecting what is good, preparing it, and digesting it.

Jesus says we must have faith. Calvin makes a penetrating statement for everyone, when he states unequivocally, "God requires of us only that we believe. There is an implied contrast between faith and men's cares and efforts here, as if He were saying men are busied to no purpose when they try to please God without faith." To understand this we must realize we are only fooling ourselves, not God, when we perform works that do not have their basis in the Lord Jesus Christ or result from our faith in Him.

When contemplating this teaching, we must recognize what Christ is stressing. It is not only that faith is the gift of God and that we may use it or not, but that faith is what God requires of us. He wants us to exhibit it daily, in all the phases of our lives. As members of Christ's body we are not along for the ride. We are participants, we are doers. It is by faith that we become members of His body, and enable His spirit to guide us as He works within us.

After Jesus gets the people to focus on God, not on themselves, He tells them that He is "the bread from heaven," saying, *I am the bread of* life; *he that cometh to me shall never hunger; and he that believeth on me shall never thirst* [John 6:35]. He also said, *And this is the will of him that sent me, that everyone which seeth the Son, and believeth on him, may have everlasting life* [John 6:40]. What does this have to do with Paul's exhortation *to be strong in the Lord, and in the power of his might* [Eph. 6:10]? Quite a bit! The people were filled one day, but were hungry the next. Our attention is to focus on God if we want to do the work of God.

Faith is what God requires of us. To understand the teachings of God and to act accordingly requires His strength, power, and might. Consider certain examples.

Ezra faced enormous difficulties during the reconstruction of Jerusalem. He was surrounded by enemies, ruins, and chaos. He was up against monumental odds. What did he say and what guided him? *The joy of the Lord is your strength* [Neh. 8:10].

Daniel says, *but the people that do know their God shall be strong, and do exploits* (take action) [Dan. 11:32]. We are to be strong in the Lord. We are to learn Christ. We are to learn what Scripture says. When we do, it means that there will be changes in how we act, what we say, and in our priorities. Your thinking changes when you know Christ as your Lord and Saviour. Think of Paul. He changed 180 degrees. Think of Peter, the apostles, Luther, Knox, Calvin, Gurnall, the Wesleys, Lloyd-Jones, and countless others.

Consider Nehemiah. He was doing the Lord's work, he was building the wall when his enemies came several times and tried to trick him, so they could harm him, and prevent him from completing the project and doing the Lord's work. He refused each and every entreaty. Finally they said to Nehemiah, *Let us meet together in the house of God, within the temple, and let us shut the doors of the temple* [Neh. 6:10].

They wanted Nehemiah to leave the work he was performing for the Lord and go into the temple. Why? So they could slay him. Nehemiah responded with these memorable words, *Should such a man as I flee* [Neh. 6:11]? To this he added, *and who is there, that, being as I am, would go into the temple to save his life? I will not go in* [Neh. 6:11]. Nehemiah continued to do the Lord's work, and the wall was finished. Further, his enemies did not do him any harm.

We may not be called upon to do the exploits of Ezra, Daniel, and Nehemiah, but we each have our encounters, our assignments, and our enemies. Therefore, we should put into practice, *The joy of the Lord is your strength* [Neh. 8:10], *but the people that do know their God shall be strong, and do exploits* (take action) [Dan. 11:32], and *Should such a man as I flee* [Neh. 6:11]?

In addition, there are New Testament examples. Paul tells Timothy to be strong and that *All Scripture is given by inspiration of God, and is profitable for doctrine, for reproof, for correction, for instruction in righteousness: That the man of God may be perfect* (complete), *thoroughly furnished* (equipped) *unto all good works* [2 Tim. 3:16–17].

When Paul met with the elders from Ephesus at Miletus he said, *Take heed . . . unto yourselves, and to all the flock, over the which the Holy Ghost hath made you overseers, to feed* (shepherd) *the church of God, . . . And now, brethren, I commend you to God, and to the word of his grace, which is able to build you up, and to give you an inheritance among all them which are sanctified* [Acts 20:28, 32].

When considering these teachings it is well to ask, why did God in His eternal wisdom provide us with the Bible? What is the purpose and the objective of it? "It was given to strengthen us, to build us up in our most holy faith. However, our faith cannot be strengthened, we cannot be built up if we do not partake of the food, if we don't go to where the food is being served, if we don't take time to eat, remember who we are and our relationship to God and to Christ," as accurately expressed by Martyn Lloyd-Jones.

What shall we do, that we might work the works of God [John 6:28]? The New Testament was written not only to present the teachings of the Lord Jesus Christ, but to keep the early believers from going wrong in doctrine. When misled in doctrine, we follow the wrong paths in our thinking and in our actions. It happens to individuals and to churches. When they go wrong in doctrine, they go wrong in their living.

What are we to do? Know the truth contained in Scripture, and revealed unto us, know what God requires, know that we have many battles to fight, know our priorities, know the work required, know Christ Himself, each and every day. What is required to do these things? Discipline, yes, discipline with a capital D. Most everyone likes a winner. Oh, but the work and discipline required to be a winner at any level is another story.

Think of the work and discipline required to have a joyful and lasting marriage. Whoever said it would be easy? What about a joyful and lasting relationship with the Lord Jesus Christ? Did He ever say it would be easy to follow Him? No! No! No! As a matter of fact, the only time the word "easy" appears in the New Testament is when Jesus says, *My yoke is easy, and my burden is light* [Matt. 11:30].

Scripture says we are to exert effort, learn, and acquire discipline. Peter says that we

> *... have obtained like* (the same kind of) *precious faith with us through the righteousness of* (our) *God and our Saviour Jesus Christ:*
> *According as his divine power hath given unto us all things that pertain unto life and godliness, through the knowledge of him that hath called us to glory and virtue:*
> *Whereby are given unto us exceeding great and precious promises: that by these ye might be partakers of the divine nature, having escaped the corruption that is in the world through lust* [2 Pet. 1:1, 3–4].

Peter reveals that through God's grace our faith is the same as that which Christ had. Further, God's divine power has given us all that we need to proceed through life and to know the godliness available from Him.

This is accomplished *through the knowledge of him* (Christ Jesus) *that hath called us to* (by) *glory and virtue* . . . . Calvin expounds upon these enlightening words, saying that Peter "now describes the way in which God makes us sharers of these great blessings, namely by revealing Himself to us in the Gospel . . . . None of the spiritual gifts can be of any use for salvation until we are enlightened with the knowledge of God by the teaching of the Gospel. He makes God the source of this knowledge because we never approach Him unless we are called, and it is therefore the calling of God and not the perception of our own minds that is the effective cause of faith. He is not speaking only of outward calling which by itself is ineffectual, but of inward calling which consists of the hidden power of the Spirit for God does not only speak to our ears by human voice, but He inwardly draws our heart to Him by His Spirit."

How are we to partake of the *exceeding great and precious promises* that are available to us of which Peter speaks? Peter states that if we are *partakers of the divine nature* there are not only things we must do, but they are to be done with all diligence, haste, speed, and earnestness. Then he tells us what they are. Yes, God bestows gifts upon us, but we are to add to them. Note what we are to add to *faith virtue; and to virtue knowledge; And to knowledge temperance* (self-control); *and to temperance patience* (perseverance); *and to patience godliness; And to godliness brotherly kindness; and to brotherly kindness charity* (love) [2 Pet. 1:5–7].

Calvin succinctly states, "He means by this that there is no place for laziness or for following the calling of God easily or carelessly, but keen zeal is a necessity, as though He were saying, 'put forth every effort and let everyone see it.'" So you think it is easy. It is not going to be done for us. We have to do it, and we cannot do it sitting in a rocking chair. If we want to do *the work of God* and to *be strong in the Lord* then we must add to these gifts pertaining unto life and godliness.

We must realize that when God begins a work in us, it is not only our responsibility to add to it, but we will be held accountable. Scripture plainly teaches "that the proper feelings are formed in us by God, and made effective by Him," according to John Calvin. Further, these various gifts are received through God's Spirit.

There is an additional truth of great importance. Peter says, *For if these things be in you, and abound, they make you that ye shall neither be barren* (useless) *nor unfruitful in the knowledge of our Lord Jesus Christ* [2 Pet. 1:8]. We are neither to store these gifts nor ignore them. We are to use them and to add to them as stated above. The strength and power to do so is available from God if we beseech Him and exert the necessary effort.

We need to look at these terms more closely, so that we will better understand what the Holy Spirit is saying through Peter. What is meant by adding to your faith, virtue? It does not mean to add morality or conform to certain standards. The original Greek word *aretē* means first to add *the manifestation of His divine power*. Get that! The focus is on His divine power. Further, the word connotes adding vigor, energy, and the strength of soul. It clearly states we are not to be languid, lethargic, or half-hearted in our faith and in adding to it.

Next, we are to exercise effort in adding knowledge to the manifestation of His divine power. We are not to succumb to what Charles Lamb described as "the mumps and measles of the soul." We are to focus on God and knowing more about Him.

What about adding temperance to knowledge? The proper interpretation is to add self-control to knowledge. That makes a difference. Exercising self-control over our tempers, emotions, desires, and priorities requires discipline, which comes from the divine power and knowledge.

Further, add patience. It means what you think it does and more. It means that patient endurance develops from trials related to serving the Master; chastisements received from God, undeserved afflictions, running the appointed race under adverse conditions, and pursuing the course even when it is difficult. How does that grab you? You are to be refined as fine gold. You are to endure the fiery furnace and become what God wants you to become. Think. Did the apostles have an easy time? Are you always going to have an easy time as you acquire more knowledge about the Triune God, increase in faith and walk with the Lord Jesus?

What does it mean to add godliness to patience? "Being conscious of walking in the sight of God and with God, no matter where we are going or what we are doing. This again is something which we have to do, and we have to remind ourselves of it," as expressed by Lloyd-Jones to offer us encouragement. Remember, God said to Abraham, *I am the almighty God; walk before me, and be thou perfect* (blameless) [Gen. 17:1]. In other words, Abraham, remember who I am, you are walking in my presence, and you are to be complete according to my Word. That applies to each and every one of us.

Then Scripture says to add brotherly kindness. This is an exhortation to be kind, to think kind thoughts, and to perform kind deeds. Other thoughts and deeds are to be eliminated, ignored, or overcome.

Last, Scripture says to add charity. We are to love the members of Christ's body. It does not mean that we will like each and every one or everything they do, but we are to love them and pray for them.

The flow of Peter's teaching is amazing. It proceeds logically with its demands: faith—which God requires; virtue—bestowed by His divine power; knowledge—of God's mercy, grace, love, commands, and requirements; self-control—exhibiting patient endurance, despite obstacles and opposition; Godliness—walking daily in God's presence; and charity—reflecting joyfully God's love. *If ye love me, keep my commandments* [John 14:15]. These things we are told to add and to do, not to hand them over to God or to ignore them. Further, we are to work at them and practice them. Nowhere in Scripture are we told to relax, to go on a holiday, to be soft, or to "let go and let God."

We are to work, eat the food God provides, and *be strong in the Lord, and in the power of his might* [Eph. 6:10]. If we do these things then we will *neither be barren* (useless) *nor unfruitful in the knowledge of our Lord Jesus Christ* [2 Pet. 1:8].

Amen!

10

Responding in Faith

Finally, my brethren, be strong in the Lord, and in the power of his might [Eph. 6:10].

In Paul's command, *Finally, my brethren, be strong in the Lord, and in the power of His might* [Eph. 6:10], the Apostle emphasizes two things. They are also emphasized throughout the Old and New Testaments. First, God, His strength, power, and might; and second, our dependence upon Him, and the necessity of receiving strength from Him.

Why does Paul exhort us to *be strong in the Lord*? First, to remind us "to ask from God a supply of what in themselves they lack; and at the same time promises that, if they ask for it, the power of God will be displayed," as Calvin stated based on his knowledge and experience. Certainly, Abraham on more than one occasion looked to God for strength, power, and might, and he received it. The same was true of Moses, Joshua, and others in the Old Testament.

They were aware of God's presence, His commands, and what they should do and should not do, because God had commanded them, not because it was acceptable among the people. It was acceptable because God commanded it and blessed it. Therefore, the focus was on God and what He wanted. One thing we should grasp and cling to each day is God's presence, and we should often go to Him in prayer.

I do not mean to imply that the Israelites always did what God commanded. They did not! But the Word was proclaimed, even if only by a remnant. They knew that God had said to Moses, *Speak unto all . . . the children of Israel . . . Ye shall be holy: for I the Lord your God am holy* [Lev. 19:2]. We are the children of Israel. We are members of Christ's body. We are to *be strong in the Lord*. We are to know what Scripture says and God requires. We are to know the Lord Jesus Christ better than we know any person. Not just the miracles He performs, not just His words, sayings, and the commands that He gives, not just His actions and His obedience, but Him as the Son of God, Him as God-Man, Him as the Saviour, Him as friend and defender, and Him as our companion on life's journey.

We are to know Him. How does this happen? By spending time with Him, by listening to Him, by talking to Him, and by knowing Him. When we do this we grow and receive His blessings. However, we do not do it for that reason, but as a result of focusing on God and becoming more dependent upon our heavenly Father.

What makes it possible for us to do what we are supposed to do? Moses said in blessing the children of Israel, *As thy days, so shall thy strength be* [Deut. 33:25]. God promises to provide the strength for our days. However, we are to ask for it, and we have to apply it. It is not done for us. When the days are black, when we see darkness, when we are overcome, then we are to call upon the Lord. He will provide the strength for those days.

The author of the letter to the Hebrews says,

> *Seeing then that we have a great high priest, that is passed into* (through) *the heavens, Jesus the Son of God, let us hold fast our profession.*
> *For we have not a high priest which cannot be touched* (sympathize) *with the feeling of our infirmities* (weaknesses); *but was in all points tempted like as we are, yet without sin.*
> *Let us therefore come boldly* (confidently) *unto the throne of grace, that we may obtain mercy, and find grace to help in time of need* [Heb. 4:14–16].

Note that it says Jesus is our high priest, He is the Son of God. But it says more: that He can be touched, He can be grasped, He is aware of our infirmities, and by His grace He will provide *help in time of need*.

When it says, He is *aware* of our infirmities, what does it mean? The Greek word for *aware* means that God completely understands our infirmities, and our "want of strength," and our weaknesses. Christ knows us! Have you ever wanted to help someone, but they would not let you? Undoubtedly, you have.

We need to realize that we have infirmities, and that the Master is willing to help us in our *time of need*. Therefore, it is important to get self out of the way and to ask for His help in both the little and big things of life. God may be on His throne, but He walks with us. His grace and fatherly love should make us realize that He wants to help us in our *time of need*. When we are *aware* of the teachings of Scripture we know that this has been true through the ages. As Anselm said, "Faith seeks understanding."

There is a third factor enabling us to be strong in the Lord. Peter said to Cornelius when he entered Caesarea,

> *That word, I say, ye know, which was published* (proclaimed) *throughout all Judea, . . . after the baptism which John preached; How God anointed Jesus of Nazareth with the Holy Ghost and with power: who went about doing good, and healing all that were oppressed of the devil; for God was with him* [Acts 10:37–38].

Calvin's exposition of Peter's speech sheds additional light on being strong in the Lord. He says that "the coming of Christ into the world, His death and resurrection are the basis of our salvation, that only Christ can be offered for salvation is if we first know that He put on our flesh, and lived among men in such a way that He showed Himself to be the Son of God by certain proofs; and that He was finally fastened to the cross and raised up from the dead by the power of God . . . : [W]e must be taught the reason why he came down . . . from the glory of heaven, why He endured the death of the cross . . . . The reason for the resurrection must be taught for from it the effect and fruit of all these things is gathered, that Christ was emptied so that He might restore us, who were lost, to complete blessedness; . . . that He made atonement for our sins by the sacrifice of His death to make the Father favourable to us, that . . . He secured eternal life for us; . . . that the whole power of the Spirit was poured out on Him so that He might enrich us from His abundance.

"For the power from which Christ excelled, was from no other source but the Spirit. Therefore when the heavenly Father anointed His Son, He equipped Him with the power of His own Spirit. Peter immediately goes on to say that this power appeared in miracles, . . . that Christ testified that He was endowed with the power of the Holy Spirit so that He might do good to the world. For it was not fitting that the power of God that causes terror should be put forth in Him, but the power that would draw the world, by the pleasant taste of goodness and kindness, to love Him and long for Him."

The Lord Jesus was anointed with the Holy Ghost and His power. What about us? *In whom ye also trusted, after that ye heard the word of truth, the gospel of your salvation: in whom also after that ye believed, ye were sealed with that holy Spirit of promise, Which is the earnest* (down payment) *of our inheritance* [Eph. 1:13–14]. There is this power with which we have been anointed and sealed. It enables us to do various things. It is important to realize that this power has been given to us and is continuously available.

There are numerous records in Scripture of the Lord providing strength to His servants. *The Lord God is a sun and shield* [Ps. 84:11]. God intervened to help Elijah when he was in need. Elijah said, *Fear not: for they that be with us are more than they that be with them* [2 Kgs. 6:16]. Jesus said in Gethsemane, *And yet I am not alone, because the Father is with me* [John 16:32]. While Paul was in Corinth the Lord said to him, *Be not afraid, but speak, and hold not thy peace* (do not keep silent): *For I am with thee, and no man shall set on* (attack) *thee to hurt thee: for I have much people in this city* [Acts 18:9–10]. The Lord is aware of our infirmities and will provide help in *time of need*. However, we must be aware of our deficiencies and seek His help.

When people hear these accounts and others they say something like this: Is that true? Can it happen today? What about me? Think what would have happened if certain people had not responded in faith. Consider the following examples. Matthew tells us of the man with the withered hand. The Lord said, *Stretch forth thine hand* [Matt. 12:13]. Suppose he had not? What about the woman that touched His garment? What about the man he told, *Arise, and take up thy bed, and walk* [Mark 2:9]? What about the centurion when He told him his son was healed?

Of course, there are other incidents. But, the crux of the matter is that the Lord completely understands our infirmities and will help us. However, we must ask and exert effort. We must do something! It is not a case of "Let go and Let God" or "Hand it over to the Lord."

What does Scripture say? The men that God used prepared themselves. They spent time getting ready. They studied, they prayed, they worked, they asked, and they went forth relying upon the Lord.

How should we interpret this? Not that we have the strength and power within us, but as children of God and members of Christ's body we have a definite, positive relationship with God. Therefore, His strength, power, and might enable us to do things. A poem by John S.B. Monsell clarifies this point.

> Fight the good fight with all thy might;
> Christ is thy strength, and Christ thy right;
> Lay hold on life, and it shall be
> Thy joy and crown eternally.
>
> Run the straight race through God's good grace,
> Lift up thine eyes, and seek His face;
> Life with its way before thee lies;
> Christ is the way, and Christ the prize.
>
> Cast care aside; lean on thy guide,
> Lean and His mercy will provide;
> Lean and the trusting soul shall prove
> Christ is its life, and Christ its love.
>
> Faint not nor fear, His arm is near;
> He changeth not, and thou art dear;
> Only believe, and thou shalt see,
> That Christ is all in all to thee.

The Apostle Paul exhorts us to *be strong in the Lord, and in the power of His might* for a reason. What is it? *To stand against the wiles of the devil* and *to withstand in the evil day.* It is for our benefit.

As we conclude examining this verse, it is well to bear in mind several thoughts. Many people feel that once they accept Christ they will have a life of relative ease and that problems and difficulties will evaporate as though "There will be no fight, there will be no struggle, effort will not be required. So when they find that, on the contrary, they have grave difficulties and (are in) a mighty battle they are utterly discouraged," as appropriately described by an unknown author.

Then what happens? They become slack and lethargic. They focus their eyes inwardly instead of focusing on the Lord. The Lord tries us. He wants us to grow and to increase in strength and knowledge. The fact that we accept Christ and try to follow Him causes other people to look askance, to shun us, to make remarks, to make us uncomfortable, to tempt us, and to try us.

Peter tells the early followers, *Beloved, think it not strange concerning the fiery trial which is to try you, as though some strange thing happened unto you: But rejoice, inasmuch as* (to the extent that) *ye are partakers of Christ's sufferings* [1 Pet. 4:12-13]. That is difficult. It is hard to rejoice when we are being persecuted or maligned, especially when trying to serve God. It happened in the first century and in every one since then. When these things happen we are to look to the Lord and receive our strength from Him.

Paul wrote to Timothy advising him, *Yea, and all that will live godly in Christ Jesus shall suffer persecution* [2 Tim. 3:12]. He wrote to the Philippians informing them *Unto you it is given in the behalf of Christ, not only to believe on him, but also to suffer for his sake* [Phil. 1:29].

Luke records Paul and Barnabas preaching and *Confirming* (Strengthening) *the souls of the disciples, and exhorting them to continue in the faith, and that we must through much tribulation enter into the kingdom of God* [Acts 14:22]. "God makes trial of our faith in this way,... that we become partakers with Christ," as Calvin said for our edification.

It is important to have an understanding of what Scripture says, since it is the Word of God. It is as appropriate for us today as it was the day it was written. The Word focuses on God's strengths and our weaknesses. In so doing it enables us to grow stronger. Scripture informs us regarding what it means to be a member of Christ's body. When we understand what it says and how it helps us, then our faith increases and we become more willing to learn and to obey His commands.

Further, we begin to understand different exhortations in the Bible.

> *Ye that love the Lord, hate evil* [Ps. 97:10].

> *Know ye not that the friendship of* (with) *the world is enmity with God* [Jas. 4:4].

> *He that saith, I know him, and keepeth not his commandments, is a liar, and the truth is not in him* [1 John 2:4].

These representative verses contain strong meat, strong words, and strong truths. How are we to react to them? In obedience to Christ's command, *AND THOU SHALT LOVE THE LORD THY GOD WITH ALL THY HEART, AND WITH ALL THY SOUL, AND WITH ALL THY MIND, AND WITH ALL THY STRENGTH* [Mark 12:30].

Recall Peter's words, *Be sober, be vigilant; because your adversary the devil, as a roaring lion, walketh about, seeking whom he may devour* [1

Pet. 5:8]. Peter exhorts us to be sober and watchful mentally, spiritually, and physically. Also, to be vigilant, alert, wide awake, and on guard. This requires knowledge, understanding, and self-control. There is an important point to grasp in this verse, the phrase *your adversary the devil*. Peter says your adversary is in reality the devil. We want to personalize it and say or think that our adversary is another person. Peter states the real truth, *your adversary the devil*. May we progress to the point where we see that it is the devil who works in people and produces bad or evil works.

"The devil is not primarily our enemy, he is the enemy of God. It was against God he lifted up himself, it was against God that he rebelled; and it is against God that he wages the conflict. He uses us in our ignorance and folly to attack God. It is God who made us, and God who redeemed us at a tremendous cost; and if the devil can defeat us he defeats God," as forcefully and definitively stated by Martyn Lloyd-Jones. Hopefully, this helps us to see why Paul wants us to *be strong in the Lord, and in the power of His might* [Eph. 6:10].

Why does Paul urge us to *be strong in the Lord and in the power of His might?* So that we *may be able to stand against the wiles* (schemes) *of the devil*. "Never fear nor falter nor faint, but always be prepared through an enduement with fresh strength which enables you to be victorious from the start to the finish . . . . To assume power we must be assured of power. But that assurance will never come if we look inward at ourselves or out at the enemy," according to Ruth Paxson. Then what are we to do? She continues saying, "our strength lies in a person, and oh, what a person! Note His name. THE LORD. Ponder that name until it stands out . . . in all its singular glory and solitary grandeur. Not 'Jesus,' his personal, human name that indicates his Saviourhood, . . . not 'Christ,' His official mediatorial name, The Anointed One, indespensable as that is to us. But 'LORD,' His sovereign, kingly name that stands for His rulership . . . . The Lord, the mighty God, the blessed and only Potentate, the King of kings and the Lord of Lords.

"*And in the power of his might*. Our strength lies not only in what He is, but in what He has. Our power is in a Person whose power is extraordinary, for 'it is the *power of his might* . . . In the strength of the mighty power of the Lord we are equipped to fearlessly meet Satan and all his hosts, confident that we shall be '*able to stand,*' '*able to withstand,*' and 'able to quench all of the fiery darts of the wicked one.' Our part . .

. is calm, confident assurance of power over all the power of the enemy. We enter the warfare victors through faith in the victorious Lord, upon whom we keep our eyes fixed. Dear reader, do you know in your daily experience the conquering power of his might?"

Why does he exhort us to stand and to withstand? As stated previously, Christ is the captain of our salvation. The word *captain* means "chief leader" or "author." He is the one who provides the first of anything and everything. He is the leader in whom we have confidence, the One to whom we stretch forth the withered hand, the One whose commandments we obey *to take up thy bed and walk*, the One who is aware of our infirmities, and the One who provides strength, power, and might that we may stand and withstand.

Too often we become enmeshed in our own problems and difficulties. When we do, pray that we may think of Christ. He was tempted, chastised, rebuked, deserted, misunderstood, maligned, and persecuted. His friends and followers left Him. Yet He was obedient to the Father. He remained true and faithful to His disciples. He strengthened them and poured forth an abundant measure of His grace, mercy, and love. May we grasp and hold on to the living faith as revealed in Him.

The Apostle Paul, after his conversion, suffered many things, but he kept focusing on the Lord. Therefore, he was able to say, *Only let your conversation* (conduct) *be as it becometh the gospel of Christ* [Phil. 1:27]. May we live that way. At the end of his ministry, Paul wrote to Timothy,

> *For I am now ready to be offered, and the time of my departure* (death) *is at hand.*
> *I have fought a good fight, I have finished my course* (race), *I have kept the faith:*
> *Henceforth there is laid up for me a crown of righteousness, which the Lord, the righteous judge, shall give me at that day: and not to me only, but unto all them also that love his appearing* [2 Tim. 4:6–8].

May we think these thoughts, say these words, believe these truths, and focus on God while proceeding along life's pathway with our constant companion, Christ Jesus, and continuously responding in faith.

Amen!

11

Gird Your Loins

> *Wherefore take* (up) *unto you the whole armor of God, that ye may be able to withstand in the evil day, and having done all, to stand.*
> *Stand therefore having your loins girt about* (your waist) *with truth, and having on the breastplate of righteousness* [Eph. 6:13–14].

The Gospel is truly amazing. It reveals what God has done, is doing, and will do. Also, it reveals what we are to do and how we are to act and react. As we focus on these last verses of Ephesians, it is proper to remind ourselves about Paul and the saints and the faithful at Ephesus. Paul went there to proclaim the Gospel; he stayed three years, preached, taught, and pastored; he went into their homes; he called the Elders to meet him at Miletus; he declared the whole Gospel, not a portion of it or 99 percent of it; and he wrote this marvelous letter to instruct them and to remind them of what God had done in Christ, and what was required of them. It is important to note this latter point: *what is required of the faithful.*

We have considered in detail, Paul's exhortation to *be strong in the Lord, and in the power of his might* [Eph. 6:10]. Now it is time to examine *the whole armor of God.* Be careful to note that we are commanded to do two things: *be strong in the Lord*, and *Put on the whole armor.* When thinking of these two functions, think of both the offense and defense. You have these functions in most sports, most situations in life, and definitely in our life with the Lord Jesus Christ. When thinking offensively, we should think of His strength and His power. When thinking defensively, we should think about protecting ourselves, preventing the opposition from hurting us, or making a score, and turning aside the attack. God is concerned about our welfare, about our relationship to Him. Therefore, the Apostle defines what we are to do both offensively and defensively.

Of course, some may ask why does Paul first say, *Be strong in the Lord* and then say, *Put on the whole armor of God*? What does a football team do? First, they acquire strength and conditioning, then they put on the pads and begin to have contact. The Holy Spirit tells us first to be strong and then to *put on the whole armor of God*. Scripture says the whole armor, not just a few pieces or only one. This is most important. What is the armor that Paul is describing? Doctrine! The teachings of Christ! It is what we are to apply and to do! It is specific! It is truth, righteousness, the gospel of peace, the shield of faith, the helmet of salvation, the sword of the Spirit, and the Word of God.

We are to put on these things, we are to wear them, and they are to be part of our being. The Greek word is *enduō* and means *putting on*. Paul says to the Romans, *let us put on the armor of light* [Rom. 13:12]. Also, *Put ye on the Lord Jesus Christ* [Rom. 13:14]. Paul says to the Galatians, *Put on Christ* [Gal. 3:27]. And to the Ephesians he says, *Put on the new man* [Eph. 4:24]. The Greek word *enduō* also signifies *to get into, to become covered*. The Holy Spirit realizes we need to put on each and every identified item. Further, they are to be put on completely and fully, not partially, not half-heartedly.

"There are six pieces of armour, each of which is a source of strength and security in warfare. Five are for defensive and for offensive warfare. No part of life must be exposed, for even one vulnerable place would mean defeat. So we cannot pick and choose what parts of the armour we wish to wear. We need the whole armour all the time . . . . What a relief to know that we do not need to provide the armour! How ignorant we are of the strength and the stratagems of the enemy! How inadequately we guage our own inability and impotence! But our omniscient God, who knows all about our foe and about us, has provided an armour both suitable and sufficient," as compellingly stated by Ruth Paxson.

Yes, strength is needed, but in addition the protection of each item of armor is required and is to be used. Too often people become overconfident or ignore the teachings of Scripture. When this happens, they suffer. Paul says to the Corinthians, *Wherefore let him that thinketh he standeth* (causes himself to stand) *take heed lest he fall* [1 Cor. 10:12].

What about David and Sampson? They thought they could stand without the whole armor of God. Look what happened to them. The apostles, especially Peter and Paul, ministered among the saints and the faithful observing their characteristics, strengths, and weaknesses, and recognizing when they were strong in the Lord and when they needed *the whole armor of God*. Therefore, the apostles exhort us to be on guard, to use effectively the armor of God, and not to depend upon ourselves.

There are questions to ask and ponder. Is our dependence upon God, His teachings, and His requirements, or is it upon our own capabilities, experiences, and desires? When I focus inwardly and tell myself I can handle the situation, I usually fall. When I focus on God, beseech Him to help, and seek to obey His commands, then usually I stand and walk in His light. Unfortunately, I have to keep learning this lesson.

Why does Paul repeat his exhortation to *put on the whole armor of God*? Verse eleven says, *Put on the whole armor of God* and verse thirteen says, *wherefore take unto you the whole armor of God*. The Greek word in these two verses in *panoplia*, and it means *full armor* or *complete equipment*. God, through Christ, will make available all the protective equipment we need. However, we must put it on, every bit of it.

Paul repeats himself because it is important to emphasize the need to apply and use everything that is available. God provides for our every need. Peter says, *According as his divine power hath given unto us all things that pertain unto life and godliness, through the knowledge of him that hath called us to* (by) *glory and virtue* (the manifestation of His divine power) [2 Pet. 1:3]. God gives all these things to us. However, we have to use them and apply them. Yet what do we want to say and do? We can handle the situation. Yes, we may be a little worried or have a certain amount of anxiety, but we can apply a little common sense. Give me a little time, and I will work it out. There is no sense in crying over spilt milk, or I can use my mind, my reasoning power, and my will power. Sooner or later, we must realize the need for the whole armor of God, we must put it on, and we must use it.

Why? Because we are not just contending with ourselves, other people, or physical matter. Scripture says we are contending with principalities, powers, rulers of darkness, and spiritual wickedness. We must progress to the point where we realize when people offend us or transgress against us, that they are under the power of darkness, the evil one, the devil. It is difficult, but we must progress to the point where we pray for them in spirit and in truth.

How can this happen? By putting on the whole armor of God and having the strength to use it. This armor is not physical. It is spirit and truth. Further, we are to wrap ourselves in it.

When considering this teaching, remember the Apostle is directing it to the saints and to the faithful, not to the world at large, not to those outside the body of Christ. We are members of Christ's body. Therefore, we are to use the equipment and the weapons the Master makes available, all the equipment, not just certain pieces.

If you are going to be a good golfer, then you have to learn how to use each and every club. You have to learn to hit the ball downhill, uphill, sidehill, from the sand and from the rough. If you are going to be a good cook, you have to learn to cook the meat, the vegetables, prepare the salad, fix the dessert, and prepare the bread. You cannot pick and choose.

If you are going to be one of Christ's soldiers, you cannot pick and choose the equipment you will wear and use. You are to put on and use the truth, righteousness, gospel of peace (the gospel of unity or concord in Christ), faith, salvation, and the sword of the Spirit, all of which are the Word of God.

During recent years, a school of thought has developed that says you can pick and choose. Unfortunately, it has continued unto this day. It states that man is so intelligent, man has developed, and man has progressed. Therefore, he can pick and choose. That is not what Scripture says. It says, *put on the whole armor of God*. You need it all. Paul declared *the whole counsel of God* to the saints and faithful in Ephesus. Oh, that ministers and teachers would follow Paul's example and proclaim *the whole counsel of God*, not just part of it. It needs to penetrate the heart, the mind, and the will of the people hearing it.

When you are a member of Christ's body, you are part and parcel of His heart, mind, and will. You cannot separate yourself from any part of Him. What did Christ do during His earthly ministry? He clothed Himself with the whole armor of God. He did not pick and choose, He was neither half-hearted nor lethargic, and He exerted Himself, but in so doing He was obedient to His Father.

What is the first thing the Apostle commands us to do? *Stand therefore*. The proper interpretation is "Cause yourself to stand, by conditioning and preparing your loins for service as one of Christ's followers, and clothing yourself with His truth, as it is found in Him," as appropriately described by an unknown author. Our Lord warns His disciples to be watchful, wary, and prepared by saying to them, *Let your loins* (waist) *be girded about* [Luke 12:35].

Why does the Apostle use the figure of speech *having your loins girt about* (your waist) *with truth* [Eph. 6:14]? You have to remember that the soldiers in Paul's time wore garments that were full, long, and loose-fitting. The girdle or belt was used to gather materials so that they would not be a hindrance causing the soldier to step on the garment, or to stumble, or to have his activities impeded. Therefore, when a soldier was preparing for action he would gather his clothing together, fix it in the proper position, and secure it with the belt or girdle. These steps prepared the soldier for battle, for action, and to carry out the orders of his superior. When the belt or girdle was firmly in place the soldier had a sense of both security and preparedness. He was ready for action, to repel the enemy, and to serve his master.

When we gird our loins about with the truth as it is found in the Lord Jesus Christ, then we have more confidence and are better able to serve the Master. A natural question is, what is meant by the word *truth* in this phrase? It is more than ethical truth. It is truth in all its fullness and scope as embodied in Christ Jesus. However, some scholars want to say that a different type of truth is meant in this verse. They say it refers to truth that comes from within a person, and they quote from the Fifty-first Psalm, which says, *Thou desirest truth in the inward parts* [Ps. 51:6].

They expand this to include sincerity, candor, truthfulness, openness, honesty, and moral attributes according to man's standards. They turn from the truth as found in Christ to truth that comes from within a person. "This, they say, is the basis of everything; we have to be honest and have to have ethical truthfulness in us, which is different than knowing the truth and being clothed with it," according to Martyn Lloyd-Jones as he describes distinct differences between the two types of truth.

These propositions are contra to the teachings of our Master, the apostles, and the other writers of the New Testament. Also, they are contra to the teachings of the prophets and God's Word as recorded in the Old Testament. They remind us of the warnings issued by Paul and Peter about false prophets and teachers, and their ilk. Peter states it unequivocally,

> BUT *there were false prophets among the people, even as there shall be false teachers among you, who privily* (secretly) *shall bring in damnable* (destructive) *heresies, even denying the Lord that bought them, and bring upon themselves swift destruction.*
> *And many shall follow their pernicious* (destructive) *ways; by reason of whom the way of truth shall be evil* (blasphemed) *spoken of.*
> *And through covetousness shall they with feigned* (deceptive) *words make merchandise of* (exploit) *you:* . . . [2 Pet. 2:1–3].

We need to take to heart the words of the Lord Jesus, Paul, Peter, and others regarding the truth as it is found in Christ and in the Word of God. We are to learn and to know the truth as it is revealed in Scripture. When we become knowledgeable regarding God's Word, we should not be led astray. Yes, there is a difference between the two, as can be shown. When Jesus was tempted in the wilderness, He used *the sword of the Spirit* which is *the Word of God* and quoted from Scripture.

God is orderly, methodical, and purposeful. He does things step by step, block by block, and development by development. Therefore, He first wants us clothed with His truth as it is in Christ, so that we will be able to use the weapons He provides. We have already seen that we are to *be strong in the Lord, and in the power of his might*, not our own power and might. Therefore, it follows logically and orderly that we should put on His truth, not ours.

Why do I say this? What does Scripture reveal about this truth? John records the following occasion with the Jews who believed. *As he* (Jesus) *spake these words, many believed on him* [John 8:30]. *Then said Jesus to those Jews which believed on him, If ye continue* (abide) *in my word, then are ye my disciples indeed; And ye shall know the truth, and the truth shall make you free* [John 8:31–32]. Jesus is talking about the entire Christian doctrine, every bit of it. Paul said to the elders at Miletus, *I have not shunned to declare unto you all the counsel of God* [Acts 20:27].

Jesus tells the disciples to continue in the truth, *in my word*. It means to abide in His Word. Jesus prays, *Sanctify them through thy truth: thy word is truth* [John 17:17]. We are sanctified by God's truth as it is revealed in Christ.

Paul says to the Corinthians, *Watch ye, stand fast in the faith.* What does this mean? We are to hold steadfastly to faith in Christ, which is the truth as it is found in Him. If there was any lack of truth in Him, then there would be a lack of faith in us.

Peter says, *Wherefore gird up* (prepare) *the loins of your mind* (for action) [1 Pet. 1:13]. What is your mind to grasp? The truth as it is found in Christ.

Both Peter and Paul exhort us to gird our minds with the spiritual truth as it is found in Christ. The mind must find its rest in thee. It must be enlightened. It must proceed from darkness to light. Hopefully, these examples help. The truth as it is used by Paul "is the objective truth which I possess in a subjective manner," as expressed by Martyn Lloyd-Jones. It is knowledge of the *truth as it is in Christ Jesus*. It is the truth, which I am to grasp, but it is the truth that grabs hold of me and controls or guides my being.

Have you ever tried to do something or to solve a problem and had no success at all or only partially, or been somewhat self-satisfied with your progress or performance and then have someone come along and show you a simple trick or provide you with an important piece of knowledge? What happens? A whole new vista opens, a new light dawns. You rejoice in the new, enlarged truth. You perform as you were never able to do before. You did not develop that new truth. It was given unto you. It was revealed to you. Guess what? You are not going to let it go. You are going to keep using it.

That is the way it is with the *truth as it is in Christ Jesus*. The more you receive of it and the more you grab hold of it, then the more you will apply it in your daily walk with the Lord Jesus. No wonder the Apostle first says *having girded your loins about with truth*.

We are to continue in His Word. We are to declare and to heed the whole counsel of God. We are to be equipped. We are to know Scripture, to know the truth. We are not to be *tossed to and fro, and carried about by every wind of doctrine*. We are to know Christ, and *be filled with the Spirit*. Peter states it eloquently and meaningfully,

> *Wherefore gird* (prepare) *up the loins of your mind* (for action), *be sober, and hope to the end for* (rest your hope fully upon) *the grace that is to be brought unto you at the revelation of Jesus Christ;*
> *As obedient children, not fashioning* (conforming) *yourselves according to the former lusts in your ignorance:*
> *But as he which hath called you is holy, so be ye holy in all manner of conversation* (conduct);
> *Because it is written, BE YE HOLY; FOR I AM HOLY*
> [1 Pet. 1:13–16].

You will note that the Apostle Peter says *gird* (prepare) *up the loins of your mind, be sober*, . . . "He means that our minds are held entangled by the cares of the world and by vain desires, so that they do not rise up to God. Therefore, anyone who really wants to have this hope must learn in the first place to disentangle himself from the world, and gird up his mind so that he turns aside to vain affections. For the same reason he enjoins sobriety, which immediately follows. He commends not only temperance in eating and drinking, but rather spiritual sobriety, when we contain all our thoughts and affections so as not to be inebriated with the allurements of this world. Since even the least taste of them draws us away stealthily from God, when anyone plunges himself into them, he must of necessity become sleepy and stupid, and as a result he forgets the things of God.

"The addition, *at the revelation of Jesus Christ*, may be explained in two ways: that the doctrine of the Gospel reveals Christ to us; and . . . we see Him yet only through a glass and . . . full revelation is put off to the last day . . . . The second seems, . . . more suitable to the passage. The object of Peter is to call us away beyond the world, and for this purpose the most fitting thing was the remembrance of Christ's coming.

"He means first of all that we are called by the Lord through the Gospel to the privilege and honour of adoption, and, secondly, that we are adopted on the ground that He should in turn have us as His obedient children. . . . How far this obedience extends is shown by Peter when he forbids God's people to conform to or to comply with the desires of this world, and he exhorts them rather to conform to the will of God. . . . This cannot happen unless we are renewed and put off the image of old Adam.

"In bidding us to be *holy* like Himself, the comparison is not that of equals, but we ought to advance in this direction as far as our condition will take us. . . . We ought daily strive more and more. We ought to remember that we are not only told what our duty is, but that God also adds, 'I am he who sanctifies you,'" [see Lev. 22:9, 1b], as stressed by John Calvin.

May we gird ourselves with these truths and apply them each and every day that God gives us.

Amen!

12

The Girdle of Truth

Stand therefore, having your loins girt about (your waist) *with truth, and having on the breastplate of righteousness* [Eph. 6:14].

Several years ago when I was associated with a major company, my wife and I were the hosts for a large meeting attended by executives from the company itself and owners/ executives from other companies. At the conclusion of the session one day, before we adjourned for golf, tennis, and the beach, I made an announcement. I informed everyone that at dinner that night, which was to be a cookout, the attire would be informal, sport shirts, no coats and ties. There were approximately one hundred fifty men plus their wives, or three hundred people in total. When we arrived for the dinner that night, guess what happened?

Dick Austin came up to me and said, "Bob, didn't you say that the dress would be informal tonight, sport shirts and no ties?"

I said, "Yes, that is what I said."

Then, he said, "How come you have on a tie and a sport coat?"

I replied, "Dick, it is very simple, we were a little late coming in from playing golf, so as I dashed to the shower I said to my wife, please get me some clothes to wear tonight. So when I got out of the shower, and put on my underwear, I said where are my clothes to wear to the dinner?"

She said, "they are on the bed."

I said, "But I told everyone it was informal attire."

She said, "Wear those clothes."

So I said, "Dick, here I am."

You know what he said? "That's simple, I understand perfectly."

What does that have to do with our Scripture regarding your loins being girded with truth or clothing yourself with His truth, as it is found in Him? Everything! God provides us with His clothing, with the raiments that will aid and protect us. However, we must put them on. It is analogous to a doctor prescribing medicine for us. It will not do us any good unless we ingest it. God's armor will not do us any good unless we put it on, learn about it, become proficient in it, and use it. All four things must be done.

Probably the greatest irony perpetrated by the church at large in the twentieth century and early twenty-first century is that you can have morality or ethics, or as I prefer, the righteousness of the Bible without "*the whole counsel of God*" or the truth as it is revealed in Christ Jesus. You cannot construct a multi-story building without a foundation. There is only one foundation: *the truth as it is found in Christ!*

What is this truth with which we are to clothe ourselves? First, consider what it is not. It is not a general, vague attitude that urges people to exhibit friendship or love, or to worship together. It is more, much more than that. It is based upon particular commands, principles, and teachings that can withstand the frailties of human nature. It is the strength and power of God that enables us to put away *all bitterness, and wrath, and anger, and clamor, and evil speaking, . . . with all malice: and be ye* (become) *kind one to another, tenderhearted, forgiving one another* [Eph. 4:31–32]. It is being *filled with the spirit*. This can occur only by abiding in the truth as it is found in Christ. The clothing with which He wishes to gird us is not always what our experiences in the secular world, or teachings from it, would have us believe. It is so difficult for people to see this. Yet we have the classical example of the scribes and Pharisees.

The next thing that this truth is not, is that a person's life is more important than what he or she believes. People may say that a certain person is not a Christian, but their good deeds prove they are. Balderdash! What a person believes does make a difference. "To tell people that what a man believes does not matter as long as he lives a good life and does good is not only a denial of the Gospel, it is bound to discourage people from believing the only truth which can save them," as Martyn Lloyd-Jones forthrightly states. There is no compromise to his statement.

There are those who propose the idea that truth cannot be defined, that it is subjective, that it comes from within a person. Further, since this is true you should not criticize others, nor should you stand fast based on teachings from Scripture. When you do, people will say you are contentious, that you do not have "a Christian spirit." Also, you must not say that any teaching or interpretation is wrong, because if you do, then your actions will affect any unity that may exist. The teaching of this group says to allow anyone to believe what they like, just as long as they say their objective is to do good.

Some people put uniformity or unanimity before doctrine. They want agreement even though different parties may believe what they like. They deal with God's truth as if they were trying to agree on a political platform or candidate. Some carry this further and say that we must put aside our differences with Rome and reach agreement. Maybe the Reformers were wrong. Who can say who is right and who is wrong? You should not exclude any group regardless of what they believe or what they do. Let in the gays, let in the agnostics, and let in the atheists with their various platforms. That is not New Testament teaching! Statements are made like, "we are all one, therefore there must be unity, what difference does it make what a person believes?"

Then there are the proponents of modern knowledge. Those who say, that it was okay for the Reformers to believe what they did, or the Puritans, or the Wesleys and Whitefields, but today man is different, he is more knowledgeable.

Or it is said the New Testament is alright for the time in which it was written, but the people of that time were primitive, simple, and uneducated. They ignore the fact that the New Testament was written after the Golden Age of Greece. They ignore the truth in Corinthians:

> *For after that in the wisdom of God the world by wisdom knew not God, it pleased God by the foolishness of preaching* (message preached) *to save them that believe.*
> *For the Jews require a sign, and the Greeks seek after wisdom:*
> *But we preach* (proclaim) *Christ crucified, unto the Jews a stumbling block, and unto the Greeks foolishness;*
> *But unto them which are called, both Jews and Greeks, Christ the power of God, and the wisdom of God* [1 Cor. 1:21–24].

Calvin makes a wise and penetrating statement regarding this Scripture, saying, "This is a very fine passage, and from it we can plainly see how great is the blindness of the human mind, which surrounded by light, perceives nothing. For it is true that the world is like a theatre in which the Lord shows us a striking spectacle of His glory. However, when such a sight lies open before our eyes, we are quite blind, not because the revelation is obscure, but because we are alienated in mind, meaning that not only the will but also the power for this activity fails us. For notwithstanding that God shows Himself openly, yet it is only by the eye of faith that we can look at Him, bearing in mind that we receive only a slight inkling as to His divine nature, but enough to put us in the position of being without excuse."

It is quite clear that we are to examine Scripture. We are to ask, "How am I to put on the girdle of truth?" Paul says to Timothy,

> *Of these things put them in remembrance, charging them before the Lord that they strive not about words to no profit, but to the subverting* (ruin) *of the hearers.*
> *Study* (Be diligent) *to show thyself approved unto God, . . . rightly dividing the word of truth.*
> *But shun profane and vain babblings* (worthless talk): *for they will increase unto more ungodliness.*
> *And their word will eat* (spread) *as doth a canker* (cancer): *of whom is Hymeneus and Philetus;*
> *Who concerning the truth have erred* (strayed), *saying that the resurrection is past already; and overthrow the faith of some* [2 Tim. 2:14–18].

Paul wants the faithful to properly interpret the words of false preachers and teachers who deny Christ and are under Satan's influence. The Scripture being considered is very clear in stating that "truth is defined and error is condemned," as Martyn Lloyd-Jones acknowledges and confirms.

Paul does not claim to be the founder of it but to be a minister of it, to be the one who has adopted it, and serves it fully and completely. Earlier in his letter to Timothy, Paul speaks of *my gospel* when he says, *Remember that Jesus Christ . . . was raised from the dead according to my gospel.* Further, he says, *If we deny him, he also will deny us. Study* (Be diligent) *to show thyself approved unto God* [Selections from 2 Tim. 2:8, 12, 15]. These are strong, strong words. They contain commands that are easy to understand. But they are more than that, they require effort on our part, and they are to be followed and obeyed.

Why does Paul command us to have our *loins girt about with truth*? Ruth Paxson's answer enables us to understand the reason for that command saying, "We have seen that Satan comes to us first as a liar and deceiver, so we can understand why God provides first of all the girdle of truth for our protection. Christ, the Truth and the true God, is our armour against the attacks of Satan, the liar and deceiver."

She provides further clarification and insight regarding the girdle and the truth, that will protect us as we journey along life's pathway with all its snares, trials, tests and temptations. "The soldier's girdle was no mere ornament. It went around the body, holding other pieces of armour in place and giving the soldier freedom in movement. So this divine girdle of truth must encompass our whole life. The whole circle of truth should wholly encircle us, leaving no gaps. This will really mean the two prayers of Ephesians answered in us; the revelation of God's truth to our minds through the Spirit's enlightenment, realized in our experience through the Spirit's enlightenment, realized in our experience through the Spirit's enablement. Truth apprehended will be applied. This involves a very intimate dealing of truth with every department of our lives, which the apostle John described as 'a walk in truth.'

"Such a walk implies a stern, strict dealing with sin and self; allowing no conscious hypocrisy or insincerity; no compromise with known sin; no excuse or vindication for wrongdoing; no condoning of sins such as temper, irritability, worry or depression on the ground of physical causes or domestic circumstances. It compels us to face things just as they are and call them by their right names. He who is the truth encompasses our whole being making every part true, beginning with inward character, and ending with the outward conduct." Whoever said the life of a Christian was easy or that it did not have tis challenges?

The Apostle draws a definite distinction between being obedient to the truth and succumbing to *the wiles* (schemes) *of the devil*. Scripture draws a distinct line between the truth as revealed in Christ and the errors perpetrated by man. We are to depart from iniquity, flee youthful lusts, avoid foolish and unlearned questions, and strive not against the Lord. We are to: honor, sanctify, and be meet for the Master's use; prepare unto every good work; follow righteousness, faith, charity, and peace; be gentle unto all men; be patient and kind; and acknowledge the truth in word and deed. Why? That we may refrain from submitting to the snares of the devil.

What does this mean? We are to know and accept the truths proclaimed by Christ before we can enjoy the fruits of living in a right relationship with Him and God the Father. If we do not know what is required of us, then we will be disobedient to God, and succumb to the snares of the devil. The Apostle John says, . . . *believe not every spirit, but try* (test) *the spirits whether they are of God* [1 John 4:1]. Calvin stresses the truth that "Satan strives to infect and corrupt" the purity of Scripture "by all sorts of errors." Therefore, we are to beware, we are to be able to distinguish between true and false teachings, and we are not to listen to or be part of any teaching or group that denies that Christ is the Son of God or denies the truths regarding Him, His life, and His teachings.

The New Testament aggressively attacks false teachings and beliefs in lies. Remember, Paul wrote to the brethren in Galatia, *But though we, or an angel from heaven, preach* (tell the good news) *any other gospel unto you than that which we have preached unto you, let him be accursed* [Gal. 1:8]. Then to show the severity of what he is saying, Paul practically repeats himself, *As we said before, so say I now again, If any man preach any other gospel unto you than that ye have received, let him be accursed* [Gal. 1:9].

The apostles were not wishy-washy. Yet, in the twentieth and twenty-first centuries when people stand strong in the Word, or will not compromise Christ's teachings, others say they are negative, narrow, opinionated, or disruptive.

Again, how am I to put on the girdle of truth? How am I to know it? First, what is the authority for the truth contained, identified, and revealed in Scripture? It is not human reason, based upon modern technology or knowledge. If it were then every fifty to one hundred years the knowledge base would change. God and His truth are unchangeable. He is the same yesterday, today, and tomorrow.

Second, am I to know the truth through my feelings? If there is anything that is changeable or unreliable, it is feelings. They are constantly changing. Further, feelings are subjective, subject to what happens to us and to how well we fare day to day.

Third, is the authority for truth to be the Roman Catholic Church, or the Presbyterian Church, or the governing body of any denomination? Are the pronouncements or the traditions of churches the truth? No, the truth that is in Christ Jesus is unchangeable.

Lloyd-Jones asks a very penetrating question, "Can you see your church as she is today in the New Testament?" This is a question that we must ask. However, if we ask it, then we must be prepared to learn what the New Testament says. We must be able to distinguish between the teachings of Christ and the pronouncements of men.

You may ask, "What does this have to do with me?" Plenty! You are a member of Christ's body. You cannot hand these things over to a priest or minister. You have to deal with it. You are one of the saints and the faithful. You are neither a bystander nor a spectator. You are a participant, a combatant.

You are to grasp the New Testament teachings regarding the truth as it is found in Christ. And you have to beware of the pronouncements of men and governing church bodies. Recall Paul telling the Ephesians, *There is one body, and one Spirit, even as ye are called in one hope of your calling; One Lord, one faith, one baptism, One God and Father of all, who is above all, and through all, and in you all* [Eph. 4:4–6]. We are to clothe ourselves with the truth as it is found in the Lord Jesus Christ. Not with human reason or modern knowledge, or with feelings, or with church pronouncements, or traditions, but with the truth as it is in Christ.

What about those who speak authoritatively or from positions of authority? People will listen to them and accept their pronouncements. However, we have a responsibility to distinguish between true and false teachings. It is not something we can abrogate or ignore. It is our responsibility to know the basis of a person's authority.

Where is that authority to be found? In Scripture, the Word of God. It is the sole authority regarding matters of faith and practice. We are to be knowledgeable about the *whole counsel of God*, not just part of it.

What is the Reformed position? The Bible is the Word of God, not that it contains the Word, but that it is the Word. And that God through the Holy Spirit controlled and inspired the men who wrote the different books of the Bible.

When you think about authority, truth, the Word, and yourself, it is easy to succumb to the *wiles* (schemes) *of the devil* and say, what difference does it make? Why put forth the effort? Why bother? Think of Martin Luther. Suppose he had listened to peer pressure. Thank God he did not. It makes a difference what we believe and where we stand. We are to stand on "The impregnable Rock of Scripture," as W.E. Gladstone stated.

Why did Luther say, "Here I stand, I can do no other"? God revealed to Him that it was Scripture, the Word, that contained the truth, not the church, nor men, nor philosophers. Paul states it concisely to the Corinthians,

> *That your faith should not stand* (be) *in the wisdom of men, but in the power of God.*
> *Howbeit we speak wisdom among them that are perfect* (mature): *yet not the wisdom of this world, nor of the princes* (rulers) *of this world* (age), *that come to nought:*
> *But we speak the wisdom of God in a mystery, even the hidden wisdom, which God ordained* (predetermined) *before the world* (ages) *unto our glory:*
> *Which none of the princes* (rulers) *of this world* (age) *knew: for had they known it, they would not have crucified the Lord of glory* [1 Cor. 2:5–8].

God is what He is, *I am that I am*. God accommodates Himself to us. He reveals Himself to us bit by bit, truth by truth. He is infinite, absolute, and eternal. This we must realize. Then we can begin to grasp something of the truth as it is in Christ. *But God hath revealed them unto us by his Spirit: . . . That we might know the things that are freely given to us of God* [1 Cor. 2:10, 12]. The Holy Ghost teaches these truths, and we are to clothe ourselves with them. What does the truth of God do? Several things. May I suggest that it disturbs us, and it prods us. It also strengthens and comforts us.

Bear in mind, *All Scripture is given by inspiration of God, and is profitable for doctrine* [2 Tim. 3:16]. Peter reminds us,

> *We have also a more sure word of prophecy* (counsel of God); . . .
> *Knowing this first, that no prophecy of Scripture is of any private interpretation* (origin).
> *For the prophecy came not in old time by the will of man: but holy men of God spake as they were moved by the Holy Ghost* [2 Pet. 1:19–21].

Jesus says, *The Scripture cannot be broken* [John 10:35]. Luke records the following:

> *And he* (Jesus) *said unto them, These are the words which I spake unto you, while I was yet with you, that all things must be fulfilled, which were written in the law of Moses, and in the prophets, and in the psalms, concerning me.*
> *Then opened he their understanding, that they might understand the scriptures* [Luke 24:44–45].

At the conclusion of the Sermon on the Mount, Scripture says, *For he taught them as one having authority, and not as the scribes* [Matt. 7:29].

John says in his Gospel, *No man hath seen God at any time; the only begotten Son, which is in the bosom of the Father, he hath declared Him* [John 1:18]. What is the truth we are to put on? What is the authority? Where do we find them? In Christ Jesus as He is presented and revealed in the Word of God.

Amen!

13

The Righteousness of God

> *Stand therefore, having your loins girt about (your waist) with truth, and having on the breastplate of righteousness* [Eph. 6:14].

Life is filled with low points, high points, and in-between points. But mostly, our days, our functions, and our encounters are in-between points. We are not down in the pits nor are we on the mountaintops. The vast majority of life is spent in-between.

The Roman soldier spent most of his time: performing routine assignments and duties; preparing himself; carrying out orders; serving the Emperor; and doing many little, necessary things. He knew what was required, and he did it!

How often have you thought of yourself as Christ's soldier? Yes, we have all sung with gusto that great hymn, "Onward, Christian Soldiers," by Sabine Baring-Gould. The first verse and the refrain stir us and move us for the moment. Oh, but what truths are contained in the second and third verses. The words state clearly what we have been studying in Ephesians and the New Testament. Listen to them.

> *Like a mighty army*
> *Moves the Church of God;*
> *Brothers we are treading*
> *Where the saints have trod;*
> *We are not divided, All one body we,*
> *One in hope and doctrine, One in charity.*
>
> *Crowns and thorns may perish,*
> *Kingdoms rise and wane,*
> *But the Church of Jesus,*

> *Constant will remain;*
> *Gates of hell can never*
> *'Gainst that Church prevail;*
> *We have Christ's own promise,*
> *And that cannot fail.*

Yet the uninformed removed this magnificent, truthful hymn from our hymnals. What a travesty! Those words contain New Testament truths. We are to put them on and live by them. They are to be part and parcel of our daily living.

Charles Wesley wrote a magnificent hymn that is most appropriate as we study the whole armor of God. Let me share with you the meaningful words in "Soldiers of Christ, Arise."

> *Soldiers of Christ arise,*
> *And put your armor on,*
> *Strong in the strength which God supplies*
> *Through His eternal Son.*
> *Strong in the Lord of hosts,*
> *And in His mighty power,*
> *Who in the strength of Jesus trusts*
> *Is more than conqueror.*
>
> *Stand then, in His great might,*
> *With all His strength endued;*
> *And take, to arm you for the fight,*
> *The panoply of God:*
> *That, having all things done,*
> *And all your conflicts passed,*
> *Ye may o'ercome, through Christ alone,*
> *And stand complete at last.*
>
> *Leave no unguarded place,*
> *No weakness of the soul;*
> *Take every virtue, every grace,*
> *And fortify the whole.*
> *From strength to strength go on;*
> *Wrestle, and fight, and pray;*
> *Tread all the powers of darkness down,*
> *And win the well-fought day.*

These are strong words, accurate and true. They reflect the teachings of the New Testament and contain the truths of the Master. They talk about day-to-day happenings: going to the market, going to work, going out into the secular world, encountering the forces of the evil one, and being tempted. These are the places where the members of Christ's body are confronted by their adversary, Satan. They are engaged in a relentless, mortal battle with him. It never ceases. Therefore, as Christ's soldiers they need the whole armor of God, and they need to know how to use it.

One time while having our morning devotions we were struck by a little word and a big thought. The little word was *add*. The big thought is what we have to do as members of Christ's body in putting on the whole armor of God. Peter says,

> And beside this (But also for this very reason), *giving all diligence, add to your faith virtue; and to virtue knowledge;*
> And to knowledge temperance (self-control); *and to temperance patience* (perseverance); *and to patience godliness;*
> And to godliness brotherly kindness; and to brotherly kindness charity (love).
> For if these things be in you (are yours), *and abound, they make you that ye shall neither be barren* (useless) *nor unfruitful in the knowledge of our Lord Jesus Christ* [2 Pet. 1:5–8].

What is the Holy Spirit saying through Peter? That you have things to do. You are Christ's soldier. You are one of His disciples. Since you are, prepare yourself. You are going on active duty. You are going to be a witness. You are going to have to give an account of yourself.

Oswald Chambers states it beautifully, yet matter-of-factly, "You have inherited the Divine nature, says Peter, now screw your attention down and form habits, give diligence, concentrate. 'Add' means all that character means. No man is born either naturally or supernaturally with character, he has to make character. Nor are we born with habits; we have to form habits on the basis of the new life God has put into us . . . Drudgery is the touchstone of character. The great hindrance in spiritual life is that we will look for big things to do . . . Jesus *took a towel . . . and began to wash the disciples feet*" [John 13:4–5].

There are times when there is no illumination and no thrill, just the daily round, the common task. Routine is God's way of saving us between our times of inspiration. Do not expect God always to give you His thrilling minutes, but learn to live in the domain of drudgery by the power of God.

It is the "adding" that is difficult. Do not expect God to carry you to heaven on flowery beds of ease, and act as if you do! The tiniest detail obeyed has all the omnipotent power of the grace of God behind it. If we do our duty, not for duty's sake but because we believe God is engineering our circumstances, then at the point of obedience the whole super grace of God is ours through the Atonement.

What are we considering? Daily living, being soldiers, strength and power, applying truths, routine performance, character, obedience, the superb grace of God, and the righteousness of God in Christ. The exhortation in the last chapter of Ephesians is to put on the whole armor of God and to clothe your loins and body with truth, *having on the breastplate of righteousness.* Scripture says, *having on.* It does not say "have a breastplate," rather it says *having on the breastplate.* It is to be put on and used!

What does the Apostle mean by this particular command? The breastplate was used to protect the Roman soldier both in his front and back. It extended from the neck to the thighs. It was used to protect the heart and other vital parts of the body. The breastplate of righteousness protects the heart from Satan's attacks and the temptations that befall or confront us.

God has endowed us with feelings, affections, desires, and a will. However, they are to be developed and used according to His teachings. How is this accomplished? By the righteousness of God through the Lord Jesus Christ.

Why does Paul tell us, not ask us, to have on at all times the breastplate of righteousness? Calvin provides illumination and much food for thought saying, "he recommends *righteousness*, and desires that it should be a breastplate to protect the chest. Some imagine that this refers to free righteousness, which consists of [the] remission of sins. But to my mind this would be irrelevant here; for Paul is dealing with innocence of life. He wants us adorned, first, with integrity, and next with a devout and holy life." Ponder that today, tomorrow and tomorrow forevermore. God wants us adorned with integrity, not just on Sundays, but every day, wherever we go, whatever we do, and with whomever we associate. This will lead to what God wants—a devout and holy life for you and for me.

Before proceeding, there is a matter of the utmost importance to address. Some interpreters claim that righteousness can be interpreted as moral rectitude, or integrity, or being a just and good person. These traits may be respected by certain people. Each one is desirable, but inadequate when confronted by *the wiles* (schemes) *of the devil,* when wrestling against flesh and blood, principalities, powers, rulers of darkness, and spiritual wickedness. Human traits are inadequate in the war against Satan and cannot be depended upon. It requires the righteousness of God found in Jesus Christ. The Apostle did not rely upon those human traits, nor have the great saints and disciples throughout the ages.

Scripture reveals that there are two types of righteousness. *The righteousness which is in the law, . . .* [Phil. 3:6] and *That which is through the faith of Christ, the righteousness which is of God by faith* [Phil. 3:9]. According to the law, Saul was in the eyes of his contemporaries blameless and without spot. He did things that cultivated a life of integrity by man's standards and interpretation, because he acted according to the acceptable practices of the law. However, this was the case before Christ revealed Himself to Saul and before Saul knew his Lord and Master and became the Apostle Paul.

Years later, Paul would write from a different perspective; from knowledge acquired through study, revelation, and practice; from walking with the Master; and from subverting his will to Christ's. Then he would proclaim that, "Righteousness is obtained through faith, and resides in faith in Christ . . . The righteousness of the law must be given up and renounced, that you may be righteous through faith, and second, the righteousness of faith comes from God. It does not belong to man," as pronounced by John Calvin. There is not one part of this righteousness that comes from man, his ability, or his capability. It all comes from God.

William Gurnall describes two types of righteousness. First, there is legal righteousness, which requires a person to perform in a scrupulous, meticulous, punctilious, and careful manner every intent and letter of the law, every jot and tittle. Further, it is to be done in absolutely perfect obedience to the law, and the obedience must be perpetual. There can be no stumbling or falling. It is impossible to achieve this type of righteousness.

Second, there is the righteousness of grace. It is possible to receive righteousness in this way. The question is *how*? The righteousness of grace is received in two ways. William Gurnall identifies them as, "Imputed righteousness, which is wrought by Christ for the believer" and "Imparted righteousness, which is wrought by Christ in the believer." This righteousness of grace is wrought for the believer and in the believer. Gurnall amplifies upon this by stating, "The imputed righteousness, is the righteousness of our justification, by which the believer stands just and righteous before God and is called, . . . the righteousness of God."

This is known as justification by faith. God's standards are different from our standards. We cannot perform according to them. What does our Lord say?

> *Jesus said unto him, THOU SHALT LOVE THE LORD THY GOD WITH ALL THY HEART, AND WITH ALL THY SOUL, AND WITH ALL THY MIND.*
> *This is the first and great commandment.*
> *And the second is like unto it, THOU SHALT LOVE THY NEIGHBOR AS THYSELF* [Matt. 22:37–39].

Who can live according to those two commandments? No one! That is why God sent His only begotten Son into the world. That is why He imputed His righteousness unto us. That is why He went to the Cross and bore our sins on His body. Paul states it clearly to the Corinthians, saying, *For he hath made him to be sin for us, who knew no sin; that we might be made the righteousness of God in him* [2 Cor. 5:21]. What does this mean? He imputes His righteousness to us.

If a person owes a debt, and it is transferred to another, then it is imputed. But that is not sufficient. The person to whom the debt was transferred also pays it willingly, fully, and according to all prescribed conditions. Christ not only pays the debt, but He imputes His righteousness to me. When God looks upon me, He sees the righteousness of His Son. I have not kept the law. I cannot keep the smallest, most minute portion of it. But Christ has, and it is imputed to me. The Apostle says, *And be found in Him, not having mine own righteousness, which is of the law, but that which is through the faith of Christ, the righteousness which is of God by faith* [Phil. 3:9]. This imputed righteousness is "not only wrought by Christ, but also performed in Christ, who is God, and it is not inherent in us, though for us, so that the benefit of it redounds by faith to us, as if we had wrought it," as properly and thankfully described by William Gurnall.

"The imparted righteousness begins where the imputed righteousness leaves off. God "begins to work in me the righteousness of His own Son. He 'imparts' it to me. He makes it a part of me. He puts it into me . . . there is a new seed of life 'implanted in me.' The seed is to grow and develop within us. It is to be accepted, not rejected. We are to provide an environment in which it will grow," according to Martyn Lloyd-Jones. The Apostle Paul adds to this, saying, *Wherefore, my beloved, as ye have always obeyed, not as in my presence only, but now much more in my absence, work out your own salvation with fear and trembling. For it is God which worketh in you both to will and to do of* (according to) *his good pleasure* [Phil. 2:12–13].

What is required to grow in grace and in the knowledge of God and Christ? We need to keep adding. We are to put on, keep on, and use the breastplate of righteousness. We are to have confidence in it. We are to say with the prophet Ezra, *The joy of the Lord is your strength* [Neh. 8:10]. It is that strength that we need. How can we get it? By clothing ourselves with the truth and having on the breastplate of righteousness.

How are we to use it? We are to endeavor to walk, as Gurnall says, "In the power of holiness and righteousness in (His) life and conversation." This is to be done day in and day out. Luke says of Zechariah and Elisabeth, *And they were both righteous before God, walking in all the commandments and ordinances of the Lord blameless* [Luke 1:6]. Paul says, in addition to the above, *And herein* (this being so) *do I exercise* (strive) *myself, to have always a conscience void of* (without) *offense toward God, and toward men* [Acts 24:16].

"Righteousness is not a day or a week luxury, but a seven days a week necessity, if we are to resist Satan's temptations. . . . 'of righteousness.' . . . This breastplate of righteousness is ours when we live according to the pattern of Christ and the precepts of the Word in our relationship to men. We can then stand before Satan's accusations with a good conscience and without self-reproach. We can also stand before his temptations without yielding. But there must be no flaw in the breastplate in the form of (a) permitted wrong habit or practice. In all things, large and small, there must be strictest integrity . . . to our knowledge of God's Word and ways. A lustful desire allowed to rest in the heart can result in adultery; a love of money can lead to theft or to dishonesty in securing or handling funds. 'Nothing exposes a saint in conflict more readily than a bad conscience in his ways,' as expressed by Ruth Paxson.

What factors enable us to walk in the commandments and ordinances of the Lord? Certainly, it is neither emotionalism nor feelings. It begins with an objective recognition and acceptance of what Christ has done for us. It involves the will, the heart, and the mind. Paul says, *But God be thanked, that* (though) *ye were the servants* (slaves) *of sin, but ye have obeyed from the heart* (affections, feelings) *that form of doctrine which was delivered* (entrusted to) *you* (to your mind) [Rom. 6:17]. There you have the three components: mind, heart, and will.

Certainly, it is not "remarkable and unusual experiences," as some unknown person observed. The Apostle Paul had more than his share, with the escape from Damascus, the events in prison, the insect in the fire, the storm at sea, and others. But they were not the basis of his faith, nor what enabled him to walk according to God's commandments. As a general rule we are not to rely on experiences but on the teachings of the Master and God's truth as it is revealed in Him.

Further, it is not the functions we have performed, the deeds we have done, or the services we have rendered. Luke records Jesus saying, *So likewise ye, when ye shall have done all those things which are commanded you, say, We are unprofitable servants: we have done that which was our duty to do* [Luke 17:10]. This is the position and status of Christ's disciple. This should not be a cause for concern, but for rejoicing. Paul says to the Corinthians, *For other foundation can no man lay than that is laid, which is Jesus Christ* [1 Cor. 3:11]. We may build on it with various things, but the foundation has been laid. "Christ is the one and only foundation of the Church," as defined by John Calvin, and we are members of it.

As I walk in the commandments and ordinances of the Lord, why do I need the breastplate of righteousness? It is necessary to keep things from harming me and my relationship to God, such things as spiritual depression; trials and tribulations; distractions and discouragement; entanglements keeping me from the Word of God; perplexities, despair, and persecution; and questions regarding the authority of Christ. Any of these things can happen to the saints and the faithful. These things can overwhelm us, especially when we think we have been obedient to His commands. The devil will appeal to us, he will tempt us, and he will beguile us.

When this happens we are required to do a very difficult thing. We are to "rest in the Lord and wait patiently for Him." When we do this, we are in a state of preparedness. We are to do as our Scripture says, *having put on the breastplate of righteousness*. We are to remember who we are and who has called us to be His disciple. When considering this teaching, the hymn, "Am I a Soldier of the Cross," by that great saint, Isaac Watts, becomes more meaningful.

Am I a soldier of the cross,
A follower of the Lamb?
And shall I fear to own His cause,
Or blush to speak His name?

Must I be carried to the skies
On flowery beds of ease,
While others fought to win the prize,
And sailed through bloody seas?

Are there no foes for me to face?
Must I not stem the flood?
Is this vile world a friend to grace,
To help me on to God?

Sure I must fight, if I would reign;
Increase my courage, Lord;
I'll bear the toil, endure the pain,
Supported by thy Word.

Do we need the breastplate of righteousness? Indeed, we do!
 Amen!

14

Christ's Righteousness

Stand therefore, having your loins girt about (your waist) *with truth, and having on the breastplate of righteousness* [Eph. 6:14].

What are we? What are we called to do? What is given to us? What is required of us? Is faith in God through the Lord Jesus Christ active or passive? Does it make a difference what we believe and how we act? Why is there so much emphasis in Scripture upon "obey" and "obedience," upon "follow my commandments" and "do my will"? Why is there so little emphasis in the church today on these matters?

When considering these questions it is well to remember the special teachings of the Old Testament and to learn the truths contained in the New Testament. God called Abraham and made a covenant with him. Abraham responded in faith. He learned, he obeyed, he practiced.

God called Moses. He spoke through Moses. He gave the law through Moses. He told the people to keep His statutes and ordinances. God said, *Speak unto all the congregation of the children of Israel, and say unto them, Ye shall be holy: for I the Lord your God am holy* [Lev. 19:2].

The prophets in the Old Testament and the apostles in the New Testament talk repeatedly about being righteous, the righteous One, and righteousness. The Scripture being considered emphasizes the righteousness of God. Paul states that God has chosen us, *That we should be holy and without blame before Him in love* [Eph. 1:4].

Scripture from Genesis through Revelation calls us to be, to do, to act, to obey, and to fight the good fight. Yes, we are to respond in faith, but we are to clothe ourselves with the truth as it is found in Christ. We are part of the act. We are not spectators who go to see a performance, sit comfortably, applaud at the right time, then get up and go home. No, that is not it. We are to learn our parts and do them.

As stated previously, our relationship with the Lord Jesus Christ involves the mind, the heart, and the will. All three! Too many people think it involves only feelings and emotions. That is not what the prophets, psalmists, and apostles teach.

It is, or it should be, most important for us to know about the *breastplate of righteousness* and the *righteousness of God which is by faith of Jesus Christ unto all and upon all them that believe* [Rom. 3:22]. Further, we need to know about imputed righteousness, to know about imparted righteousness, to know that my relationship to God is based upon fact, not some faint hope or wish, but comforting and satisfying facts. This requires a positive response, even though I am a fallible sinner incapable of attaining righteousness by myself. I can only attain it through Christ Jesus and His grace.

This is something to be grasped by the mind, the heart, and the will. Then it is to be applied. Think of the words of that beautiful old hymn by Isaac Watts.

> *When I survey the wondrous cross,*
> *On which the prince of glory died,*
> *My richest gain I count but loss,*
> *And pour contempt on all my pride.*
>
> *Love so amazing, so divine,*
> *Demands my soul, my life, my all.*

Why does the Apostle exhort us to have *on the breastplate of righteousness*? God's covenant with Abraham calls for a special relationship with Him. We are to be holy. We are to be righteous through the imputed and imparted righteousness of Christ.

We are to realize and accept Paul's statement, *For all the promises of God in him are yea, and in him Amen, unto the glory of God by us. Now he which stablisheth* (establishes) *us with you in Christ, and hath anointed us, is God* [2 Cor. 1:20–21]. In this verse, *stablish* means "to make firm," "to make secure." That is the way we are to be. We are to be like a boat securely tied to its moorings. No matter what happens, no matter what storms occur, the rope will hold fast. God is the mooring. Christ is the rope. We are the boats.

The prophet, Isaiah, tells of the Messiah's coming saying,

> AND *there shall come forth a rod* (shoot) *out of the stem* (stock) *of Jesse, and a Branch shall grow* (bear fruit) *out of his roots:*
> *But with righteousness shall he judge the poor, . . . reprove* (decide with uprightness) *. . . the meek of the earth: . . . smite* (strike) *the earth . . . , and slay the wicked.*
> *And righteousness shall be the girdle* (belt) *of his loins, and faithfulness the girdle* (belt of his waist) *of his reins* [Isa. 11:1, 4–5].

Righteousness comes from and through the Messiah. "No one except the Messiah can and will establish it among his people . . . it is a gift of God!" as Markus Barth exclaims in adoration of the Lord Jesus and God His Father.

Paul realized and understood that each piece of armor is a gift from God that is to be used. Further, and this is important, Paul understood from the law, the prophets, the psalmists, the apostles, and the teachings of the Master that righteousness is a gift that is to be added to day by day and year by year. But there is a catch to this righteousness. Yes, it is a gift! But there is a condition. You are to use it. You are not to exchange it, you are not to throw it away, and you are not to hide it. You are to use it!

Karl Barth declares incisively that "Paul never speaks of a faith that is quietistic in regard to ethics, and passive in situations that demand decisions and action." Paul states clearly that we are to exhibit *obedience to the faith . . . for his name* [Rom. 1:5]. *God will show forth His righteousness in those who respond in faith and obedience.*

It was a great honor for an officer, or another individual, to receive a breastplate in recognition of their performance and ongoing contributions. However, it was obligatory upon the recipient to continue performing his duties ineffably. The same is true today of those *who respond in faith and obedience,* and receive the breastplate of righteousness. When our Lord talked about the faithful and wise steward, what did He say? *For unto whomsoever much is given, of him shall much be required* [Luke 12:48]. The honor is great, but the duty is a great responsibility!

Contrary to popular opinion, *the life in Christ is one of demands, requirements, obedience, and fighting the good fight of faith.* It is not a life of ease and rest, where you go merrily on your way. First, throughout life we are confronted by the fact of sin, whether we accept it or not. Sin is in us, and it is in others. It affects our relationship to God, to others, and to ourselves. Sin is a fact. It cannot be ignored.

The only way we can be in a right relationship with God, others, and ourselves is to be completely dependent upon the Lord Jesus Christ and His righteousness. Achieving this relationship is dependent upon the grace of God and responding in faith with our minds, hearts, and wills. If you do not, you will succumb to *the wiles* (schemes) *of the devil*, and he will get the best of you each and every time. The only way to repel the devil is through the Word of God and the Lord Jesus Christ. The author of the letter to the Hebrews sheds additional light on this matter, saying,

> *Seeing then that we have a great high priest, that is passed into* (through) *the heavens, Jesus the Son of God, let us hold fast our profession.*
> *For we have not a high priest which cannot* (sympathize) *be touched with* (our weaknesses) *the feeling of our infirmities; but was in all points tempted like as we are, yet without sin.*
> *Let us therefore come boldly* (confidently) *unto the throne of grace, that we may obtain mercy, and find grace to help in time of need* [Heb. 4:14–16].

This Scripture affirms that Christ is our high priest. He takes our infirmities. He grants us mercy. He provides help in the time of need. His righteousness is imputed and imparted to us. All this comes from the throne of grace, where we obtain His mercy and His grace. Paul states it a little differently, saying that we need to *have on the breastplate of righteousness*.

The Apostle John says,

> *And hereby we know that we are of the truth, and shall assure* (persuade) *our hearts before him.*
> *For if our heart condemn us, God is greater than our heart, and knoweth all things.*
> *Beloved, if our heart condemn us not, then have we confidence toward God.*
> *And whatsoever we ask, we receive of him, because we keep his commandments, and do those things that are pleasing in his sight* [1 John 3:19–22].

John speaks to those who get down on themselves or who do not feel that they are honoring or praising God as they should, and as a result they condemn themselves. It is at times like this that we are to focus our eyeballs outwardly toward God and not inwardly toward our emotions and feelings. Remember, God looks on our motives. He observes our prayer life, our obedience to His commands, our conduct, our treatment of others, our dependence on Him, and how we walk with the Lord Jesus. Praise God that the truth is that our relationship with Him depends upon our faith in the Lord Jesus Christ, not on our works.

How do we know that we are of the truth? When we receive an understanding of our righteousness through faith and the truth as it is revealed in Christ. It is in this way that our hearts are assured. "There can be no genuine assurance before God unless His spirit produces in us the fruit of love," as John Calvin insightfully observed. These verses reveal that the godly "truly and sincerely fear God and desire to submit to His righteousness. However, the ungodly, those who have an evil conscience, those who do not fear God, and worship Him, they are not heard when they do call upon God," as John Calvin continued to expound clearly and forcefully. Though this may not sound nice, it is supported by Scripture.

In Matthew, Jesus says, *Depart from me, ye cursed, into everlasting fire, prepared for the devil and his angels* [Matt. 25:41]. The Apostle John says, *Whatsoever we ask, we receive of him, because we keep his commandments, and do the things that are pleasing in his sight* [1 John 3:22]. What is the Apostle John saying? "That godliness and the sincere worship of God cannot be separated from faith," according to John Calvin. We are to do the things pleasing to God. That leads us to the next point.

God wants us to be "a holy people," to know His will and to do it. What did God do to make this possible? He sent His Son into the world, *Who gave himself for us, that he might redeem us from all iniquity, and purify unto himself a peculiar* (his own special) *people, zealous of good works* [Titus 2:14]. "Had man kept his primitive righteousness, Christ's pain and pains would have been spared. It was because of man's lost holiness that he came to recover ... both God and man, between whom Christ comes to negotiate, call for holiness. God's glory and man's happiness; neither of which can be attained except holiness be restored to man," as clearly stated by William Gurnall. Christ undertakes to make His people "holy as God is holy."

These two factors, sin and to be a holy people, require that we put on *the breastplate of righteousness*. That is the only way to be protected and to become holy. A poem by Augustus Toplady sums it up beautifully:

> *A debtor to mercy alone,*
> *of covenant mercy I sing;*
> *Nor fear with Thy righteousness on*
> *my person and off'ring to bring.*
> *The terrors of law and of God*
> *With me can have nothing to do,*
> *My Saviour's obedience and blood*
> *Hide all my transgressions from view.*

When encountering opposition, temptation, or doubt we need to bear this thought in mind.

What happens when we put on and keep on the breastplate of righteousness? Do we enter into some utopia? Do we become perfect or attain some ideal position? Do we retire to a life of ease? The answer to these and similar questions is a resounding "No!" The only thing not appearing in the New Testament is that we achieve perfection, become infallible, and all our troubles go away.

Yes, we have a right relationship with God, but we are still fallible. We put on the new man, but the old nature is still there. Consequently, we can stumble and fall. We say with Paul, *For that which I do I allow* (understand) *not; for what I would* (want to do), *that do I not; but what I hate, that do I* [Rom. 7:15]. Though we believe the Gospel and have faith in the Lord Jesus Christ we still need to *have on the breastplate of righteousness* and use it. John's First Epistle throws further light on this subject.

> *If we say that we have fellowship with him, and walk in darkness, we lie, and do not* (practice) *the truth:*
> *But if we walk in the light, as he is in the light, we have fellowship one with another, and the blood of Jesus Christ his Son cleanseth us from all sin.*
> *If we say we have no sin, we deceive ourselves, and the truth is not in us.*
> *If we confess our sins, he is faithful and just to forgive us our sins, and to cleanse us from all unrighteousness.*
> *If we say that we have not sinned, we make him a liar, and his word is not in us* [1 John 1:6–10].

In these verses, the Apostle John uses the word *cleanseth* or *cleanse*. It is a verb used in the present tense to signify that the cleansing action is continuous. "It means that the blood of Christ keeps on cleansing us! Though we do not do as we would, and do as we would not, the cleansing keeps occurring. It does not stop," as affirmed by Martyn Lloyd-Jones in a loving, heartwarming way. The Apostle amplifies upon this in the next chapter when he says,

> MY little children, these things I write unto you, that ye (may not) sin not. And if any man sin, we have an advocate (intercessor) with the Father, Jesus Christ the righteous.
> And he is the propitiation for our sins: and not for ours only, but also for the sins of the whole world [1 John 2:1–2].

In these two verses John clearly states what Christ does for us. The flesh is weak. Therefore, it is important to know, as Calvin said, that "men should be carefully warned that righteousness and salvation are obtained by Christ's death that we may become God's holy possession!" That is why we have an advocate with the Father. We are far from being righteous, but His righteousness is imputed and imparted to us. This is done for all those truly believing in Him that are members of His body.

Then John tells us to *abide in Him* and to *know that He is righteous* and to *know that every one that doeth* (practices) *righteousness is born of him* [1 John 2:27, 29]. The Apostle wants to make us aware of the living presence of Christ and for us to have "a real sense of His power which begets confidence," according to John Calvin. It is one thing to feel something, but it is entirely different to know it and to have complete confidence in it. That is why Calvin thoughtfully says, "The godly calmly wait for Christ and do not dread His presence."

Our relationship to God is a fact, it is a legal one, it is according to the law. It is based upon God's grace and incorporates God's love, mercy, and justice. God is faithful, just, and holy. He has completely provided for us in our relationship with Him so that we may be righteous, holy, and free from sin in His sight. The Apostles John, Peter, and Paul are in complete agreement on this. They are in concord that our standing before God is not based upon what we do or our own goodness and righteousness.

What are we to do? We are to have on the breastplate of (Christ's) righteousness, know what it is, use it, and keep it shiny and in good repair. In addition, we are to know about our relationship with Christ and God, do as we are commanded to do, know the love of God for us, and do our duty as Christ would have us do it. Yes, we are to respond in faith. But faith requires action. It requires putting on the whole armor of God and having on the breastplate of righteousness.

John Calvin makes a very penetrating statement when commenting on John's statement, *If ye know that he is righteous* [1 John 2:29]! He says that the Apostle John, "By many arguments proves that faith is joined to a holy and pure life. First that we are spiritually begotten in the likeness of Christ. From this it follows that no one is born of Christ save He who lives righteously."

Therefore, in closing, focus on the meaningful words of that thoughtful hymn by William Longstaff, "Take Time to Be Holy."

> *Take time to be holy, Speak oft with thy Lord;*
> *Abide in Him always, And feed on His Word.*
> *Make friends of God's children; Help those who are weak;*
> *Forgetting in nothing His blessing to seek.*
>
> *Take time to be holy, The world rushes on;*
> *Much time spend in secret with Jesus alone;*
> *By looking to Jesus, Like Him thou shalt be;*
> *Thy friends in thy conduct His likeness shall see.*
>
> *Take time to be holy, Let Him be thy Guide,*
> *And run not before Him, Whatever betide;*
> *In joy or in sorrow, Still follow thy Lord,*
> *And, looking to Jesus, Still trust in His Word.*
>
> *Take time to be holy, Be calm in thy soul;*
> *Each thought and each motive Beneath His control;*
> *Thus led by His spirit To fountains of love,*
> *Thou soon shalt be fitted For service above.*

It is a great responsibility *having on the breastplate of righteousness.* Amen!

15

Stand and Go Forth

> *Wherefore take* (up) *unto you the whole armor of God, that ye may be able to withstand in the evil day, and having done all, to stand.*
> *Stand therefore, having your loins girt about* (your waist) *with truth, and having on the breastplate of righteousness* [Eph. 6:13–14].

Numerous parts of Scripture are more appealing than others. It is much more popular to proclaim, "God is love," than to state what is required of the true believers who are members of Christ's body. It is more popular to tell the Christmas story than to confront church members with the fact of sin, disobedience, and unrighteousness. Also, it is more popular to state that a loving God will call and accept everyone, whether they exhibit or profess any faith or not, than to remind people that the Master stated, *For many be called, but few chosen* [Matt. 20:16].

Man, including governments and supreme courts, cannot make decrees or rulings that will determine developments or happenings in the spiritual realm. It is our responsibility to read and examine all Scripture, to understand it, to become knowledgeable, and to know what is required of us. There are many things we do not know, yet we may assume certain thoughts, ideas, or possibilities.

Our Lord's high priestly prayer in John 17 provides certain truths that should enable one to better understand His teachings and to serve Him. The Lord Jesus prayed,

> *I pray for them: I pray not for the world, but for them which thou hast given me, for they are thine.*
> *And all mine are thine, and thine are mine; and I am glorified in them.*

> *I have given them thy word; and the world hath hated them, because they are not of the world, even as I am not of the world.*
> *I pray not that thou shouldest take them out of the world, but that thou shouldest keep them from the evil* (one).
> *They are not of the world, even as I am not of the world.*
> *Sanctify* (set) *them* (apart) *through thy truth: thy word is truth* [John 17:9–10, 14–17].

In this prayer, the Lord presents some very distinct and definite contrasts. He specifically prays for those given to Him by the Father who believe God sent Him into the world. "He openly declares that He does not pray for the world, for He is solicitous only for His own flock which He received from the Father's hand." Also, "Christ expressly declares that they who are given to Him belong to the Father," as John Calvin faithfully expounds upon God's Word.

Christ specifically states that He has given the believers *thy word* and what happened? *The world hated them* [John 17:14]. Why does Christ give us His Word? Why does He pray for us? "That Christ's joy may be fulfilled in us," as expressed by Calvin. There is a definite purpose in Christ's actions, prayers, and truth. It is to fulfill the Father's will and to produce joy in us. Either we become obedient to Christ or to the world. We have a choice by God's grace.

The Master, in His high priestly prayer, does not pray to the Father that we be taken out of the world, or that a fence be erected around us, or that we have a special position. He does not pray that we have a life of ease or pleasure or that all our troubles, afflictions, problems, harassments go away and never reappear. Nor does he pray to remove all anxieties or negative circumstances from our lives. Though those things may beset us, our focus is to be upon the object of our faith, none other than the Lord Jesus Christ Himself. Our eyeballs are not to be turned inwardly, but to seek, search, and find the Lord of the universe. His strength will sustain us. God wants us to be strong in the faith. *My grace is sufficient for thee: for my strength* (power) *is made perfect in weakness* [2 Cor. 12:9].

In the Book of Revelation, the Lord Jesus says to the members at Sardis, *For thou hast a little strength, and hast kept my word, and hast not denied my name.* [Rev. 3:8] A little strength will enable us to keep His Word. But we must know it and not deny it. In His high priestly prayer the Lord Jesus prays that we are sanctified and states very appropriately, *Thy word is truth* [John 17:17].

People, including ministers and teachers, talk about our Lord's beautiful prayer on the night He was betrayed, but they do not grasp, or they overlook or ignore the abundant truths contained in these twenty-six verses.

The seventeenth verse is particularly critical. People talk about sanctification, but they fail to read, study, and hear the Word that is truth. Ministers do not proclaim the full Gospel. Teachers do not present the full truth. The hearers want to pick and choose. You will note that the Lord Jesus did not say part of *thy word is truth* or that only certain prophets spoke the truth. Here in this prayer, the obedient Son, the obedient servant, said unequivocally, *Thy Word is truth,* not just portions of it.

What does Christ mean by this? Calvin supplies the answer saying, "Christ expressly says that the truth by which God sanctifies His sons exists nowhere but in the Word." What is meant by the Word? It is "the teaching of the Gospel, which the apostles had already heard from the mouth of their Master, and which they were afterwards to proclaim," as explicitly stated by John Calvin. Paul says in referring to the church *That he* (Christ) *might sanctify* (set it apart) *and cleanse it* (the church) *with the washing of water by the word* [Eph. 5:26]. It is God who sanctifies, but He does it through His Word.

What is the relationship between these truths contained in Christ's prayer and Paul's exhortation to *Stand therefore, having your loins girt about* (your waist) *with truth, and having on the breastplate of righteousness* [Eph. 6:14]? We are to stand: in the world; in our relationship to Christ; in the Word of truth; and in the knowledge of God. When we make this commitment, there are certain truths to bear in mind. We are to stand in the light and not in the darkness. *Ye were sometimes* (once) *darkness, but now are ye light in the Lord: walk as children of light* [Eph. 5:8]. Paul says to the Philippians, *For our conversation* (citizenship) *is in heaven: from whence also we look for the Saviour, the Lord Jesus Christ* [Phil. 3:20].

We are to aspire to live in the light and to travel in it on the heaven-bound road. Though we are exposed to the things of the world, we are to focus on the things of Christ and the Word of truth. The eleventh chapter of Hebrews reminds us incisively of the people of God who walked in the light and focused on the truths of God. The letter's author states repeatedly what the men of the Old Testament did by faith though they faced obstacles, opposition, and impossible tasks. Their eyes were turned outwardly toward God and serving Him.

The last two verses of this magnificent chapter say, *And these all, having obtained a good report* (testimony) *through faith, received not the promise: God having provided some better thing for us, that they without* (apart from) *us should not be made perfect* (complete) [Heb. 11:39–40]. What is the Holy Spirit telling us? That the full light of the Gospel should have a positive impact upon our faith, beliefs, attitudes, actions, and practices. "A tiny spark of light led them to heaven, but now that the sun of righteousness shines on us what excuse shall we offer if we still hold to the earth or the things of the world?" as Calvin in his inimical way enlightens us.

God's grace bestows much light upon us and should provide us with more abundant faith since we are aware of what God has done in and through Christ Jesus. We should exhibit our gratefulness to God's grace by walking in the light and learning the truth as contained in God's Word. This requires effort and obedience. Obedience to the commands of the Lord and a positive response to the apostles' exhortations.

Many times we are disobedient or nonresponsive because we do not want to miss out on something, or we do not want to be ridiculed, maligned, disliked, or considered a religious freak. What about the men of faith in the eleventh chapter of Hebrews? What about Paul, Peter, John, and Timothy? They had to choose between faith in God through Christ and being obedient to the Word of truth, or accepting the ways of the world.

When considering these teachings it is well to bear certain things in mind.

First, regarding the things of the world, "Worldliness is not confined to flagrant sinning," as noted by Martyn Lloyd-Jones. What do we mean by the things of the world? It is the things that keep God and Christ out of our lives or keep us from obeying His commands. They may seem proper in and of themselves, or it may be said, "everyone is doing it," but if the effect is to keep out the Lord Jesus Christ then we must turn our backs on it and move from darkness to light. This includes the acceptable and respectable things of society as well as those that are not, including being politically correct.

We are called to be holy, because the Lord our God is holy. We are called to be transformed into the image of God and to grow,

> *Till we all come in* (into) *the unity of the faith, and of the knowledge of the Son of God, unto a perfect* (complete) *man, . . .*
> *That we henceforth be no more children tossed to and fro . . . with every wind of doctrine, . . .*
> *But, speaking the truth in love, may grow up into him in all things, which is the head, even Christ* [Eph. 4:13–15].

Further, as Paul says, *Set your affection* (mind) *on things above, not on things on the earth* [Col. 3:2]. We are not called to change the world or society. We are called to serve the Lord and to become holy. We are sojourners, travelers, and pilgrims on earth. Our home is with the Lord. It is the place where we are going and where we will reside forever and ever.

There is a little-discussed Word of truth in the last chapter of the Bible, which says,

> *Blessed are they that do his commandments, that they may have right to the tree of life, and may enter in through the gates into the city.*
> *For without* (outside) *are dogs, and sorcerers, and whoremongers* (sexually immoral), *and murderers, and idolaters, and whosoever loveth and maketh* (practices) *a lie.*
> *I Jesus have sent mine angel to testify unto you these things in the churches* [Rev. 22:14–16].

This is a powerful statement! Jesus makes it clear that we are to obey His commandments, if we want to *enter in through the gates into the city.* Only those who through faith strive to learn and obey His commandments will enter through the gates. If we want to enter through the city *whose builder and maker is God* then we are to respond in faith to God through Christ and become obedient. We are to prepare ourselves for service above.

Therefore, we may ask, what are we to do? How are we to respond? The Apostle John is direct and to the point,

> *This then is the message which we have heard of him, and declare unto you, that God is light, and in him is no darkness at all.*
> *If we say that we have fellowship with him, and walk in darkness, we lie, and do not* (practice) *the truth:*

> *But if we walk in the light, as he is in the light, we have fellowship one with another, and the blood of Jesus Christ his Son cleanseth us from all sin* [1 John 1:5–7].

"If we claim (profess) that we are church members (go to church) having fellowship with God, yet walk in darkness (according to the ways of the world), then we are liars in whom there is no truth," as forcefully stated by Martyn Lloyd-Jones. It is difficult to misunderstand those words, especially if we have on the breastplate of righteousness.

What does the Apostle Paul say near the close of this meaningful letter? *Wherefore take* (up) *unto you the whole armor of God, . . . and having done all to stand. Stand therefore, . . . having on the breastplate of righteousness.* [Eph. 6:13–14]. You will note the words *wherefore* and *therefore* are used. When Paul says *wherefore* he is saying *on account of* or *because of* the things which I have been telling you. Then the Apostle says, *stand therefore . . . having on the breastplate of righteousness.*

The Apostle begins the fourth chapter saying, *I, THEREFORE, the prisoner of the Lord, beseech ye that you walk worthy of the vocation* (calling) *wherewith ye are called* [Eph. 4:1]. Paul made this statement after presenting the doctrine of our Lord Jesus Christ in the first three chapters. It is through doctrine that Paul tells the followers how they are to walk and to act. He does something similar in Romans where he says, *I BESEECH you therefore, brethren, by the mercies of God, that ye present your bodies a living sacrifice, holy, acceptable unto God, which is your reasonable* (rational) *service* [Rom. 12:1]. This verse is not only interesting, it is applicable to having on the breastplate of righteousness. "We are to seek for righteousness only from God; . . . and the sum of all our blessings is laid up for us and daily offered to us, in none but Christ." Further, "the soul is regenerated, . . . by that saving knowledge of God and of Christ," as proclaimed by John Calvin. If we are to live our lives according to the Word of truth then we are to know the teachings contained in Scripture. It is not a case of feelings or philosophy. It is a case of doctrine and truth.

In his letter to the Romans, Paul was concerned that the saints would not properly "worship God with a sincere heart . . . until they properly understand how much they are indebted to His mercy. And, that we should have a voluntary and cheerful love of righteousness," according to Calvin. The Apostle wanted to convey to the Romans and us that, "a godly mind is not formed by precepts or sanctions so much as by a serious meditation upon the divine goodness towards itself," as divinely revealed by Calvin. That reminds me of the old adage: "A man is not what he thinks he is, but he is what he thinks."

The Apostle says, *Present your bodies a living sacrifice, holy, acceptable to God*. We are to respond in faith, focusing our attention on God and the truth in His Word. When doing this we are to realize as members of Christ's body that we are to become holy, for the Lord our God is holy. Therefore, we are to examine the Word of truth and strive to apply it, because He will provide the strength to overcome our weaknesses. In order to live our lives in accordance with the will of God, it stands to reason that we must know the teachings contained in His Word.

People talk about going to worship God, spending one hour a week or a month in a sanctuary, and they call that worshipping God. That is not what the Apostle is talking about. "God is properly worshipped only when we regulate all our actions according to His command, . . . since He values obedience more than sacrifice," as John Calvin states with penetrating words.

Unfortunately, many people miss the point. They do not understand that they are to know the Word of truth and to apply it obediently. This leads to *having on the breastplate of righteousness* and to serving the Master. If you do not apply Christ's teachings they will be of no value to you.

If we are serious about worshipping God, then we must remember Paul's words earlier in this letter when he says, *This I say therefore, and testify in the Lord, that ye henceforth walk not as other Gentiles walk, in the vanity* (futility) *of their mind* [Eph. 4:17]. Then the Apostle proceeds to describe how we are to apply the Word of truth as we *put on the new man, which after God is created in righteousness and true holiness* [Eph. 4:24].

Applying these teachings continues throughout the fourth and fifth chapters and into the sixth chapter. After presenting these words of truth, the Apostle pulls it all together, saying,

> *Finally, my brethren, be strong in the Lord, and in the power of his might.*
> *Put on the whole armor of God, . . .*
> *Stand therefore, having your loins girt about* (your waist) *with truth, and having on the breastplate of righteousness* [Eph. 6:10–11, 14].

When considering these words it is well to remember the truths spoken by our Lord and Master in His high priestly prayer,

> *I pray for them: I pray not for the world,*
> *I have given them thy word; and the world hath hated them.*
> *Sanctify* (set) *them* (apart) *through thy truth: thy word is truth:*
> ... [John 17:9, 14, 17].

In closing, remember the words of Paul to the Romans, *And be not conformed to this world: but be ye transformed by the renewing of your mind, that ye may prove what is that good, and acceptable, and perfect, will of God* [Rom. 12:2]. We are to be renewed in the mind. Our hearts and our minds are to know the will of God and the Word of truth. Therefore, *we are to walk with Him . . . having on the breastplate of righteousness.* May we have the strength, courage, and resolve to stand in the light of His Word.

Amen!

16

Choices, Decisions, Priorities

And your feet shod with the preparation of the gospel of peace [Eph. 6:15].

How many choices have you made today and this past week? What priorities do you have today and did you have this past week? Probably a lot more than you can remember. Our lives are filled with choices, decisions, and priorities. The question is, what guides or determines your choices, decisions, and priorities? Basically, it is going to be either the experiences and teachings of the world, or the truth as revealed in the Lord Jesus Christ and proclaimed through the Word of God. There is a significant difference between the two. The former is in accord with our experiences and associations, and is impacted by peer pressure. It requires little additional effort. The latter is different. It requires learning the teachings of our Master, obeying His commands, and relinquishing one's self to His Spirit.

Joshua said, *Choose you this day whom ye will serve* [Josh. 24:15]. We are to choose between the straight gate and the broad way, between God and mammon, between false prophets and true ones, between building on rock or on sand. Our Master says, *Ye have not chosen me, but I have chosen you, and ordained* (appointed) *you, that you should go and bring forth fruit, and that your fruit should remain* [John 15:16]. We have to decide if we are going to accept and obey our Lord's commands or reject and ignore them. This reaction to the Word and to the Word made flesh contributes significantly to the priorities each of us establishes and toward which we exercise varying degrees of effort. Choices, decisions, and priorities influence greatly how we put on the whole armor of God and how we use it.

This brings us to the third item in God's armor. You will note that Scripture says, *Stand therefore, . . . And your feet shod with the preparation of the gospel of peace* [Eph. 6:14–15]. Our feet are very important. They carry us about, enable us to get to places, and help us to do things. Probably the only way we can ever realize how important they are is not being able to use them.

Ask a person who was in the infantry how important feet and shoes are. He will tell you in no uncertain terms. Those of us who are in God's army need to have our feet properly shod so that we may be Christ's obedient soldiers. "God has told us we would have temptations, trials, testings, so we must be prepared to stand the strain of the slippery paths of temptation and the stony hills of adversity and affliction . . . as we walk through this disordered world there are a thousand things to bruise and wound us . . . , but as good soldiers of God we are to have on the whole armor of God in our fight against Satan and his forces," as divinely assessed by Ruth Paxson. The battle with Satan continues throughout our lives, until we meet our Master face to face.

"How were the feet of the Roman soldiers, with whom Paul spent so much time, shod? They wore very substantial sandals fastened around the ankle with a strong thong or latchet. Another characteristic of this sandal was that it had hobnails or studs on the bottom. Why? To hold firm, to have sure footing, to keep from sliding, slipping, tumbling, falling, and to protect the feet from injury. A common practice in the warfare of that time was to place in the ground just above or below the surface sharp objects that would pierce the feet of the enemy and disable him. In addition to protection, the sandals provided mobility to the soldiers. Mobility is one of the greatest capabilities available to an army, and to the soldiers of Christ.

"If we are to serve our Master according to His commands, it is important for our feet to be properly shod. How is this to be accomplished? *With the preparation of the gospel of peace* does not mean to prepare yourself by putting on your sandals or shining your shoes. It means making sure the equipment is in a state of readiness and in good repair. Not only is the equipment to be ready for use, but the person using it is to be in a state of readiness" as accurately and meaningfully described by Martyn Lloyd-Jones.

Why does the Apostle tell us to be in a state of readiness? Some ministers and teachers proclaim that the reason for being in a state of readiness is to be able to take the Gospel to others and to evangelize them on short notice. That is not what the Apostle is teaching. Why do I say that? Note the context. The Holy Spirit guided Paul to describe the armor of God so that we may stand and withstand *against the wiles* (schemes) *of the devil . . . against principalities, against powers, against the rulers of darkness . . . against spiritual* (hosts of) *wickedness* [Eph. 6:11-12]. We are to be prepared and ready against all those things. This is not, repeat not, the occasion where we are called to go forth and evangelize. Scripture needs to be interpreted according to the context in which it is presented.

We are called *to be strong in the Lord, and in the power of his might* [Eph. 6:10]. Therefore, we are to be equipped and in a state of readiness to stand against whatever evil, obstacles, or opposition may come our way. We are to have confidence in our equipment, *the gospel of peace.* How our spiritual feet are shod makes a difference in how we stand and withstand.

It reminds me of a professional football championship game in the 1930s between the New York Giants and the Chicago Bears. The temperature was extremely cold, below freezing. The playing field was a sheet of ice. During the first half the players were slipping, sliding, and falling since they could not maintain their balance. Steve Owens, the Giants coach, had the owner of a sporting goods store bring his players tennis shoes at half time. They put them on, took to the field, and won the game since their feet *were shod with the preparation* for the icy field.

The Apostle calls us to stand fast in the Gospel. We are to know it, believe it, defend it, and be resolute according to God's grace in revealing His Holy will to us. Unfortunately, in the church today there is much emphasis on unity, actually meaning uniformity. There is emphasis on being affable, pleasant, nice, and compromising, instead of putting *on the new man, which after God is created in righteousness and true holiness*, and on becoming *kind one to another, tenderhearted, forgiving one another, even as God for Christ's sake hath forgiven you* [Eph. 4:24, 32].

Do you know where you stand? Are you equipping your spiritual feet? "Do you really believe that the Bible is the Word of God? Are you ready to stand for the deity of Christ, for His Virgin birth? For the miracles? Are you ready to stand for the resurrection of Christ as a literal fact? Are you ready to stand for the person of the Holy Spirit? Are you ready to put on the new man . . .To be filled with the Spirit? To submit yourselves one to another in the fear of Christ? To be strong in the Lord, to put on *the whole armor of God*? "Can you say with Luther 'Here I stand; I can do no other?'" as Martyn Lloyd-Jones asks in a direct and penetrating way.

Luther had to learn to stand and withstand, and so do we. Yes, there are choices to be made, decisions to be reached, and priorities to be established. If you remain wishy-washy, you cannot be a member of Christ's body or one of his disciples. *For the Son of God, Jesus Christ, who was preached among you by us, . . . was not yea and nay, but in him was yea* [2 Cor. 1:19].

What does this mean? That the Word proclaimed was "nothing but Christ who is the eternal and immutable truth of God. That his (Paul's) teaching of Christ was not changeable or ambiguous, so as to present Christ in different shapes at different times . . . , to please men, present Christ under different false disguises, and teach a thing one day and the next retract it, out of fear. Such was not Paul's Christ nor the Christ of any apostle . . . For the only true Christ is He in whom can be seen this invariable and perpetual 'yea' which Paul here declares to be characteristic of Him," as explicitly stated by Calvin, in providing sage advice for preachers and teachers.

How we stand, how we have our spiritual feet shod, is determined to a large extent by choices, decisions, and priorities. Are we on the Lord's side or on mammon's? Are we yea and nay? Do we betray our Lord, or do we obey our Lord? Are we learning the teachings of Christ or not? Are we watching and praying, lest we enter into temptation? Do we realize that temptation is anything that keeps us from God? Why do we consider these questions? Why should our spiritual feet be shod?

Please note that Paul says, *And no marvel; for Satan himself is transformed* (transforms himself) *into an angel of light* [2 Cor. 11:14]. Think on that! "If Satan can transform himself, what will his ministers do?" Calvin asks. The devil wants to get us into trouble. He wants to come between Christ and us. He will try anything and do anything. That is one reason we must put on God's armor and equip ourselves.

The enemy is not always discernible. The devil does not always appear ugly and foul and harsh and cruel. He can be most pleasant, affable, and ingratiating. Many are deceived by these changes. Affability is what most people mean by saintliness today. So nice, they say, so pleasant. "I talked to the man, and he was so kind." But the question is, what does he believe? The important question in this realm is not whether a man is nice or not. The question is, what is he saying? What does he say about the truth? "Ah, but he is so nice," people say. "He never says an unkind word about anyone. Therefore he must be a wonderful Christian," says the believer who does not have his feet shod with the preparation of the Gospel of Peace," as faithfully expressed by Martyn Lloyd-Jones in these several quotes.

What other factors can come between God and us? What things can impede the church and have a negative effect upon it?

There are people who are lifeless or sluggish in the church, yet they occupy positions of authority. Also, there are people who are dull or uninteresting and do not present the full Gospel, only selected portions.

There are people who have followed a particular routine for years. They go to church and participate because they always have. They really do not know why they go, except that it is expected of them. Or it is part of their works! These people are without a real understanding of the Christian message. In reality, these people are excess baggage.

Think of David and Goliath. The Israelites wanted to dress David in Saul's armor. It did not fit. He did not know how to use it. So what did David say? I cannot use Saul's armor; I must use my own method of fighting.

> *David said unto Saul, I cannot go with these; for I have not proved them. And David put them off him.*
> *And he took his staff in his hand, and chose him five smooth stones....*
> *Then said David to the Philistine . . . but I come to thee in the name of the Lord of hosts* [1 Sam. 17:39–40, 45].

It is clear that David would not fight in armor that did not fit and with which he was not familiar.

What did David rely upon? The Lord of hosts, the God of Israel. David said, *My heart is fixed* (steadfast), *. . . I will sing and give praise* [Ps. 57:7]. David had decisions to make and priorities to establish. He equipped himself, he picked up his sling, and he selected five smooth stones. He placed his confidence in God. *David hasted* (hastened*), and ran toward the army to meet the Philistine* [1 Sam. 17:48]. David had a right relationship with God. Though he was only a lad, the relationship had been developing over the years. There is an important lesson to learn here. Our strength does not depend upon numbers, but "In (our) relationship to God, and (our) ability to respond to His every suggestion, His every stimulus, His every move," as observed and noted by Martyn Lloyd-Jones. Our wills are to respond to His every command.

What do we need to do to have our feet shod with the proper equipment and to have the proper footing, so that we can stand firm wherever our feet may hit the ground and have the mobility necessary to respond to any command? In addition to having firmness and mobility in our spiritual feet, we need adaptability. We need to adapt the Gospel message to current situations, by always presenting the basic truths of Scripture.

One of the best analogies is warfare. The objective is to defeat the enemy and to occupy the territory. Over the years methods and material have changed, but certain principles remain constant, such as firmness, resoluteness, mobility, and adaptability.

Certainly, the Gospel is as relevant today regarding the needs of the people as it was two thousand years ago, and when proclaimed, it will meet the needs of individuals today. It is not for the purpose of trying to change society as a whole, but for bringing us one by one into a right relationship with the Lord Jesus Christ, where we willingly obey His commands. Changes in society will come about only then.

Unfortunately, too many times the church at large deals with the wrong problems. How are we to make choices and decisions and to establish priorities? Scripture says have *your feet shod with the preparation of the gospel of peace.* What does this require? What are we to do? What are we to achieve and realize? Peace with God, so that we do not have any doubts about our salvation. Romans states it very well, *THEREFORE being justified by faith, we have peace with God through our Lord Jesus Christ: By whom also we have access by faith into this grace wherein we stand, and rejoice in hope of the glory of God* [Rom. 5:1–2].

We must understand and accept the fact that our sins are forgiven, and we are reconciled to God. Paul says to the Thessalonians, *And the very God of peace sanctify you wholly: and I pray God your whole spirit and soul and body be preserved blameless unto the coming of the Lord Jesus Christ* [1 Thess. 5:23].

We are also to achieve peace within ourselves. Paul says to the Romans, *And we know that all things work together for good to them that love God, to them who are called according to his purpose* [Rom. 8:28].

This is difficult. This is hard. It takes time to reach the point in life where we can accept "That the troubles of this life are so far from hindering our salvation that they rather assist it," as truthfully stated by John Calvin. Oh, that we may reach that point. Paul says, *Be careful* (anxious) *for nothing; but in everything by prayer and supplication with thanksgiving let your requests be made known unto God* [Phil. 4:6]. Whoever said it would be easy? Peace within is not easy. The opposition, Satan, does not want us to have it.

Further, we are to realize peace with others. *If it be possible, as much as lieth in* (depends on) *you, live peaceably with all men* [Rom. 12:18]. This is desirable, but as Calvin points out, there are two cautions. First, "We are not to strive to attain the favor of men in such a way that we refuse to incur the hatred of any for the sake of Christ . . . there are, . . . some who, . . . are nonetheless hated even by their nearest relations on account of the Gospel. The second caution is that good nature should not degenerate into compliance . . . Since, therefore, it is not always possible to be at peace with all men, he has added two exceptive phrases, if it be possible, and as much as is in you both. We shall have to determine what the exception is on the basis of duty required by godliness and love."

As new creatures in Christ it is well to bear in mind Paul's admonition to,

> *Put on therefore, as the elect of God, holy and beloved, bowels of mercies* (tender mercies), *kindness, humbleness of mind, meekness, long-suffering;*
> *Forbearing* (Bearing with) *one another, and forgiving one another, if any man have a quarrel against any: even as Christ forgave you, so also do ye* [Col. 3:12–13].

Having your *feet shod with the gospel of peace* requires much preparation and application. It requires choices, decisions, and establishing the right priorities.

May God, by His grace, give you the power, strength, and might to do, according to His will.

Amen!

17

Shield of Faith

Above all, taking the shield of faith, wherewith ye shall be able to quench all the fiery darts of the wicked (one) [Eph. 6:16].

The armor of God is divided into two categories: items we are to have on and items we are to take up. The three items we are to have on are *Having your loins girt about* (your waist) *with truth, Having on the breastplate of righteousness,* and *Your feet shod with the preparation of the gospel of peace* [Eph. 6:14–15]. The three items to take up when engaging Satan and his legions are: *The shield of faith; The helmet of salvation;* and *The sword of the Spirit* [Eph. 6:16–17].

The first three are attached to the body, the second three are not. The first three suggest being in a state of readiness. The second three suggest activity, because they are not taken up until the person goes into battle.

The sixteenth verse contains the exhortation *Above all, taking the shield of faith*. The reason is *Wherewith ye shall be able to quench all the fiery darts of the wicked* (one), Satan. What do the two little words *above all* mean? Do they mean that *the shield of faith, the helmet of salvation,* and *the sword of the spirit* are more important than the first three items? The words *above all* introduce the next three items and tell us they are as important as the first three.

It is well to remember that we are to *put on the whole armor of God, that ye may be able to stand against the wiles* (schemes) *of the devil* [Eph. 6:10]. The battle is against a person, the wicked one, the evil one. It is not against something abstract, or impersonal, or imaginary. As noted several times, Scripture contains numerous contrasts. There is no greater contrast than that of Satan, who is wicked and evil, with God who is holy, righteous, and just. That is the most significant contrast.

What are we called to be? Paul states it clearly and accurately in the first chapter of this letter, *That we should be holy and without blame before him in love* [Eph. 1:4]. To become this way requires knowing that the evil one is a personal being. "There would be no evil in the world if there were no evil persons, there would be no evil human beings unless there were spiritual beings who entered into God's creation, tempted man and seduced him in the calamity of the Fall," as incisively proclaimed by Martyn Lloyd-Jones.

We are also to know that God the Father, the Lord Jesus Christ, and the Holy Spirit are personal beings. It is not enough to affirm this fact in our creeds or know about them. No, that is not enough. We are to know them in a personal way. We are to be comfortable with them, yet we are to be pricked by them. The rose gives forth beauty, joy, fragrance, and radiance and signifies faith, hope, and love, but it will prick you if you do not treat it with respect. Further, it will not produce and provide enrichment if you do not nourish and cherish it, if you do not feed, water, and prune it.

After we put on the three items of protective armor, what is the first thing that the Apostle tells us to take up? *The shield of faith*! Why? What does Satan want to do? He wants to separate us from God or keep us separated from God. How are we saved? How do we come into a right relationship with God and the Lord Jesus Christ? *By faith*! But remember faith is the gift of God. *For by grace are ye* (you have been) *saved through faith; and that not of yourselves, it is the gift of God* [Eph. 2:8]. Further, the author to the Hebrews says, *Looking unto Jesus the author* (originator) *and finisher* (perfector) *of our faith* [Heb. 12:2].

What does it mean that Jesus is the author and finisher of our faith? The word *author* means *the Chief Leader, the originator, the one who takes the lead and provides the first occasion. Finisher* means *the end, complete, perfect, perfection, perfector.* The Lord Jesus Christ is the beginning and the end of our faith. It is in Him and Him only that our faith begins, ends, and is made complete and perfect.

In this verse, please note the active verb in *taking the shield of faith*. There is nothing passive about it. There is not the slightest hint of letting someone else do it for you. You are the one to take it. What is this faith of which we are to take hold? It is a faith that exercises two basic truths.

First, it has a "confident reliance on God. It is the act by which he lays hold on God's proffered resources and becomes obedient to what God prescribes. Further, it abandons all self-interest and self-reliance, and trusts God completely," as appropriately described by W.A. Whitehouse.

Second, it is the Old Testament truth whereby "a person who has faith is himself made firm and reliable. However, it is God's act that brings about 'loyalty to God which is found in a man of faith.' Further, God creates and nurtures within a person a belief that is firm and trustworthy, even though the individual previously had been helpless and unstable," as acknowledged by W.A. Whitehouse.

The "confident reliance on God" is not to be confused with fatalism, which means submitting to fate and accepting the inevitability of developments, events, and relationships. It is nothing of that sort. It is faith, which is the gift of God, accompanied by His actions in delivering what He has promised. God will provide, or he will withhold. A prime example is Abraham.

> Was not Abraham our father justified by works, when he had offered Isaac his son upon the altar?
>
> Seest thou how faith wrought (was working) with his works, and by works was faith made perfect (complete)?
>
> And the Scripture was fulfilled which saith, ABRAHAM BELIEVED GOD, AND IT WAS IMPUTED (accounted) UNTO HIM FOR RIGHTEOUSNESS: and he was called the Friend of God.
>
> Ye see then how that by works a man is justified, and not by faith only. . . .
>
> For as the body without the spirit is dead, so faith without works is dead also [Jas. 2:21–24, 26].

Other examples are given in the Gospels and in the letters of Paul, Peter, and John.

This active faith is exhibited by directly cleaving to God, and, as Whitehouse says, "by having a confident trust in the unseen reality of God's present help." But there is more to it. "The faithfulness of God himself and the faithful service of the one who is anointed by God. The good fight of faith could not be fought by any man if he had to rely upon his own faith: *I believe; help thou my unbelief* [Mark 9:24]. The faith to which victory over the world is given is as much born from God [1 John 5:4] as is the brotherly love among men is founded upon and preceded by the love of God for men," [1 John 4:10, 19] as expressed with clarity by Markus Barth.

Further, it can be expressly stated that the faith we are considering is not an historical faith or a miraculous faith, but as William Gurnall says, it "is a justifying faith." What do we mean by this? Think about Judas Iscariot. He had knowledge of the scriptures and Christ's teachings. However, it cannot be said that he had a justifying faith.

Second, a "Justifying faith is not assurance." Gurnall states it simply and beautifully, "assurance is rather the fruit of faith, than faith itself. It is in faith as the flower is in the root. Faith, in time, after much communion with God, acquaintance with the word, and experience of his dealings with the soul, may flourish into assurance. But, as the root truly lives before the flower appears, and continues when that hath shed its beautiful leaves, and is gone again; so doth true justifying faith live before assurance comes, and after it disappears."

What then is a justifying faith? Faith focused upon God's mercy and what He has done through the Lord Jesus Christ. Paul's prayer in the first chapter of Ephesians states it most appropriately,

> *The eyes of your understanding being enlightened; that ye may know what is the hope of his calling, and what* (are) *the riches of the glory of his inheritance in the saints,*
> *And what is the exceeding greatness of his power to us-ward who believe, according to the working of his mighty power* [Eph. 1:18–19].

It is the fact that Christ was crucified for me, as He was for the world, that results in my debt being paid, my being pardoned, and my receiving eternal life.

Why does the Apostle compare faith to a shield? The other pieces of God's armor are fitted for certain parts of the body, *Your loins girt about* (your waist) *with truth, The breastplate of righteousness, Feet shod with the . . . gospel of peace,* and *The helmet of salvation* [Selections from Eph. 6:14–15, 17]. However, the shield of faith is intended to defend the whole body.

What was the shield like? It was a rather large item approximately the same length as the soldier carrying it. "People of high rank used the services of a shield bearer," according to Markus Barth. Originally, the large shields were made of wood and leather, later they were made of metal, bronze, iron, or even gold. The shield was a highly prized item.

The soldiers "counted it greater shame to lose their shield, than to lose the field, and therefore when under the very foot of their enemy, they would not part with it, but esteemed it an honor to die with their shield in their hand," as accurately described by William Gurnall.

This attitude toward the shield was reinforced by the mother's attitude. Gurnall observes that, "when the mother gave her son a shield as he went off to war it was with the understanding that he should either bring his shield home with him, or be brought home upon his shield. She had rather see him dead with it, than come home alive without it."

The shield of faith not only is to be taken up, but it is to be grasped and held on to wherever one goes, no matter what opposition or obstacles may be encountered. A soldier is not to let go of it. *But without faith it is impossible to please him: for he that cometh to God must believe that he is, and that he is a rewarder of them that diligently seek him* [Heb. 11:6]. The object of our faith is God, and we are to please him *That Christ may dwell in your hearts by faith* [Eph. 3:17].

What effect does it have when taking up the shield of faith to thwart or rebuff attacks? Scripture says, *ye shall be able to quench all the fiery darts of the wicked* (one) [Eph. 6:16]. It does not say, "you may be able," but that *ye shall be able*. Further, you will quench or hinder not just some, a few, or many of the fiery darts, but all of them. Whose darts will be quenched? The wicked one's.

It is interesting that the Apostle Paul calls them *the fiery darts of the wicked*. These darts are the temptations the devil uses against men and women. What are the characteristics of these fiery darts?

They are swift. Satan does not need much time to tempt a person. They fly secretly and at times it is difficult or impossible to see them coming. They come when least expected. Think of Peter who was adamant that he would stand by his Lord. Then a few hours later, he was pierced by a fiery dart.

Darts have a wounding and killing nature. They can maim a person, incapacitate him, or kill him. They are not play toys. They have an inflaming quality that cause people to sin and to act against the will of God.

The question is, how does faith enable one to quench all the fiery darts? It enables the believer to see the temptation for what it is and to see the consequences of submitting to it. Faith enables the believer to distinguish between that which is temporal, and that which is permanent. Faith provides the believer with, "The ability to apply quickly what we believe so as to repel everything the devil does or attempts to do to us. Faith is not merely an intellectual belief or theory . . . Faith is always practical. Faith always applies the truth," as appropriately and meaningfully described by Martyn Lloyd-Jones.

The author of Hebrews further enlightens us, saying, *NOW faith is the substance* (realization) *of things hoped for, the evidence* (conviction) *of things not seen* [Heb. 11:1]. Faith provides us with an understanding of God's fatherly care. William Gurnall imparts additional knowledge and strength, stating that "Faith takes away the fuel that feeds . . . temptation." Faith prompts the believer to discover the lives of the saints and faithful who have gone before and who have had to overcome difficulties, obstacles, and temptations. Faith enables us to *quench all the fiery darts of the wicked* (one).

How are we to use this *shield of faith* to defend ourselves? First and foremost, we must ask God for help. We must lay claim to His promises. Therefore, we must know the teachings contained in His Word.

Next, we are to go to God in prayer. Paul's prayer in the third chapter of Ephesians can guide us. He prays that God . . . *grant you, according to the riches of his glory, to be strengthened with might by his Spirit in the inner man; That Christ may dwell in your hearts by faith; . . . And to know the love of Christ, which passeth knowledge, that ye might be filled with all the fullness of God* [Eph. 3:16–17, 19]. Further, we are to pray to God expectantly. However, we may have to learn how to pray. This requires time, effort, and understanding. Yes, we are to ask and to expect, but we are to be guided by God's will, as given in the Word written and the Word incarnate. That puts a different connotation on praying expectantly.

In closing, remember Abraham. The object of his faith was always God. It always pointed to God, never to himself. Martyn Lloyd-Jones powerfully describes the faith of Abraham and other "great heroes of the faith," saying, "The secret of Abraham was that his faith led him to God, and God's character and promises; and when he relied upon them, all was well. We are told about the great heroes of the faith in Hebrews 11, that out of weakness they were made strong; always by faith! Not faith in faith, but faith in God! They were men who believed God, they accounted him able to do that which he had promised. That was their secret." May it be ours, also.

The shield of faith is available to us. We are to take it and use it. But as we do, we are to bear in mind that God said to Abram when he was being attacked and tired and exhausted, *Fear not, Abram: I am thy shield, and thy exceeding great reward* [Gen. 15:1]. Our shield is God and his power, not our own capabilities, our own strength. The Lord Jesus Christ said, *My grace is sufficient for thee: for my strength* (power) *is made perfect in weakness* [2 Cor. 12:9].

We are to take *the shield of faith*. It is provided by God, and it leads to Him. *Let us therefore come boldly* (confidently) *unto the throne of grace, that we may obtain mercy, and find grace to help in time of need* [Heb. 4:16].

May God bless to us the understanding of His Word and the application of it. May our faith in God increase and remain firm. May our shield of faith *quench all the fiery darts of the wicked* (one), Satan.

Amen!

18

The Helmet of Salvation

(The Door of A'chor)

And take the helmet of salvation, and the sword of the Spirit, which is the word of God [Eph. 6:17].

God provides for us in a most excellent way! Consider God's provisions, His storehouse, His promises, and His blessings. When focusing upon God's armor, it is well to consider the context in which they are made available.

We must not forget that God through Christ wants us to *be strong in the Lord, and in the power of his might;* ... [Eph. 6:10] and ... *be able to stand against the wiles* (schemes) *of the devil* [Eph. 6:11]. We must realize the conflicts besetting and bedeviling us are not just with people, but with the rulers of darkness and spiritual wickedness that control individuals and cause them to do or say as they do. Therefore, God provides the necessary armor. It is our responsibility to learn about the different pieces, how to use them, and to properly use them in our daily lives.

It is imperative to accept the truth that everything does not come up roses all the time. When we become Christ's disciples, it does not mean that all conflicts will be eliminated in our daily living, or that everyone will like or love us, or that we will walk every hour under a cool, bright sun, or a radiant full moon. No, in our relations with others, there will be trials and conflicts. There will be clouds, and we may not be able to see the sun or the moon. "In the Bible clouds are always connected with God or Christ. If there were no clouds, we should have no faith or no hope. The clouds are a sign that He is there . . . God cannot come near without clouds, He does not come in clear sunshine," as Oswald Chambers reminds us.

It is not that God wants to teach us something in our trials, conflicts, or the demands placed upon us. It may be that He wants us to unlearn something. His purpose in the clouds is to simplify our belief and to enable us to stand in our relationship to Him. Our relationship with Him is to grow and to become more dependent, more obedient, and more knowledgeable regarding His commands, teachings, and being.

Is there anyone save Jesus only in the clouds that gather along your path? If so, it will get darker; you must get to the place where there is no one, save Jesus only. Where is that simple, easy faith that does not require much of me? *It is not in the New Testament.* The New Testament is filled with conflict, rejection, and opposition in addition to love, mercy, and righteousness.

What does God in Christ want me to do? To accept, to act upon, and to appropriate the strength that is available from Him and to focus upon Him no matter how thick or black the cloud may be. This is not easy, but we are called to be heirs, members of the body, saints, and the faithful. Therefore, we are to strive to do so. Remember, we are called to be and to do!

What about the helmet of salvation, the hope of salvation? Of course, when you think of a helmet you think of your head and your mind. Jesus says, THOU SHALT LOVE THE LORD THY GOD WITH ALL THY HEART, AND WITH ALL THY SOUL, AND WITH ALL THY MIND [Matt. 22:37]. The author of Hebrews says, FOR THIS IS THE COVENANT THAT I WILL MAKE WITH THE HOUSE OF ISRAEL . . . I WILL PUT MY LAWS INTO THEIR MIND [Heb. 8:10]. Peter says, *Wherefore, gird up* (prepare) *the loins of your mind, be sober* (watchful) *and hope . . . for the grace* (rest your hope fully upon the grace) *. . . of Jesus Christ* [1 Pet. 1:13].

Paul says, FOR WHO HATH KNOWN THE MIND OF THE LORD . . . BUT WE HAVE THE MIND OF CHRIST [1 Cor. 2:16]. To the Philippians Paul says, *Let this mind be in you, which was also in Christ Jesus* [Phil. 2:5]. And Paul writes to the Ephesians saying, *And be renewed in the spirit of you mind* [Eph. 4:23]. Christ and the teachings of the New Testament are concerned with the human mind: yours and mine.

It needs to be protected! It needs to be prepared. It needs to be enriched and enlightened. It needs to have understanding. "Knowledge of full salvation in Christ is absolutely essential for the Christian warrior. If he has any doubt of his own salvation, how can he effectually win a sinner to Christ? And in these days of manifold Satanic counterfeits, how can he discern the false from the true?" as described by Ruth Paxson in these direct and penetrating words and questions.

The mind is integral and paramount to being in a right relationship to God in Christ, putting on the helmet of salvation, and knowing the hope of salvation. In this section of Scripture, the Apostle is concerned with the attitude of the saints and faithful regarding their faith in Christ and the negatives encountered in walking *worthy of the vocation* (calling) *wherewith ye are called*. He realized the saints and the faithful would be tormented by disappointments, disheartenments, weariness, tiredness, opposition, and hopelessness. Therefore, the Apostle says to the Galatians, *And let us not be weary in well doing: for in due season we shall reap, if we faint not* (do not lose heart) [Gal. 6:9].

Paul reminds the Corinthians that,

> *We are troubled* (hard pressed) *on every side, yet not distressed* (crushed); *we are perplexed, but not in despair;*
> *Persecuted, but not forsaken; cast* (struck) *down, but not destroyed;*
> *Always bearing about in the body the dying of the Lord Jesus, that the life also of Jesus might be made manifest in our body* [2 Cor. 4:8–10].

Paul tells us in these verses that although we face various difficulties in this life, God's positive, comforting, and encouraging words remain. Why? Because we are living by faith in the Lord Jesus Christ. We are to look to Him, be guided by Him, and have confidence in Him.

Paul's life was far from easy. Though trials, tribulations, and temptations come our way, John Calvin encourages us, enlightens us, and strengthens us in our walk with Jesus, saying, "The Lord comes to our aid. Many foes are in arms against us but in God's keeping we are safe. In a word, though we are brought so low that all seems over with us, yet we do not perish. The last possibility he mentions is the most serious of all. You see how he turned to his own advantage every charge that the wicked (one) brings against him."

These people were told to look to the promise, to look to Christ with their minds, not their emotions. Peter reminds us, *The Lord is not slack* (slow) *concerning his promise* [2 Pet. 3:9].

How are we to deal with these matters? We are *to stand against the wiles* (schemes) *of the devil* and to *Put on the whole armor of God*. Another portion of Scripture supports these teachings. Paul says to the Thessalonians, *But let us, who are of the day, be sober, putting on the breastplate of faith and love; and for a helmet, the hope of salvation* [1 Thess. 5:8]. In addition, Luke reminds us, *AND he* (Jesus) *spake a parable unto them to this end, that men ought always to pray, and not to faint* (lose heart) [Luke 18:1].

The question should be asked, what is the hope of salvation? William Gurnall answers this question appropriately, saying, "Hope is a supernatural grace of God, whereby the believer, through Christ expects and waits for all those good things of the promise, which at present he hath not received, or not fully." This is a meaningful, wonderful description of hope.

Yes, we are to remember that God through Christ doth provide for those times when His disciples encounter disappointments, disheartenments, weariness, tiredness, opposition, and hopelessness. It is a difficult lesson to learn. But by God's grace we will.

Why do these things persist when we are members of Christ's body, when we have been told that things would get better? What can we expect? The words of Rustum in Matthew Arnold's "Sohrab & Rustum" should provide us with comfort, courage, and hope.

> *For now in blood and battles was my youth,*
> *And full of blood and battles is my age;*
> *And I shall never end this life of blood.*

Martyn Lloyd-Jones amplifies upon this, saying, "He says to himself, I have been fighting ever since I have become a Christian; and I am still fighting. Is there no end to it? That means that the devil is attacking and trying to get him to feel that the whole thing is vain and useless."

There are statements of conditions that are less than ideal in Galatians and Second Corinthians. But don't stop there! Go on to the promise, to the reaping, to the advantages, to Christ Jesus. Do not stop with the clouds! Go to the sunlight or moonlight. Go to Christ!

There are other illustrations of discouraged, disillusioned Christians, saints, and the faithful in Hebrews and Second Peter. Peter says, *But the God of all grace, who hath called us unto his eternal glory by Christ Jesus, after ye have suffered a while, make you perfect, stablish* (confirm), *strengthen, settle you* [1 Pet. 5:10]. Note what he is saying: it is the grace of God through the Lord Jesus Christ that has called us and watches over us even as we suffer through difficulties and periods of doubt. It is then that we are to remember His promise to *make you perfect, stablish* (confirm), *strengthen, settle you.*

We are to bear these truths in mind when considering Matthew 24, Mark 13, and Luke 21, where our Lord warns His followers that they will have trials and tribulations. On the other side of the coin, they think that being a saint or faithful follower is something magical and that once you become a member, your problems and troubles disappear. However, as Christ points out, it is not like that. He talks about obedience, knowing His Father's will, redemption, sanctification, and promises.

How is the helmet of salvation to be used? The hope within the faithful follower should stir him or her "to high and noble exploits," as William Gurnall boldly states. When this hope is present it makes one anxious and zealous to know God and to please him. It creates an impatience in the faithful follower to better serve the Lord, to grow in a right relationship with Him, and to strengthen that relationship. How true this is!

Peter expounds by going straight to the point, *Blessed be the God and Father of our Lord Jesus Christ, which according to his abundant mercy hath begotten us again unto a lively* (living) *hope by the resurrection of Jesus Christ from the dead* [1 Pet. 1:3]. It is a living, lively hope. It is active, it realizes the promises, and it is not dull and lifeless. It is expectant, it sees a little, and then sees more and more. The more is based upon the promise.

The prophet Hosea helps us understand the hope of serving the Lord, of living, growing, expecting, and obeying, when he says, *And I will give her her vineyards from thence, and the valley of Achor for a door of hope* [Hos. 2:15]. The prophet alludes to the time when the Israelites were coming out of the wilderness after forty years and entering the promised land. They did not take it all at one time. They entered by Achor, which God made possible. He gave it to them, and they possessed it. However, God did not let them look on it as an area to be possessed and where they were to stay. No! He made them look on it as a door of hope through which they would pass and take the land promised to them. Yes, they would have obstacles and resistance, *but they had the promise.*

This particular principle applies to each of us. There are times when we wander in the wilderness or encounter opposition, but then a door of hope opens, maybe ever so slightly, maybe wide. We are to pass through it expectantly, trustingly, and obediently, knowing God has provided an A'chor for us. It should not only strengthen and comfort us, it should lead us forward into new areas.

Think of the Apostle Paul. He had many enemies at Ephesus and much opposition. But he writes to the Corinthians on a positive note, saying, *But I will tarry at Ephesus until Pentecost. For a great door and effectual* (one) *is opened unto me, and there are many adversaries* [1 Cor. 16:8–9]. *Effectual* in this instance means "active" and "powerful in action." This is how the door was opened for Paul in Ephesus. Once there, the Gospel was made effectual as a result of his entering into the city. Paul entered Ephesus by a door of A'chor provided by God. He had hope, he used his mind, he saw the promise, he proclaimed the Gospel, and he pastored to the people despite many adversaries. The body of Christ grew and was strengthened, even though it was not a bed of roses for Paul.

They had to remember the teachings, they had to use their minds, and they had to apply the truths received from Christ to their daily lives. They were to remember God saying to Joshua, *I will not fail thee, nor forsake thee* [Josh. 1:5]. They knew that God did not say, "I will make it easy for thee."

What should our attitude be toward this helmet of salvation? Remember, God provided it as part of the whole armor of God. Therefore, first of all, we are to be thankful for it.

We should endeavor to live up to our hopes. The promise is there. But we must go through the clouds; we must go through the door of hope. We must *walk worthy of the vocation* (calling) *wherewith we have been called*. Our minds should guide our footsteps as we become more knowledgeable and enlightened about the teachings of Christ and endeavor to apply them.

We should strengthen our hope. It should be exercised, fed, and watered. It should be nourished. The author of Hebrews reminds us of what is required, saying, *And we desire that every one of you do show the same diligence to the full assurance of hope unto the end: That ye be not slothful* (sluggish), *but followers* (imitators) *of them who through faith and patience inherit the promises* [Heb. 6:11–12].

We are to show diligence in the full assurance of hope. We are not to be slothful but follow in the footsteps of Paul and the other saints who, despite many adversaries, remained firm in their faith and inherited the promises of God. Calvin enforces this saying, "You must now apply yourself with not less zeal to progress in your faith, so as to show God its firm and full certainty." *If we are to strengthen our hope, then we must study the word diligently and apply it.*

Paul exhorts the Romans, *Now the God of hope fill you with all joy and peace in believing, that ye may abound in hope, through the power of the Holy Ghost* [Rom. 15:13]. John Calvin provides further enlightenment and food for thought, saying, "The Lord in no way measures his precepts according to our strength, or the power of free will, nor does he instruct us in our duty, so that we may place reliance on our own powers and prepare ourselves to render obedience. Rather, the precepts which he gives us require the assistance of His grace to stimulate us to an assiduous desire for prayer . . . It is only when we embrace what we are taught calmly, gladly and with one mind, that we are really prepared for faith." This is a powerful statement that we should grasp and cling to with thanksgiving.

We are to embrace the true teachings of Scripture; we are to know what Christ taught directly and through the apostles. Why? *That ye may abound in hope.* It is in this way that hope is confirmed and strengthened in the faithful. How does this happen? *Through the power of the Holy Ghost.*

In conclusion, bear in mind that the Apostle John says,

> BEHOLD, *what manner of love the Father hath bestowed upon us, that we should be called the sons* (children) *of God: therefore the world knoweth us not, because it knew him not.*
> *Beloved, now are we the sons* (children) *of God, and it doth not yet appear what we shall be: but we know that, when he shall appear, we shall be like him; for we shall see him as he is.*
> *And every man that hath this hope in him purifieth himself, even as he is pure* [1 John 3:1–3].

We are to become holy and without blame. This happens through Christ by the grace of God and the power of the Holy Ghost. The God of hope "will stir and stimulate us to the pursuit of purity, for it leads us straight to Christ," as John Calvin boldly assures us. Yes, there are clouds to pass through. Our minds are to be used. There is a door of hope.

There is an A'chor to pass through. There is effectual power, and there are promises to inherit even though there be many adversaries. For we are called by a God of hope who provides the power of the Holy Ghost.

Therefore, put on the helmet of salvation. Have the living, active hope to become pure, as He is pure, as you pass through your door of A'chor.

Amen!

19

The Sword of the Spirit

And take the helmet of salvation, and the sword of the Spirit, which is the word of God [Eph. 6:17].

Apparently, the Apostle Paul respected the armor with which the Roman soldiers protected themselves, the manner in which they prepared it, and their ability to use it. Also, he respected their ability and skill to use the one item that could be used offensively or defensively, the *sword of the Spirit*. By this I do not mean to infer that Paul had great respect or admiration for the Roman Empire, or its emperor, or how it used its power and military might.

It appears the Apostle observed the soldiers with admiration for their proficiency, ability to learn, dedication, commitment to practice, and willingness to deny themselves. The Apostle says, in addition to the other items, *take . . . the sword of the Spirit, which is the word of God.*

The first thing we notice is that Scripture says to take up a sword. Normally, when you think of a sword you think of it as an offensive weapon, of the Cavalry riding in the movies with their swords exposed, or of a military figure offering his sword to his victorious opponent as a symbol of peace.

The Greek word used for *sword* is *Machaira*. It denotes two things. One is a short, straight sword that was used both offensively and defensively. It was a very effective weapon, sharp and pointed. It could cut and penetrate. Also, it was "A symbol of jurisdiction, over life and death, but also (over) persecution and senseless bloodshed," as Markus Barth describes it.

Paul knew full well that the Roman soldier or officer could use the sword to defend himself or to attack an enemy. What else did Paul know?

That he himself, as well as the saints and faithful, needed to protect themselves and to route the enemy when Satan and his forces attacked.

James says, *Resist the devil, and he will flee from you* [Jas. 4:7]. We are to resist the devil's attacks and to cause him to flee. Each of us has been, is being, and will be subject to these attacks. Therefore, we need to be prepared, knowledgeable, skillful, and obedient. How are we to resist the devil and cause him to flee? By our own capabilities? By placing confidence in ourselves? No! No! No! What does Scripture say? *And take . . . the sword of the Spirit, which is the word of God* [Eph. 6:17].

That seems rather simple, does it not? Yet, there are erroneous interpretations of *to take . . . the sword of the Spirit*. The first one is that the Spirit is the Word of God. Martyn Lloyd-Jones properly and forcefully states, "Nowhere in the Scripture is the Holy Spirit described as the Word of God. That description is confined solely to our Lord Jesus Himself. The Holy Spirit is not the sword."

Second, The New English Bible translates this phrase thusly, "For sword, take that which the spirit gives you—the words that come from God." This interpretation opens the door to almost any type of explanation or usage.

What is the Apostle saying in this verse? Lloyd-Jones states it explicitly, "Take up the sword which the spirit Himself provides for you, that is to say, the Word of God; in other words the scriptures, the Bible."

The Scripture being considered shows how our Lord responded to the devil's temptations after he had been in the wilderness *forty days and forty nights*. He specifically quoted Scripture. He did not use words that were given him at that particular moment. He knew Scripture, He recalled Scripture, He depended upon Scripture, and He used Scripture! Each time Satan attacked the Lord Jesus, he was routed by *the sword of the Spirit, which is the word of God* [Eph. 6:17]. That is the weapon the Lord used to route His adversary.

Ruth Paxson provides further amplification and clarity through the following statement: "The sword is God's own utterance given to us in His written Word, inspired by the Spirit, revealed to us by the Spirit, used by the Spirit in us to sanctify and cleanse, and then wielded by the Spirit through us to defeat the devil." Not only are we to accept the Lord Jesus as our Lord and Saviour, we are to do as He did and be obedient to His commands. Why are we told to put on the whole armor of God and to take up *the sword of the Spirit, which is the word of God* [Eph. 6:17]?

Note, it is *the sword of the Spirit, which is the word of God,* that comes from God. It does not come from anyone else or anywhere else. It comes from God. Therefore, we have a tremendous responsibility to know it and to know how to use it. Paul writes to Timothy, *All Scripture is given by inspiration of God* [2 Tim. 3:16]. The Apostle "commends the scripture because of its authority, and then because of the profit that comes from it. To assert its authority he teaches that it is inspired of God . . . and we know that God has spoken to us and are fully convinced that the prophets did not speak of themselves," as beautifully and straightforwardly stated by John Calvin.

There now follows the second part of his commendation, that Scripture contains the perfect rule of a good and joyful life. This again requires knowing Scripture and how to use it. "The Law and the prophets are not teachings handed on at the pleasure of men or produced by men's minds as their source, but are dictated by the Holy Spirit," as John Calvin properly claims.

There is another important teaching that says,

> *We have also a more sure word of prophecy; whereunto ye do well that ye take heed, as unto a light that shineth in a dark place, until the day dawn, and the day star arise in your hearts:*
> *Knowing this first, that no prophecy of the Scripture is of any private interpretation* (origin).
> *For the prophecy came not in old* (at any) *time by the will of man: but holy men of God spake as they were moved by the Holy Ghost* [2 Pet. 1:19–21].

What does Peter mean? The Old Testament prophecies are not the private statements or interpretations of the prophets! The prophecies did not come *by the will of man*. But the holy men of God spake as they were moved by the Holy Spirit. God was the one that guided the prophets and the other writers of the Old Testament.

What enables us to understand the Word? The Holy Spirit. Paul illuminates this by saying, *We have received, not the spirit of the world, but the spirit which is of God; that* (in order that) *we might know the things that are freely given to us of God* [1 Cor. 2:12]. It cannot be known any other way. Paul amplifies upon this, saying, *Not in the words which man's wisdom teacheth, but which the Holy Ghost teacheth; But the natural man receiveth not the things of the Spirit of God, for they are foolishness unto him: neither can he know them, because they are spiritually discerned* [1

Cor. 2:13-14]. "The Holy Spirit enables us to understand the Word," as stated by Martyn Lloyd-Jones. It does not depend upon innate ability, scholarship, or education, but upon the Holy Spirit working within us and properly interpreting the Word.

There is a relationship between the Word and the Spirit. They go together. They should not be separated. There needs to be the proper balance between the two, neither is to dominate or to be absent. Basically, the Quakers placed full emphasis on the Spirit and ignored the Word or said that the Word was not important. Then there are others who ignore or discount the Holy Spirit and place all their interest and emphasis upon the Word. Consequently, the Holy Spirit is forgotten.

What is needed by the saints and the faithful? "What is needed is the Spirit opening the Word, and opening my mind and opening my heart," as thoughtfully described by Martyn Lloyd-Jones. When the Spirit and the Word work within an individual, that person can grow in the Lord and in the knowledge of the Lord. Also, he or she can stand against *the wiles* (schemes) *of the devil.*

The question has been asked: Why did the Holy Spirit, in guiding Paul, lead him to list *the sword of the Spirit* last? Why was it not listed earlier? The reason being: "To let us know how necessary the graces of God's spirit are to our right using of the Word. Nothing (is) more abused than the Word. And why? Because men come to it with unsound and unsanctified hearts," according to William Gurnall as he properly enlightens our hearts and minds. Therefore, God's grace is necessary so we can learn how to properly use the Word.

Second, each member of Christ's body needs the Word of God and needs to know how to use it. He may have the other pieces of armor, *the Breastplate of righteousness*; *the Shield of faith*; and *the Helmet of Salvation.* But that person needs the *sword of the Spirit*, . . . *the word of God* [Eph. 6:17].

Further, it needs to be used. A person may grow in his or her faith, may walk more closely with the Lord Jesus, and may become more knowledgeable and increasingly obedient. Yet, when these things that are good and desirable happen there is still another need, the need to know the Word better and better and the need to pray that the Holy Spirit will interpret it aright in one's heart and mind.

Please remember that the Word of God comes to us in two ways. First, we can never forget the opening verse of John's Gospel, *IN the be-*

ginning was the Word, and the Word was with God, and the Word was God [John 1:1]. To this it is appropriate and necessary to add, *And he was clothed with a vesture* (robe) *dipped in blood: and his name is called The Word of God* [Rev. 19:13]. Here we have Christ identified as the Word of God, but in a different way than our Scripture for this message. In John's Gospel, the Lord Jesus is called the Word, "Because first He is the eternal wisdom and will of God, and secondly, because He is the express image of His purpose," as suitably described by John Calvin.

Third, the Word of God is declared to us through men. It pleased God to accommodate us by declaring and revealing His Word, His truth, and His teachings through certain people. This Word has become the Holy Scripture, the Word of God. It is in this way that God has delivered His Word unto the saints and faithful. This should enable us to better understand the following Scripture: *And are built upon the foundation of the apostles and prophets, Jesus Christ himself being the chief corner stone* [Eph. 2:20].

Holy Scripture can be divided into four parts:

> Historical—relating how God revealed himself so that there could be a record of the creation, the call of Abram, and subsequent events;

> Prophecies—containing the predictions of the things that would come and what would be fulfilled;

> Doctrinal—revealing who God is, what His nature and being are like, and providing knowledge about Him and His Son; and

> Precepts and commands—to guide us in our relationship with God, and applying His commands and teachings to our daily living.

Why is the Word of God called *the sword of the Spirit*? First, God is the author of it. He formed, fashioned, and forged it. Second, as William Gurnall wisely informs us, "The Holy Spirit is the only true interpreter of the Word." Third, it is the Holy Spirit that gives the Word efficacy and power within each person.

There are people who may have knowledge of Scripture or who profess to know what Scripture is saying, but the Holy Spirit does not interpret it properly in their hearts and minds. Think of the Pharisees and scribes. They knew the Word but did not interpret it properly. They were the obstacle and would neither consider nor think of changing or modifying their preconceived ideas and mind-set.

Luke records Jesus' encounter with the lawyer who tried to tempt Him by asking, *What shall I do to inherit eternal life* [Luke 10:25]? What did Jesus do? He told the lawyer to do something. He referred him to Scripture saying, *What is written in the law? how readest thou* [Luke 10:26]?

The Apostle John relates the incident of the Jews wanting to stone Jesus for blasphemy, for wanting to make Himself God. How did Jesus respond to their accusations? By saying, *Is it not written in your law, I SAID, YE ARE GODS* [John 10:34]? What did Jesus do on this occasion? He defended Himself. He routed his adversaries. He used *the sword of the Spirit*.

People want to attack or discredit the Lord Jesus Christ and His teachings. The way to respond is not with our own thoughts, ideas, and experiences, but with the Word of God. They will not want to hear what the Word says, because it is a sharp, telling, piercing sword.

Think of Luther. He exposed the Word to the people in the face of tremendous opposition. What happened? The Word and the Holy Spirit worked amongst the people. They responded in faith. They began applying the teachings of Scripture. It should be noted in light of John Leith's book, *The Reformed Imperative*, that Luther maintained, "The Church is not above the Scriptures. The standard by which you judge even the Church is the Scriptures."

This is very interesting when considering two developments, the decline in church membership among the so-called main line denominations, and the Roman Catholic Church opening the Bible to her members and encouraging them to read it. Why have these developments occurred? They are interrelated. Possibly, this explanation will shed some light on both developments. Martyn Lloyd-Jones recorded "the words of a dignitary of the Roman Catholic Church, . . . said privately to a Protestant who put the question to him as to why they had changed their policy. His reply is worth noting. He said, "I will tell you why we have changed our policy. There is no longer any need for us to be afraid of the Scriptures, for this reason, that you Protestants no longer believe in the Scriptures. It is you Protestants with your destructive criticism of the Scriptures that have undermined the confidence of the people in the Scriptures. So we are able to say that it is we alone who are standing for the Scriptures." That is quite a mouth full.

Let's face it, Holy Scripture has been criticized: the Word has been ignored; ministers, teachers, and officers have said it is too difficult to learn Scripture; there has been a reliance upon philosophy, science, and modern knowledge; there has been a reliance on the secular world's standards; the Catechisms have been removed and put on a shelf; and all the negatives that have been having an impact for two thousand years are being propounded.

What is needed to repel the negative attacks and to route the adversary? *And take . . . the sword of the Spirit, which is the word of God* [Eph. 6:17]. You can have all the other armor of God, but if you do not *have the sword of the Spirit* and use it, you are not a soldier in Christ's army. It is our responsibility, and it is an awesome one, to proclaim and teach the Word and to use *the sword of the Spirit, which is the word of God* [Eph. 6:17].

Some may wonder what is the difference between having *your loins girt about* (your waist) *with truth* and *the sword of the spirit, which is the word of God* [Eph. 6:14, 17]. The former is directed to the central truth of salvation, while the latter is directed toward a detailed knowledge of Scripture. We are to know that we have been redeemed and are in a right relationship to God through Christ. Equally important, we are to know Scripture in detail and how to apply it.

William Gurnall asks a penetrating question, "Will this faith ever carry thee to heaven that is not able to bring thee out of hell?" Ponder that question!

We need the whole armor of God; the truth of salvation; the breastplate of righteousness; the gospel of peace; the shield of faith; the helmet of salvation; and the sword of the Spirit, that is the Word of God. Our Master used each and every one. So must we! The saintly Ruth Paxson firmly admonishes Christ's followers with the following sage advice and encouragement: "This will require of us a constant, systematic study of God's word, that our sword may be easily and quickly unsheathed, and that just the needed part of it may be used at the right time and in the right way." May we heed her words.

Amen!

20

Stand Therefore—Praying Always

Praying always with all prayer and supplication in the Spirit, and watching thereunto with all perseverance and supplication for all saints [Eph. 6:18].

What did the Roman soldier do after he had put on his armor and had taken up the different pieces? He looked to his superiors for orders, commands, supplies, training, and guidance. What does the football player do when he receives his equipment and prepares to take the field? He listens for instructions, he follows orders, he uses his ability but looks for and accepts assistance, and he knows he cannot do it by himself.

What are those who say they are Christians to do? Our Master's words in Scripture make several things clear. Some we may like to hear, and some we may not. He is the true vine; we are merely the branches. He gives the life and growth in several ways.

He prunes the branches. He does it to each of us because we need it. Why? Because we go in the wrong direction or do not do as he wants us to do. Calvin says, "He removes unfruitful branches, so they can be thrown into the fire and burned. He gets rid of them." He takes away the branches that do not bear fruit. The meaning, in this phrase, is directed toward those who are not really members of Christ's body, "but those who . . . are merely professed followers, giving only the appearance of being joined to the vine." (Vine's expository dictionary of new testament words).

Christ tells us we are to abide in Him and He will abide in us. It is in this way we bring forth fruit, much fruit, desirable fruit. . . . *the fruit of the Spirit is love, joy, peace, long-suffering, gentleness* (kindness), *good-*

ness, faith (faithfulness)*, Meekness, temperance* (self-control)*: against such there is no law* [Gal. 5:22-23]. Christ adds a few poignant words to the branches of the vine saying, . . . *for without me ye can do nothing* [John 15:5].

He reveals that He is the vine, that His father is the husbandman, and that you are to produce fruit or something is going to happen: you will get your wings clipped, you will get an "AA" (Attitudinal Adjustment), or you will be cut off and wither away. Jesus makes it clear that the unfruitful branches will be removed. He also makes it clear that without Him, or apart from Him, we cannot really bear fruit that is "pleasing to God," according to John Calvin. Jesus speaks plainly in emphasizing to His disciples that if you do not abide in Me, you will be cut off, gathered up, and cast into the fire and burned.

The strength and nourishment to produce fruitful branches comes from being part and parcel of the vine. If we are not truly connected to the vine or if we are cut off, we will wither away. In addition, the Master gives the conditions for abiding in Him. First, it is an ongoing relationship; it is never-ending. It is not a stop-and-start, or on-again, off-again situation. Second, His words are to abide in us. This requires effort and diligence. If we do not learn, study, remember, use, and apply His words, how can they abide in us? They cannot. Third, by faith we are to take root in Him and His words. They are to be nourished and cherished, so that they will grow and multiply.

The Greek word for *words* as used in *If ye abide in me, and my words abide in you, ye shall ask what ye will, and it shall be done unto* (for) *you* [John 15:7] is not only interesting, it is enlightening. The word is *Rhēma*. What is significant about it? It denotes "that which is spoken," or "uttered in speech or in writing." This is not too significant. It is used by Paul in his letter to the Romans to speak of the Gospel and to identify *the word of Christ* or *the word which preaches Christ*. Again, this is not too significant.

> THE WORD IS NIGH (NEAR) THEE, EVEN IN THY MOUTH, AND IN THY HEART: *that is, the word of faith, which we preach;*
> *So then faith cometh by hearing, and hearing by the word of God.*

> *Have they not heard? Yes, verily,* THEIR SOUND WENT INTO ALL THE EARTH, AND THEIR WORDS UNTO THE ENDS OF THE WORLD [Rom. 10:8, 17–18].

Again, this is not too significant. However, the significance of *Rhēma* is that the same word is used in Ephesians 6:17 whereby we are to *take the sword of the Spirit, which is the word of God* and the reference in Ephesians and John 15:7 "is not to the whole Bible as such, but to the individual Scripture which the Spirit brings to our remembrance for use in time of need, a prerequisite being the regular storing of the mind with Scripture," as stated in *The Vine's expository dictionary of new testament words.*

If these two conditions are met: abiding in Christ; and His Words abiding in us; the Lord Jesus says, *Ye shall ask what ye will, and it shall be done unto* (for) *you* [John 15:7]. This does not mean that you have license to ask for any and every thing, or that your requests do not have boundaries and limitations. Remember, the Master is speaking to His disciples, to the saints and the faithful, not to those outside His body. Calvin properly states, "He (God) limits His people's wishes to that principle of praying aright which subjects all our affections to the will of God."

What happens if we abide in Him and His words abide in us? *The Father will be glorified! Think on that!* Then, He lays down another condition. We are to keep His commandments, so that we can continue to live in Him and follow Him. His Word is to light our pathway and to be a light unto our feet.

It may seem impossible to obey Christ's commandments and to continue in His love. When Christ says this, please keep in mind Calvin's exposition of this verse that, "the desire to live a good and holy life, which Christ wants us to do, does not at all exclude the chief article in His teaching, namely, the free imputation of righteousness, by which through the kindness of forgiveness our duties are pleasing to God, although in themselves they deserve to be rejected as imperfect and impure. Therefore, believers are regarded as keeping His commandments when they apply themselves to them, though they be far distant from the mark." This is a beautiful, comforting, and heartwarming exposition!

He has spoken these truths for two reasons, that His joy may remain in us and that our joy may be full. His joy will continue in us, as long as we abide in Him. Further, our joy, not happiness, covetousness, desires, or wants, but joy, will be substantial and full. This does not mean that we will never experience fear, anxiety, grief, and sadness, but that our joy will be in the Lord.

Why are we spending time considering the Lord Jesus' teaching about the parable of the vine and His words that follow, when we are studying the whole armor of God? The Lord Jesus taught His disciples in spirit and in truth. The apostles built upon the foundation, with Jesus Christ being the chief cornerstone. There is a definite relationship between the Master's parable of the vine that He told to His disciples and Paul's exhortation to the Ephesians to *put on the whole armor of God*, including to *take . . . the sword of the spirit, which is the word of God* [Eph. 6:11, 17].

When the Roman soldiers were outfitted and equipped they needed something else. When the football players receive their equipment they need something else. When we receive the whole armor of God there is still something missing. Therefore, the Apostle does not complete this sentence until he provides the ingredient that ties it all together and makes each item an effective piece of armor.

What does Paul tell us to do now that we have put on the armor and taken up the pieces? He makes a specific yet all-encompassing statement saying, *Praying always with all prayer and supplication in the Spirit, and watching thereunto with all perseverance and supplication for all saints* [Eph. 6:18]. The word *all* is used four times in this phrase. It is directed toward every aspect of life as long as it continues. Prayer is to be part of our living through all the days, months, and years allocated to us; it includes all types of prayer—public, private, short, long, spur-of-the-moment, contemplated, thanksgiving, and petitions. It covers the whole range of living whether it be physical, mental, or emotional, and whether it involves the head, heart or body. And it involves all the saints and faithful, all the members of the community of believers, including the weak ones, the strong ones, and those in between.

Markus Barth expounds further on the command to be *praying always* when he says, "Nothing less is suggested than that the life and strife of the saints be one great prayer to God, that this prayer be offered in ever new forms however good or bad the circumstances, and that this prayer not be self-centered but express the need, and hope of all the saints."

When rereading this eighteenth verse and Markus Barth's exposition, you begin to realize not only the significance of it, but that it is a command to be followed each and every day of our lives. It is not an onerous command, but a joyful one. The Holy Spirit, through the Apostle Paul, says after taking up *the sword of the Spirit, which is the word of God* that we are to be *Praying always*. It means all the days allotted to us, whether they are filled with strife and all its unpleasantness or filled with joy, peace, and contentment.

What is included in the *Praying always* command? Commands that will contribute to enriching our relationship with the Lord Jesus Christ. Therefore, we are to obey Paul's command, which includes the continuous, never-ending process of praying; all kinds and types of prayers, whether long or short, or while walking, standing, sitting, or kneeling; praying through the Spirit in the name of the Lord Jesus; being alert to the needs of others while praising God; persevering in prayer; and *Praying always* for all the saints.

Why does the Apostle exhort us in this manner? Martyn Lloyd-Jones tells us clearly, concisely, and convincingly that there is one very important thing each of us is to do every day when he says, "The armor which is provided for us by God cannot be used except in fellowship and communion with God. Every single piece, excellent though it is in itself, will not suffice us, and will not avail us, unless always and at all times we are in a living relationship to God and receiving strength and power from Him."

The Apostle Paul realizes that although we have put on all this armor it will not protect and serve us unless we remain in continuous communication with God. Our dependence is not to be solely on the different pieces of armor. It is to be upon God, and this comes through prayer.

When considering this eighteenth verse bear in mind that this section begins with the admonition, *Finally, my brethren, be strong in the Lord, and in the power of his might* [Eph. 6:10]. We are also told to *stand therefore* having on and taking up the whole armor of God.

Now we are exhorted to be *Praying always*. What does this mean? Georgina Dufoix answers this question in a loving, thoughtful way, boldly saying, "We are to remain connected to the Lord Jesus no matter where we are, what we are doing, or what the conditions may be. We are to stay connected through prayer." Wherever we may be, whatever we may be doing, we are to be in communion with God. Whether we are in periods of prosperity or periods of poverty. Whether the days are ordinary or marked by stress, strain, and crisis.

"Praying *always* is to have the spirit in such unbroken communion with the Lord that all things, at all times, in all places, may be carried to Him in the upward look and inward attitude, even if no words are spoken. It implies also the outstretched hand of complete dependence both on ordinary days and in sudden crises. But preparedness against Satan's wiles requires the wisdom and strength that comes only through definitely-stated times set apart for prayer.

"Satan fears nothing as he fears a saint who knows how to prevail with God in prayer and release the omnipotent power of God against him. So he will use every devise to keep us from praying. He will cause physical fatigue and lethargy; unfit us mentally for prayer through the cares and burdens of the home and of business; and destroy our power in prayer through doubt, discouragement, and depression," as meaningfully described by Ruth Paxson.

Our Lord spent much time in prayer from the beginning to the end of His ministry. Scripture reveals that the Lord Jesus prayed often. Apparently, the disciples were impressed with His prayer life, because he tells them, *after this manner therefore pray ye* [Matt. 6:9] and then provides them with what we fondly call the Lord's Prayer.

His frequency of prayer and his attitude towards it is supported by Luke, *AND he* (Jesus) *spake a parable unto them to this end, that men ought always to pray, and not to faint* (lose heart) [Luke 18:1]. Note it says, *men ought always to pray*. What is the relative importance of prayer in our lives? Martyn Lloyd-Jones provides a personal, thoughtful, understandable statement on the importance of prayer in our daily lives, saying, "It is more important than knowledge and understanding. Do not imagine that I am detracting from the importance of knowledge or understanding. They are vitally important. There is only one thing . . . more important, and that is prayer. The ultimate test of my understanding of the scriptural teaching is the amount of time I spend in prayer. As theology is ultimately the knowledge of God, the more theology I know, the more it should drive me to seek to know God. Not to know about him, but to know Him . . . If all my knowledge does not lead me to prayer there is something wrong somewhere."

The Apostle Paul is bringing this magnificent letter to a close, yet he is compelled to provide us with important details. He tells us we are to be *Praying always*. What does he mean? We are to use all types of prayer on a continuing basis. Whether we are walking, sitting at home, at work, or playing. It may be an ejaculation, a groan, a cry, or a more orderly, formal prayer. The Apostle is saying, go ahead and pray. Do not allow self to get in the way or the devil to keep you from praying when you want to or feel the need to do so.

Our prayers are to include every type: praise, adoration, worship, thanksgiving, and requests. Remember, *Be careful* (anxious) *for nothing; but in everything by prayer and supplication . . . let your requests be made known to God* [Phil. 4:6]. How are we to pray? In the Spirit. *For through him we both have access by one Spirit unto the Father, and be filled with the Spirit* [Eph. 2:18, 5:18]. *Likewise the Spirit also helpeth our infirmities* (weaknesses): *for we know not what we should pray for as we ought: but the Spirit itself maketh intercession for us with groanings which cannot be uttered* [Rom. 8:26]. The Spirit Himself will take our weaknesses and inadequacies and lift us up. The Spirit will help us and strengthen us.

Why does Paul say *In the Spirit*? Because we worship God in the Spirit and in the truth. Jude says, *But ye, beloved, building up yourselves on your most holy faith, praying in the Holy Ghost, Keep yourselves in the love of God, looking for the mercy of our Lord Jesus Christ unto eternal life* [Jude 20–21]. We are not to pray as the Pharisees, but *in the Spirit*. Nor are we just to say a prayer or to repeat a prayer, but we are to pray *in the Spirit*. What does this mean? The Holy Spirit creates it, directs it, empowers it, and enables it. The Holy Spirit will give us the words, the thoughts, and the ability. He will work within us individually, and He will work within us collectively.

You may say, "I don't know how to pray or what to pray." That reminds me of what Lee Trevino, the golfer, said about his golf game, "The more I practice, the luckier I get."

Paul admonishes us to be *praying always* and then adds the charge, *watching thereunto with all perseverance and supplication for all saints*. Paul knows how to meddle in our affairs. Once again, Paxson provides clarity by expounding upon Paul's words through the power of the Holy Spirit saying, "we are members of one another, bound together in Christ in a union so real that if one member suffers, all the members suffer, therefore the members should have the same care one for another. The whole body of Christ suffers defeat to the degree that the individual members are defeated and the victory of the Church over the Satanic foe is dependent on the victory of every Christian. Herein lies the responsibility of each saint for all saints. Not all Christians are appropriating their wealth in Christ, or walking worthily of their high calling, or standing victoriously against Satan. Many are grieving the Spirit by still walking according to the world and the flesh, thereby giving place to the devil! So few are enlightened by the Spirit; praying in the Spirit; strengthened by the Spirit; and filled with the Spirit. Does not each saint share the blame in so far as he has failed to pray for all saints?" It is our responsibility to be enlightened; to pray always; to be strengthened; and to ask the Holy Spirit to do these things as He fills us with His power.

The Apostle Paul prayed often. He went from the point where as a Pharisee he said or repeated prayers to praying in the Spirit. He got himself out of the way and let the Holy Spirit take over. Think. Here is Paul, writing to the Ephesians a relatively short letter. Yet he offers two prayers *in the Spirit*. He prays that they receive *the spirit of wisdom and revelation in the knowledge of him: . . . and that their understanding being enlightened; that ye may know what is the hope of his calling, . . . and what* (are) *the riches of the glory of his inheritance in the saints, And what is the exceeding greatness of his power to us-ward who believe* [Eph. 1:17–19].

Then we have what may be called the Apostle's prayer. He prays fervently for the saints and faithful,

> *Be strengthened with might by his Spirit in the inner man;*
> *That Christ may dwell in your hearts by faith; that ye, being rooted and grounded in love,*
> *May be able to comprehend* (understand) *with all saints what is the breadth* (width), *and length, and depth, and height;*
> *And to know the love of Christ, which passeth knowledge, that ye might be filled with all the fullness of God* [Eph. 3:16–19].

The Apostle prays for our needs, not our wants. May we do likewise.

In so doing may we remember, *men ought always to pray, and not to faint* (lose heart) [Luke 18:1]. *Praying always, Praying without ceasing*, and praying *in the Spirit*. Yes, we abide in Him, and His words abide in us. Yes, we have put on the whole armor of God, but there is one more thing, praying and knowing God.

Therefore, I leave you with these words that were made available by Martyn Lloyd-Jones:

To keep your armor bright,
Attend with constant care,
Still walking in your captain's sight,
And watching unto prayer.
Amen!

21

Hearing, Obeying, Persevering

> *Praying always with all prayer and supplication in the Spirit, and watching thereunto with all perseverance and supplication for all saints;*
> *And for me, that utterance may be given unto me, that I may open my mouth boldly, to make known the mystery* (hidden truth) *of the gospel,*
> *For which I am an ambassador in bonds* (chains): *that therein I may speak boldly, as I ought to speak* [Eph. 6:18-20].

Three characteristics of our Lord Jesus Christ have been emphasized in previous messages, even though He exhibited numerous favorable traits, i.e. humility, love, wisdom, and many others, during His earthly ministry. Those propounded are obedience, prayer, and communication. By the latter I mean listening as well as speaking. These characteristics were true of Paul and the other apostles. Scripture contains many references to obeying, praying, hearing, and speaking the truth.

Paul brings this magnificent letter to a close by telling his brethren in Christ what they are to do after putting *on the whole armor of God.* They are to be active in their faith by *Praying always . . . in the Spirit, and watching thereunto with all perseverance and supplication for all saints; And for me* (Paul) *. . . , that I may open my mouth boldly, to make known the mystery* (hidden truth) *of the gospel; That therein I may speak boldly, as I ought to speak* [Eph. 6:18-20]. These are the commands given by Paul. They are not requests. He informs us of our duty, and how we are to perform it. He also needs our prayers to continue fulfilling his ministry for Christ Jesus.

Why does Paul complete these beneficial teachings in this way? The overriding reasons are wanting us to know God and the Lord Jesus in a personal, intimate way; to grow and become stronger in our faith; to have our spiritual lives enriched and enlightened; and to walk in the light and love of Christ Himself, His commands, and teachings.

We are to be obedient according to these last verses by *watching thereunto*. We are not only to accept the commands and teachings of Christ, but we are also to exert ourselves, to put forth the effort, and to exhibit *all perseverance and supplication for all the saints*. There is an obligation imposed upon us as members of Christ's body to pray and to watch. Fulfilling this commitment is beneficial, as appropriately described by William Gurnall with these words, "A Christian (is) to watch . . . that he may keep the Lord's charge and do the duty imposed upon him as a Christian . . . This is not a temporary duty, but for his whole lifetime." Martyn Lloyd-Jones expands upon this obligation, saying, "Prayer is a duty, but it is much more than a duty. It should be a delight, it should be the ultimate expression of the Christian life."

The Roman soldier on duty was to watch, to be alert. So is the football player when he takes to the field. What about the members of Christ's body? Day in and day out they are to be watching. Ruth Paxson defines *watching thereunto* properly as "permitting no laziness or self-indulgence that unfits for prayer; . . . watchful for everything that feeds and fosters the prayer life, and on guard against anything that enfeebles or hinders it."

Why are we to watch by praying? Prayer is an act of worship. In prayer we go to God. We petition Him, we ask Him, and we are in His presence. In our prayers we either honor or dishonor God. Therefore, we are to watch how we pray. If our prayers are to be effective, they are to be lifted in a holy manner, expecting Him to hear and answer our prayers.

Yes, we are to watch before praying, but also while praying and after praying. This is difficult but necessary. I know when I am praying that my mind wanders, and I become distracted, and then I have to get back on course. It takes *watching thereunto*.

How are we to *watch thereunto*? *With all perseverance*. This is a hard, challenging command. Why does the Apostle say this? The Greek word for *perseverance* means *to continue steadfastly and to give unremitting care to it*. This signifies strength of purpose and the ability to achieve that which the Apostle is exhorting us to do. It requires the commitment to achieve despite unfavorable circumstances or conditions. The apostles said in the early days after the resurrection, *But we will give ourselves continually to prayer* [Acts 6:4].

Paul encouraged the Romans with these words, *Rejoicing in hope; patient* (persevering) *in tribulation; continuing instant* (steadfastly) *in prayer* [Rom. 12:12]. He exhorted the Colossians to, *Continue* (persevere) *in prayer* [Col. 4:2]. These exhortations apply to everything and in anything. There is no way to escape these admonitions. This should enable us to better understand and accept Calvin's enlightened words when he says, "When everything flows on prosperously, when we are easy and cheerful, we have hardly any thought of praying; in fact, we never flee to God, unless driven by distress. Paul therefore desires us to let no season pass, without remembering to pray; so that praying at all seasons is the same as praying both in prosperity and adversity."

Praying *with all perseverance* needs to be tempered by a certain understanding. First, we are to continue praying steadfastly until one of two things happen: the object of our prayer is received or it is removed, and in effect our petitions are denied.

Second, we are to realize that God may intentionally delay answering our petitions or may seem to deny them. Why is this so? It is not because He does not hear us or is not interested in us. He may want to see how earnest we are. He may want us to develop a habit that will sustain and prepare us. As William Gurnall so effectively states, it may be that, "He lays blocks before the wheel of their prayers, to try their mettle—how well they draw, when it comes a dead pull, and the mercy comes not at their prayer."

Yet you may well ask, why does God seem to withhold His answer? James explains it very well, saying,

> *Take, my brethren, the prophets, who have spoken in the name of the Lord, for an example of suffering affliction, and of patience.*
> *Behold, we count them happy* (blessed) *which endure. Ye have heard of the patience* (perseverance) *of Job, and have seen the end of* (final result intended by) *the Lord; that the Lord is very pitiful* (compassionate), *and of tender mercy* [Jas. 5:10–11].

Calvin provides additional light, saying, "Should any man imitate his (Job's) patience, no doubt he will likewise feel the hand of God come at last to his relief... God did not allow his servant Job to be vanquished for he endured his pains with patience: So the patience of no man will be wasted...Why does the Apostle so greatly commend the patience of Job, who . . . showed considerable signs of impatience. The answer is, that even though on occasion he lapses through weakness of the flesh, . . . yet he always comes back to entrusting himself wholly to God, and offering himself to his restraining and controlling arm."

Yes, Job is credited with having great patience, but the glory belongs to God, who turns adversity into triumph. God will do His part if we will do ours by *obeying, praying, and persevering*. God will reveal Himself through His love, mercy, and righteousness.

What other reasons are there for praying and watching *with all perseverance*? The advantages for those who persist in praying and watching are: they will come to know God and the Lord Jesus better and better; their understanding and knowledge will increase; their confidence will grow based upon Jesus Christ Himself, the chief cornerstone; and they will be better prepared and strengthened to *walk worthy of the vocation* (calling) *wherewith ye are called* [Eph. 4:1]. In addition, what may have seemed to be a duty, obligation, or chore is now embraced as a joy and delight. In addition, one desires the time and opportunity to go to God in prayer.

It is well to ask, what is it to pray? Is it to beg or ask alms or favors? Hardly! It starts with acknowledging who God is and that He is holy, righteous, and faithful. He promises to answer His children's prayers, but the time is of His own choosing. God is not unfaithful! Our faith and belief need to be enlightened and strengthened because God is faithful!

For whom are we to be *praying . . . and watching thereunto with all perseverance and supplication for all saints* [Eph. 6:18]? All the saints! Each and every one. Why? Because we are all members of Christ's body. The following explicitly states,

> *That there should be no schism* (division) *in the body; but that the members should have the same care one for another.*
> *And whether* (if) *one member suffer, all the members suffer with it; or one member be honored* (glorified), *all the members rejoice with it* [1 Cor. 12:25–26].

The members of Christ's body share in both afflictions and happiness. Calvin was well aware of the fact that all true believers have challenges, adversities, and disappointments. Therefore, he shares his wisdom with us because God's truths were revealed to him and he feels compelled to emphatically state, "There is no room for envy or scorn in it. There is nothing that (fosters) harmony better than this feeling for each other where each one realizes that he is enriched by the benefits of others every bit as much as they, and that when they suffer loss, he is impoverished along with them."

Each saint and faithful follower has a responsibility for all the others. However, they all do not exercise it. Unfortunately, too many do not walk worthy of their calling, or are uninformed, or do not appropriate the riches of Christ. Why? Because they do not realize what Scripture is saying, especially in Ephesians, that you may be enlightened by the Spirit; that you may be strengthened by the might of the Spirit, that you might be filled with the Spirit, and that you might pray always in the Spirit.

For what are we to pray regarding all the saints? That they may know Christ, His grace, His glory, and His love. This should be first. Further, that they may boldly proclaim the Gospel, by their words and their actions, to those with whom they may come into contact, remembering Paul's words *that I may speak boldly, as I ought to speak* [Eph. 3:20]. Our boldness is to be in accord with Christ's love, grace, and firmness. We should pray according to the examples given by Paul, the other apostles, and our Lord Jesus.

We are not to be narrow, selfish, or exclusive in our prayers. We are to pray for all the saints, those we like and those we do not. That is not all! We are to pray for the lives of the saints, individually and collectively. If there are some we do not particularly care for, we are to pray for them. God works through the saints; therefore, we need to pray that their hearts, minds, and souls will be open to His will. We are to pray for love and unity among the saints according to Christ's commands and teachings. This is difficult, yet it is necessary. Recently, some people were having a discussion about a few members of their Church. I said you have to pray for them. They said they could not; I said you must.

Paul does not end his sentence or his teaching on this note. He continues by saying, *and for me*. He wants them *praying always, watching thereunto with all perseverance* for himself. Here is this great Apostle asking the saints and the faithful to pray for him. He knew what he was doing. He knew he needed their prayers. He knew that strength and enlightenment would come from their prayers. Ruth Paxson's words explain why Paul asked for and received the prayers of others, "Though undaunted, he was not self-confident. He needed strength and courage . . . to faithfully fulfill his duties . . . ."

What did he ask that they pray for in his behalf? That he be released from prison? That he receive physical comfort? No! Not for anything that could be considered a personal benefit or blessing.

What did he ask them to pray for?

> . . . *that I may open my mouth boldly, to make known the mystery* (hidden truth) *of the gospel.*
> . . . (And although) *I am an ambassador in bonds: that therein I may speak boldly, as I ought to speak* [Eph. 6:19–20].

Period—end of sentence—end of exhortation—end of message!

Talk about being explicit! Paul told them exactly what he wanted them to pray for concerning himself.

> *How that by revelation he made known unto me the mystery* (hidden truth); *as I wrote afore* (before) *in few words,*
> *Whereby, when ye read, ye may understand my knowledge in the mystery of Christ*
> *Which in other ages was not made known unto the sons of men, as it is now revealed unto his holy apostles and prophets by the Spirit* [Eph. 3:3–5].

Paul wants them to pray that the Gospel will be preached boldly and that the Gospel will be made known. Consider Paul's exhortation, *FINALLY, brethren, pray for us, that the word of the Lord may have* (run) *free course and be glorified* [2 Thess. 3:1]. Paul wants them to pray that he will present the whole Gospel and keep nothing back, that he will carefully and fully present it.

Unfortunately, today there are ministers and teachers who want to pick and choose, who do not present the whole Gospel for fear that they might offend someone or some group. They want to be politically correct, whereas Christ Himself, Paul, Peter, and the other apostles were anything but politically correct.

Paul recognized full well that the whole Gospel was to be made known to them. When Paul was addressing the Elders from Ephesus at Miletus he said,

> *For I have not shunned to declare unto you all the counsel of God.*
> *Take heed therefore unto yourselves, and to all the flock, over which the Holy Ghost hath made you overseers, to feed* (shepherd) *the Church of God, which he hath purchased with his own blood* [Acts 20:27–28].

Paul presented the Gospel in the following ways:

- he gave details as to how they were to walk;
- he taught them the miracles, teachings, and truths of Christ and Him crucified;
- he did not hesitate, he did not apologize, he proceeded on course;
- he proclaimed the whole Gospel, all aspects of it;
- he wanted them to hear it, because he knew if they heard it that it would change their lives;
- he knew that the Word of God would strengthen them to face the adversities of life;
- he wanted them to be able to handle the triumphs and defeats of life; and
- he wanted them to serve God and the Lord Jesus Christ, not to be men pleasers.

We are to pray that the Gospel will be proclaimed by preachers and teachers boldly and honestly, with assurance and certainty that it is the Word of God.

Remember Paul's magnificent, meaningful statement *That we henceforth be no more children, tossed to and fro, and carried about with every wind of doctrine, by the sleight* (trickery) *of men, and cunning craftiness, whereby they lie in wait to deceive* [Eph. 4:14]. That statement is sandwiched between *Till we all come in* (into) *the unity of the faith, and . . . knowledge of the Son of God, unto a perfect* (mature) *man, unto the measure of the stature of the fullness of Christ*: and *But speaking the truth in love, may grow up into him in all things, which is the head, even Christ* [Eph. 4:13, 15].

Think of the wisdom Paul received from the Holy Spirit. He stresses faith and knowledge to become a perfect man in the stature of the fullness of Christ before warning them about every wind of doctrine, sleight of men, and cunning craftiness, prior to speaking the truth in love so that they may grow up into Him in all things, even Christ.

What do we need to watch for in preachers and teachers? First, William Gurnall provides an accurate description of the type person against whom we are to be always on guard, "the vainglorious person, the one who wants to make known his or her ideas, who is witty or wishes to orate instead of making known the Gospel and opening Scripture so it can be applied."

Second, is the abstruse person who clouds the issues and makes the simple truths complex. One commentator with insight put it this way, "The places on which they treat were plain till they expounded them. Their text was clear till their obscure discourse darkened it." As you well know, it is not always the deepest water that is the darkest or murkiest.

Third, is the merely moral person, who preaches or teaches the moral code or law or duties, but stops short of the Lord Jesus Christ, the Son of God, through whom there is forgiveness of sins, a new life, righteousness, and life everlasting. They forget that the whole purpose of Scripture is to reveal and make known the Lord Jesus Christ.

These people ignore Paul saying,

> *Unto me who am less than the least of all saints, is this grace given, that I should preach among the Gentiles the unsearchable riches of Christ;*
>
> *And to make all men see what is the fellowship of the mystery* (ways of God in grace), *which from the beginning of the world hath been hid in God, who created all things by Jesus Christ* [Eph. 3:8-9].

Paul also says, *Yea, woe is unto me, if I preach not the gospel* [1 Cor. 9:16]!

Gurnall states an important, illuminating truth, "God never laid it upon thee to convert those he sends to thee, No; to publish the gospel is thy duty, to receive it is theirs." Preachers and teachers need to remember what Paul knew so well that God judged him according to the content of the message he proclaimed and his faithfulness in delivering it. He judges us by our: faithfulness in hearing the Word and applying it; obedience to His commands and teachings; and perseverance in praying for all the saints.

May the Word be proclaimed boldly. May we hear it boldly. May we live it boldly. Remember, after the Apostle Paul came to know the Lord Jesus Christ he became obedient, he listened, he communicated, and he prayed. He knew his duty, and he did it. May we do likewise.

Amen!

22

Ambassadors of Christ

> *For which I am an ambassador in bonds* (chains): *that therein I may speak boldly, as I ought to speak.*
> *But that ye also may know my affairs, and how I do, Tychicus, a beloved brother and faithful minister in the Lord, shall make known to you all things:*
> *Whom I have sent unto you for the same purpose, that ye might know our affairs, and that he might comfort your hearts.*
> *Peace be to the brethren, and love with faith, from God the Father and the Lord Jesus Christ.*
> *Grace be with all them that love our Lord Jesus Christ in sincerity. Amen* [Eph. 6:20–24].

The Apostle Paul brings to a close this magnificent letter, affectionately known as the "Holy of Holies," reminding the Ephesians that he is Christ's ambassador even though he is in bonds. He asks them to pray that he might open his mouth boldly to make known the mystery of the Gospel.

He prays that he may speak boldly, as he ought to speak, as an ambassador, that they may know of his affairs and that he might comfort their hearts. Paul is ever bold in proclaiming the Gospel and ever loving in caring for the saints.

When we embarked upon this journey through Ephesians, it was to acquire more knowledge about God, our heavenly Father, to increase our faith in Him and His Son, Christ Jesus, and to grow in our relationship with them. Therefore, it is appropriate to go back and examine the precepts upon which we established the foundation and *builded* (being built) *together for a habitation* (dwelling place) *of God through the Spirit* [Eph. 2:22].

What benefits should we receive from walking through Ephesians? First, we are given an understanding of what God has done and is doing for *the called out*, the saints of God, and the faithful in the three initial chapters. Second, the last three chapters inform us as to how we are to walk as the sons and daughters of God; how we *may grow up into him in all things* [Eph. 4:15]; and how we are to act as new creatures in Christ and to *BE . . . followers of God, as dear children* [Eph. 5:1]. Third, the Apostle Paul wants us to receive an intimate knowledge of Christ and prays that this will happen. He prays that we know Christ no matter what our circumstances or condition may be and that we become Christ-centered, not self-centered.

Why did Paul want this for the saints and the faithful? Because he did not want them to be misled, but that they would *. . . henceforth be no more children, tossed to and fro, and carried about with every wind of doctrine, by the sleight* (trickery) *of men, and cunning craftiness* [Eph. 4:14]. Therefore, Paul presented the eternal truths of God in Christ in the first three chapters and the application of these truths by the saints and faithful in the last three.

Paul describes not only the fruits of hearing and believing the Gospel, but also the duties and responsibilities that the saints and faithful have as disciples, as *the called out*.

The Apostle emphasizes that you cannot separate the Gospel from daily living. We are to grab hold of the Lord Jesus Christ, and respond affirmatively to His commands in faith and obedience. We are to understand the truths of God as they are revealed. How are we to do this? By communicating with God, by hearing what He has to say, and by praying. It is interesting that Paul concludes this letter with an emphasis upon praying.

Paul does *not* talk about his experiences, his years of service, his labors and difficulties, his accomplishments, or his adversaries. He encourages the saints and faithful regarding the Gospel; coming closer to God and His Son, our Lord; man communicating with God; being obedient and faithful; and having a personal relationship with Christ by maturing in the Lord.

Probably some have wondered what would be covered in these final pages, and have echoed the Greeks' question regarding Paul, *What will this babbler say* [Acts 17:18]? Bearing this in mind, one thing this *babbler* has strived to do is to present the Gospel of Jesus Christ as proclaimed in Scripture, not his own ideas or thoughts, but the Gospel as Paul received it from Christ through the Holy Ghost. Another demand has been to present everything contained in this letter, so that a better understanding of Christ's teachings may be obtained as well as a willingness to obey His commands. So here we are, at the close of the letter. Where do we go from here?

Before proceeding to the conclusion, consider the Lord's words at the end of Matthew's Gospel,

> *Then the eleven disciples went away into Galilee, into a mountain where Jesus had appointed them.*
>
> *And when they saw him, they worshipped him: but some doubted.*
>
> *And Jesus came and spake unto them, saying, All power* (authority) *is given unto me in heaven and in earth.*
>
> *Go ye therefore, and teach* (make disciples of) *all nations, baptizing them in the name of the Father, and of the Son, and of the Holy Ghost:*
>
> *Teaching them to observe all things whatsoever I have commanded you: and lo, I am with you alway, even unto the end of the world. Amen* [Matt. 28:16–20].

The eleven disciples obeyed and went into Galilee.

Some disciples expressed fears or doubts after the first Easter morning. John Calvin, in his characteristic manner, provides clarity, insight, and strength for us as he relates how the Lord Jesus removed the disciples' fears, doubts, and hesitations, and replaced them with His power so that they would obey His commands and serve Him in every facet of their lives. This same power and understanding is available to each believer today. Hear Calvin's admirable words as to what happened to the original disciples and what will happen to each and every believer, "In my opinion, the sense is that some [of the disciples] hesitated at first until Christ approached them nearer and more intimately. When they knew him in truth and certainty, then they worshipped Him. There is no doubt that His approach took away all their doubts. Before relating that the office of teaching was laid upon them, Matthew says that Christ spoke first of His power, and rightly so . . . The Apostles would never be persuaded to undertake such a task of difficulty unless they knew that their Champion sat in heaven, and that supreme power was given to Him."

What did the Master command His disciples to do? *Go . . . therefore, and teach* (make disciples of) *all nations* [Matt. 28:19]. What were they to teach them? *Teaching them to observe all things whatsoever I have commanded you* [Matt. 28:20]. And then what did He say? Here is what you do? Here is the money? No, no, no! He stated his authority and removed their doubts. He commanded them and gave them responsibilities. He promised them, and He fulfilled His promises. It was then that they responded in faith. "Jesus gave his commandments in the course of his earthly ministry," as Edward Schweizer reminds us.

What were the disciples to teach? All that the Lord Jesus had taught and commanded them. What does this have to do with concluding our study of Ephesians? Everything! Undoubtedly we have questions, concerns, and doubts, and we do not know exactly what to do. Where do we start? Exactly at the same place where the disciples started, *Teaching them to observe all things whatsoever I Have commanded you* [Matt. 28:20]. How do we do that? By understanding the teachings, by grasping hold, and by becoming Christ-centered, not self-centered.

There is a lesson to learn. When the disciples were downcast, disheartened, and distressed they learned to wait, to listen, to hear what was being said and more. They learned to go, to do, to apply, and to focus elsewhere.

What happened after Jesus departed? Peter and John healed a lame man. This caused much consternation among the people and the rulers. As a result the rulers decreed,

> *. . . that they speak henceforth to no man in this name* (Jesus).
> *And they called them, and commanded them not to speak at all nor teach in the name of Jesus.*
> *But Peter and John answered and said unto them, Whether it be right in the sight of God to hearken unto you more than unto God, judge ye.*
> *For we cannot but speak the things which we have seen and heard.*
> *And now, Lord, behold their threatenings: and grant unto thy servants, that with all boldness they may speak thy word,*
> *By stretching forth thine hand to heal; and that signs and wonders may be done by* (through) *the name of thy holy child* (servant) *Jesus.*

> *And when they had prayed, the place was shaken where they were assembled together; and they were all filled with the Holy Ghost, and they spake the word of God with boldness* [Acts 4:17–20, 29–31].

What should we learn from this happening? What is our duty when confronted by enemies, undesirable circumstances, and political correctness? We must continually pursue our duty and our responsibilities as Christ's disciples. We are "to seek help at the hands of God" and be "not dismayed nor diverted . . . from . . . our duty," as John Calvin emphasizes our responsibilities and duties in serving the Lord Jesus.

Peter and John had no hesitancy in going to God and relying upon Him. They were encountering opposition, but they knew from whence cometh their help. For what did they ask? Relief from the threatenings? No! They prayed, *Lord, . . . grant unto thy servants, that with all boldness they may speak thy word* [Acts 4:29]. And what happened? *The place was shaken where they were assembled together; and they were all filled with the Holy Ghost, and they spake the word of God with boldness* [Acts 4:31]. Luke informs us that they were filled with the Holy Spirit, and they acted with boldness.

Note the significance of the situation. The apostles communicated with God. They prayed to Him! They grasped Him! They were obedient to Him! They were filled with the Holy Spirit! And *They spake the word of God with boldness* [Acts 4:31]!

How are we to conduct ourselves? The same way. "We learn from this that we rightly acknowledge the benefits of God as we ought, when we are . . . encouraged to pray that he will confirm what he has begun . . . Paul asks the faithful to pray to the Lord that his mouth may be opened [Eph. 6:19], although his voice already sounded in every place. Therefore, the more we are aware of being helped by the Lord, we should learn to ask for still greater progress . . . We must constantly pray that (The Gospel) may be continued to us," as John Calvin sums it up clearly and concisely.

This does not mean that we can go about doing as we wish or want in a bold manner. It means we are to act boldly when acting in accordance with Christ's commandments, communicating with God, and praying as His disciples. Acting boldly implies responsibility, not license. The boldness which the apostles had was as "The child of prayer, it was not bred in them, but granted from heaven unto them," according to William Gurnall in describing their prayer.

Why is responsibility involved? Paul states it explicitly, *For which I am an ambassador in bonds* (chains) [Eph. 6:20]. Paul was a minister, a disciple. What are we? Members of Christ's body, heirs, *joint-heirs*, disciples, and preachers and teachers. What is involved in being an ambassador? It means representing the one for whom you are an ambassador with dignity, commitment, fervor, understanding, and obedience. The ambassador is to do the will of the one who sent him. The ambassador swears allegiance and fealty to the one who has called, appointed, and sent him.

What does God do with His ambassadors? He gives them instructions, provides for them, and supports them. Paul expresses it thoughtfully saying,

> *Whatsoever things were written aforetime* (beforehand) *were written for our learning, that we through patience* (perseverance) *and comfort of the scriptures might have hope.*
> *Now the God of patience and consolation* (comfort) *grant you to be likeminded one toward another according to Christ Jesus:*
> *That ye may with one mind and one mouth glorify God, even the Father of our Lord Jesus Christ* [Rom. 15:4–6].

Paul wants the saints and faithful to imitate Christ, to do as they have been commanded, and to be His disciples. "There is nothing in Scripture which may not contribute to your instruction and the training of your life," according to Calvin's learned understanding and interpretation of Scripture.

We are to learn what Scripture offers and to realize that such knowledge is conducive to advancing godliness. Paul exhorts the Romans, *Now the God of patience and consolation* (comfort) *grant you to be likeminded one toward another according to Christ Jesus* [Rom. 15:5]. It is Christ who calls the signals. Therefore, if we are his ambassadors, we are to obey His commands.

What are people to do when God's ambassadors speak? They are to listen to their message when it is the message of their Lord and King. They are to respond in faith and obedience.

What are the duties of ambassadors? To honorably discharge their responsibilities; to do nothing that will stain or mar the dignity, honor, and glory of their King; to be loyal subjects; to become holy because *I the*

Lord your God am holy [Lev. 19:2]; to follow instructions; to know the Word; to proclaim the Word; and to obey Christ's commands. Paul says, *I am pure* (innocent) *from the blood of all men. For I have not shunned to declare unto you all the counsel* (will and determination) *of God* [Acts 20:26–27].

What example does Paul provide as an ambassador that we should follow as disciples? First, the purpose of the Father is to be made known. "With God there (are) no surprises and no emergencies. The Word made flesh was not an afterthought of God. (His) eternal purpose encompasses God's relationship to the saints and faithful, and how they (you and me) are to become like him and be with him now and forever," as Ruth Paxson provides additional illumination and states what we are *to become*.

Second, the characteristics and traits of Jesus Christ are presented throughout this magnificent letter as well as our responsibilities in witnessing to Him and proclaiming God's Word. We are to be ever mindful of the truths presented by the Apostle Paul:

- *An Apostle of Jesus Christ;*
- *Adoption . . . by Jesus Christ;*
- *Who first trusted in Christ;*
- *Quickened us together with Christ;*
- *Created in Christ Jesus unto good works;*
- *Jesus Christ himself being the chief corner stone;*
- *The unsearchable riches of Christ;*
- *Who created all things by Jesus Christ;*
- *That Christ may dwell in your hearts by faith;*
- *To know the love of Christ;*
- *But ye have not so learned Christ;*
- *Forgiving one another even as God for Christ's sake hath forgiven you;*
- *Walk in love, as Christ also hath loved us;*
- *Christ shall give thee light;*
- *Submitting yourselves one to another in the fear of Christ;*
- *Subject unto Christ;* and
- *Servants of Christ, doing the will of God from the heart.*

[Selections from Paul's Letter to the Ephesians]

Christ is alive and present throughout this entire letter. He is the focal point.

Third, God's purpose is revealed in and through His Son. His purpose works in us by and through the Holy Spirit. We are to *be filled with the Spirit.*

Paul concludes this wonderful, meaningful letter saying, *Peace be to the brethren, and love with faith, from God the Father and the Lord Jesus Christ* [Eph. 6:23]. Markus Barth amplifies upon this with his remarkable statement that, "Brotherly love is a gift of God, not an achievement over which man exercises control . . . It indicates that the peace which God has created brings forth two things, 'love' for thy neighbor and 'faith' in God." Paul wanted the Ephesians to be in accord among themselves. Calvin points out that "faith produces love and is its bond," and that peace, love, and faith are the gifts of God bestowed through His Son.

Paul reminds us at the end of this letter that our weaknesses require *praying always,* and that the real gifts of life come from God the Father through the Son and that our strength is in them. The final verse says, *Grace be with all them that love our Lord Jesus Christ in sincerity. Amen* [Eph. 6:24]. The word *sincerity* means *incorruption* or *incorruptible.* We are to love Him in spirit and truth.

"Looking back over the Grand Canyon of Scripture four great truths suffuse a glory light over it like an afterglow. Interwoven and interpenetrated, they reveal the Trinity at work linking eternity with time, heaven with earth, glory with grace, God with man, the Saviour with the sinner, Christ with the Church.

"The purpose of the Father stretches from the eternal past . . . to the eternal future. [It] encompasses God's relationship to men, both sinners and saints; to angelic beings, both evil and good; and to Satan and his hosts. It centres in His Son for whom in the eternal ages of the past He chose a company of saints to be His Body and His Bride who would be in Him, become like Him and be with Him now and through all the ages upon ages to come.

"One luminous person fills and floods the Grand Canyon of Scripture with the heavenly glory light—the Person of the God-man, our Lord Jesus Christ. The Jesus of history is not in view here. The Saviour of the gospels has gone from the Cross to the Throne and is seated there at the Father's right hand. The light that suffuses the Grand Canyon of Scripture is the glory of the crowned Victor; of the holy Head of the

Church in whom dwelleth all the fulness of the God-head bodily; and of the One to whom the Lordship overall things in heaven and upon earth is given.

"In Christ—how simple the words! How superb the truth! All Christians, of whom the Church consists, made one with the glorified Christ so that His position is their position; His possession their possession; His privileges their privileges; His power their power; His plenitude their plenitude. 'In Christ—then Into Christ in all things.'

"The outworking of the Father's purpose is in the Son. The inworking is by His Spirit. Access to the unsearchable riches in Christ . . . is made possible only by the mighty power of the Holy Spirit. The fulness of God the Father made available in the fulness of the Son is made actual through the fulness of the Spirit. 'Be ye filled with the Spirit,'" as beautifully described by the ineffable Ruth Paxson.

Thus we conclude our walk through the Holy of Holies and begin *Walking With Jesus* as His disciples.

Amen!

Outline Questions

Chapter 1

ASSURANCE, CHANGE OR OPPOSITION

> *Finally, my brethren, be strong in the Lord, and in the power of his might.*
> *Put on the whole armor of God, that ye may be able to stand against the wiles (schemes) of the devil.*
> *For we wrestle not against flesh and blood, but against principalities, against powers, against the rulers of the darkness of this world (age), against spiritual (hosts of) wickedness in high places* [Eph. 6:10–12].

Who does the Lord Jesus impact?

How do people react to the Lord Jesus Christ?

What happened after Lazarus came forth?

How does Calvin describe unbelief?

What do we really want from Christ?

What happens when we receive assurance?

How does Satan use his wiles with respect to assurance?

Why was it that Jesus' *disciples went back, and walked no more with Him*?

What motivated the Pharisees to oppose Jesus?

What was the prophesy uttered by Caiaphas?

What happens when we receive assurance?

What does Thomas Brooks say about Satan and his enmity?

How are we to examine ourselves?

What is the condition of the person who has assurance and is changed by Christ?

What assurance did Paul want?

Chapter 2

BELIEVING AND REJOICING IN ASSURANCE

> THEREFORE *being justified by faith, we have peace with God through our Lord Jesus Christ:*
>
> *By whom also we have access by faith into this grace wherein we stand, and rejoice in hope of the glory of God.*
>
> *And not only so, but we glory in tribulations also: knowing that tribulation worketh patience;*
>
> *And patience, experience* (character); *and experience, hope:*
>
> *And hope maketh not ashamed* (does not disappoint); *because the love of God is shed abroad in our hearts by the Holy Ghost which is given unto us* [Rom. 5:1–5].

What factors contribute to our uneasiness and unrest?

What does the Apostle John mean when he says, *"that ye may believe"*?

In whom are we to rejoice?

Why do people accept either the teachings of God or the world regarding assurance?

How is the righteousness of God received?

How does Satan make us question the assurance that is available?

How are we to handle Satan's attacks and torments?

Are we to focus our attention on self or on the Lord Jesus Christ?

What impact do *the wiles of the devil* have upon us?

How did the father receive the prodigal son?

Why does the Apostle John stress the fact that some people *went out from us, but they were not of us*?

What three categories do the people fall into who profess belief in the Gospel?

Why do we pray that God will exercise *thy mighty grasp of me*?

Chapter 3

QUENCH NOT THE SPIRIT

> *I have yet many things to say unto you, but ye cannot bear them now.*
> *Howbeit when he, the Spirit of truth, is come, he will guide you into all truth: for he shall not speak of himself* (on his own authority); *but whatsoever he shall hear, that shall he speak: and he will show you things to come.*
> *He shall glorify me: for he shall receive of* (what is) *mine, and shall show* (declare) *it unto you* [John 16:12–14].

What does the Comforter do?

Why did Jesus provide the gift of the Comforter?

What does the designation "Comforter" mean?

How does Otto Weber define sin?

What does the Greek word for "righteousness" mean?

Why will there be judgment?

Where did Paul believe the emphasis should be placed?

What does the Lord Jesus make plain regarding the Holy Spirit?

Why does Paul say, *Quench not the Spirit*?

What does *Quench not the Spirit* mean?

How do we quench the Spirit?

What does *be filled with the Spirit* mean?

What qualities are evident when the fire of the Spirit is fanned rather than quenched?

What remarkable gift does the Lord Jesus give us?

Chapter 4

WHENCE KNOWEST THOU ME

> Jesus saw Nathanael coming to him, and saith of him, Behold an Israelite indeed, in whom is no guile!
> Nathanael saith unto him, Whence knowest thou me? Jesus answered and said unto him, Before that Philip called thee, when thou wast under the fig tree, I saw thee.
> Nathanael answered and saith unto him, Rabbi, thou art the Son of God; thou are the King of Israel.
> Jesus answered and said unto him, Because I said unto thee, I saw thee under the fig tree, believest thou? thou shalt see greater things than these [John 1:47–50].

Regarding what things is Scripture very explicit?

Why did Jesus say to Nathanael, *Behold an Israelite indeed, in whom is no guile?*

What did Jesus do in addition to meeting Nathanael's need?

What did Nathanael do?

What happens when a person is led by the Spirit and does not quench it?

What should we remember regarding Nathanael?

To whom is the promise of the Holy Spirit given?

What are additional *wiles of the devil*?

What are we to do when the Holy Spirit comes?

What keeps us from responding to Jesus' call to *come and see*?

What happens when we become discouraged?

What does Paul say about anxiety?

What did Calvin say about anxiety and God's mercy?

Why are we to have a sound mind?

Chapter 5

SELF

> Finally, my brethren, be strong in the Lord, and in the power of his might.
> Put on the whole armor of God, that ye may be able to stand against the wiles (schemes) of the devil.
> For we wrestle not against flesh and blood, but against principalities, against powers, against the rulers of the darkness of this world (age), against spiritual (hosts of) wickedness in high places [Eph. 6:10–12].

What did God say to Moses that is also true today?

What is the message of the hymn "Just As I Am"?

How do we come to Christ?

How does God use Christ's followers?

What are the requirements for working with God?

What happens when we concentrate on God?

Outline Questions

What keeps us from concentrating on God?

What did Jesus look for in people?

Who provides the gifts given to each and every one of us?

How does self get in the way and keep us from focusing on God?

What was the condition of the Laodicians?

On whom does Paul want us to depend?

What defects are exhibited by self?

What questions should we ask regarding the impediments that self generates?

To whom does Paul ascribe the contributions he was able to make during his ministry?

What characteristics did Christ exhibit in His ministry?

Chapter 6

THINGS APPOINTED

> *And it came to pass, that, as I made my journey, and was come nigh unto Damascus about noon, suddenly there shone from heaven a great light round me.*
>
> *And I fell unto the ground, and heard a voice saying unto me, Saul, Saul, why persecutest thou me?*
>
> *And I answered, Who art thou, Lord? And he said unto me, I am Jesus of Nazareth, whom thou persecutest.*
>
> *And they that were with me saw indeed the light, and were afraid; but they heard not the voice of him that spake to me.*
>
> *And I said, What shall I do, Lord? And the Lord said unto me, Arise, and go into Damascus; and there it shall be told thee of all things which are appointed for thee to do* [Acts 22:6–10].

What were Paul's guiding lights after his encounter on the road to Damascus?

Are you constantly aware of who you are and what you are to do?

What did Jesus mean when He said to Peter, Follow me?

What are we called to do?

What did Paul say after Christ had called him?

What did the Lord Jesus say to Paul?

What may we learn from Paul's encounter with Christ?

How do we grow in grace?

What every day things affect us and keep us from a right relationship with God?

What does righteousness mean?

What priorities does Paul want us to embrace?

What does Paul exhort us to do?

How can we do the appointed things?

Chapter 7

THE BATTLE CALL

> *Wherefore take unto you the whole armor of God, that ye may be able to withstand in the evil day, and having done to all, to stand* [Eph. 6:13].

What are the contrasts in Paul's life and in his letter to the Ephesians?

What do you have to do to stand on God's side?

What are we to learn?

How are we to pray?

What are we to do regarding the whole armor of God?

Why do we receive a battle call?

To whom was Paul writing?

What does the Apostle tell us to do?

Why did the Holy Spirit guide Paul to write these enlightening words?

Why do we need to be strong in the Lord?

What are we to do about our weaknesses?

What happens when people accept Christ?

To what type of life are we called?

What was Paul's first priority after Christ called him?

What is required of us, as noted by Paul, in the closing verses of this letter?

Chapter 8

A DIVINE VISIT

> And when she had thus said, she turned herself back, and saw Jesus standing, and knew not that it was Jesus.
> Jesus saith unto her, Woman, why weepest thou? whom seekest thou? She, supposing him to be the gardener, saith unto him, Sir, if thou have borne him hence, tell me where thou hast laid him, and I will take him away.
> Jesus saith unto her, Mary. She turned herself, and saith unto him, Rabboni; which is to say, Master.
> Jesus saith unto her, Touch me not; for I am not yet ascended to my Father: but go to my brethren, and say unto them, I ascend unto my Father, and your Father; and to my God, and your God
> [John 20:14–17]

Where was Mary Magdalene's focus?

What happened to the two men on the road to Emmaus?

What did Mary and the two men receive?

What are we to do?

What is revealed to us?

Why should we *be strong in the Lord, and in the power of his might*?

What do we need in order to obey the Lord's commands?

Who are we to follow?

How does God strengthen us?

How does God quicken us?

How does the Gospel come unto us?

What does the Word of God keep telling us about the Comforter?

Why are these things brought to our attention?

What are we to do according to Scripture?

What poignant things does Paul tell us to do in Philippians?

Of what is the Bible full as noted by Lloyd-Jones?

How are the teachings we hear to be tested?

What meaningful truths are expressed in "Spirit of God, Descend upon my Heart"?

Chapter 9

DISCIPLINE

> *Finally, my brethren, be strong in the Lord, and in the power of his might* [Eph. 6:10].

How are we to do the works of God?

What is going to fill us?

What does God require of us?

What does Christ mean when He says, *Labor not for the meat which perisheth, but for the meat which endureth unto everlasting life*?

How does Paul's exhortation *to be strong in the Lord, and in the power of His might* relate to *I am the bread of life, he that cometh to me shall never hunger, . . . and shall never thirst*?

What are we to do?

What is required to do these things?

What are we to add to the gifts God bestows upon us?

What does Calvin say we are to do?

What is it that we are not to do?

What does the word *virtue* mean as used by Paul?

What does Peter tell us we must do if we are to be *partakers of the divine nature*?

Why are we to add self-control to knowledge, and patience to self-control, and godliness to patience, and charity to godliness?

What is amazing about Peter's command?

Chapter 10

RESPONDING IN FAITH

> *Finally, my brethren, be strong in the Lord, and in the power of his might* [Eph. 6:10].

Why does Paul exhort us to *be strong in the Lord, and in the power of His might*?

Of what were Abraham, Moses, Joshua, and other Old Testament figures aware?

What makes it possible for us to do as we are supposed to do?

What does it mean when Scripture says God is aware of our infirmities?

With what have we been anointed and healed?

How does God provide strength to His servants?

What do we observe about the men and women God used in Scripture?

What does the poem by J. S. B. Monsell say we are to do?

Why does God make a trial of our faith?

How are we to react to God's truths?

Who is our adversary?

Why does Paul exhort us to stand and withstand?

Who is the Captain of our salvation?

Where and only where was Paul's focus after his conversion?

Chapter 11

GIRD YOUR LOINS

> *Wherefore take unto you the whole armor of God, that ye may be able to withstand in the evil day, and having done all, to stand.*
> *Stand therefore, having your loins girt about with truth, and having on the breastplate of righteousness;*
> *And your feet shod with the preparation of the gospel of peace;*
> *Above all, taking the shield of faith, wherewith ye shall be able to quench all the fiery darts of the wicked* (one).
> *And take the helmet of salvation, and the sword of the Spirit, which is the word of God:*
> *Praying always with all prayer and supplication in the Spirit, and watching thereunto with all perseverance and supplication for all saints* [Eph. 6:13–18].

What did Paul do regarding Christ and the Ephesians?

What are we commanded to do?

What is God's concern regarding each follower of Christ?

What armor is Paul describing?

What are we to do when encountering opposition?

What is the whole armor of God?

Why does Paul repeat himself?

What do we want to say and do?

To what point are we to progress as believers in Christ?

To whom is the Apostle directing his words?

What did Christ do during His earthly ministry?

Why and when did the Roman soldiers girt their loins?

What is meant by the word *truth* as it is used in this instance?

Whose *truth* are we to put on?

What are we to do regarding the whole counsel of God?

What does Peter say we are to do?

Chapter 12

THE GIRDLE OF TRUTH

Stand therefore, having you loins girt about with truth, and having on the breastplate of righteousness [Eph. 6:14].

What are we do to with the raiments God provides?

When does God's armor best serve us?

What is the *truth* with which we are to clothe ourselves?

With what teachings are we not to clothe ourselves?

What does Calvin say about Christ crucified and the blindness of the human mind?

How is one to put on the girdle of *truth*?

What distinction does Scripture draw between the *truth* revealed in Christ and the errors perpetrated by man?

What are we to know in order to have a right relationship with Christ and God?

What does Scripture say about false preaching and teaching and those who propound that message?

What are your thoughts regarding Lloyd-Jones's question, "Can you see your church as she is today in the New Testament?"

Where is the authority for preaching and teaching?

What is the Reformed position regarding Holy Scripture?

Where are we to stand according to W. E. Gladstone?

Why did Luther say, "Here I stand, I can do no other"?

What does the *truth* of God do to us and for us?

Chapter 13

BREASTPLATE OF RIGHTEOUSNESS

Stand therefore, having your loins girt about with truth, and having on the breastplate of righteousness [Eph. 6:14].

What truths are revealed in "Onward Christian Soldiers" and "Soldiers of Christ Arise"?

What are we to do with the truths revealed in the New Testament?

What does Peter say we are to *add*?

What does the Holy Spirit say through Peter?

How does Oswald Chambers describe Peter's statement?

How are we to use *the breastplate of righteousness*?

Why are we to put it on?

How is the righteousness of grace received?

How is imparted righteousness received?

How are we to endeavor to walk in this life?

What enables us to walk according to God's commands and ordinances?

Upon what foundation are we to build?

Why does one need *the breastplate of righteousness*?

What does it mean to be a soldier of the Cross?

Chapter 14

OF THE TRUTH

Stand therefore, having your loins girt about with truth, and having on the breastplate of righteousness [Eph. 6:14].

What did the prophets and apostles have in common?

What does our relationship with the Lord Jesus involve?

What does Scripture call us to do?

Why does Paul exhort us to have *on the breastplate of righteousness*?

From whom does righteousness come?

What is righteousness?

What are we to do with righteousness?

Of what is the life in Christ composed?

What happens when we wear *the breastplate of righteousness*?

How do we know that we are *of the truth*?

What type of people does God want us to be?

What two factors require our putting on *the breastplate of righteousness*?

What happens when we put on and keep on *the breastplate of righteousness*?

What does the word *cleanse* mean as used by the Apostle John?

What does faith require?

Who is born of Christ?

What is the basis of our relationship to God?

What is required of us according to the admonition to *take time to be holy*?

Chapter 15

STAND AND GO FORTH

> *Wherefore take unto you the whole armor of God, that ye may be able to withstand in the evil day, and having done all, to stand. Stand therefore, having your loins girt about with truth, and having on the breastplate of righteousness* [Eph. 6:13–14].

What is our responsibility regarding Scripture?

What truths are contained in Jesus' high priestly prayer?

What does Christ present in His prayer?

Why does Christ give us His Word?

For what does Christ *not* pray?

What does *Thy word is truth* mean?

How and where are we to stand?

What are we to bear in mind when choosing between faith in God through Christ and accepting the ways of the world?

What is meant by the things of the world?

How does God sanctify?

What are we not called to change?

What does Jesus say in the twenty-second chapter of the Book of Revelation regarding those who obey Christ's commandments and those who do not?

Who will *enter in through the gates into the city*?

From whom are we to seek righteousness?

How are we to present ourselves to God?

How does the Apostle say we are to worship God?

What are we to remember from Christ's high priestly prayer?

Chapter 16

CHOICES, DECISIONS, PRIORITIES

> *And your feet shod with the preparation of the gospel of peace* [Eph. 6:15].

How *do* we make choices, reach decisions, and establish priorities?

Whom do you choose to serve?

Why does Paul say, *Stand therefore . . . and your feet shod with the preparation of the gospel of peace*?

How were the Roman soldiers feet shod?

Why does the Apostle Paul command us to be in a state of readiness?

What are you ready and prepared to stand for and to withstand regarding God, Christ, the Holy Spirit, and the whole Gospel?

What questions must we answer in the affirmative regarding the equipping of our spiritual feet?

What determines if we are on the side of the Lord or of mammon?

What are we to realize regarding temptation?

How does Satan appear?

What factors can come between God and ourselves?

What did David say to Saul?

Upon what does our strength depend?

What are we to do to have our feet shod with the proper equipment?

How is the Gospel to be proclaimed?

How *are* we to make decisions and establish priorities?

With whom are we to have peace?

What does the *gospel of peace* require?

Chapter 17

SHIELD OF FAITH

> Above all, taking the shield of faith, wherewith ye shall be able to quench all the fiery darts of the wicked (one) [Eph. 6:16].

Why are we to put on *the whole armor of God*?

What is the contrast between Satan and God?

What does Lloyd-Jones say about evil in the world?

Into what two categories can the *whole armor of God* be divided?

Why are we to take up *the shield of faith*?

Who is the author and finisher of our faith?

What is the faith of which we are to take hold?

How is assurance realized?

What is a justifying faith?

Why does the Apostle Paul compare faith to a shield?

What are we to do with the *shield of faith*?

What are the characteristics of the fiery darts?

How does faith enable one to quench all the fiery darts?

How are we to use the *shield of faith*?

What was Abraham's secret?

What are we to bear in mind when taking up the *shield of faith*?

Chapter 18

THE HELMET OF SALVATION

> *And take the helmet of salvation, and the sword of the Spirit, which is the word of God* [Eph. 6:17].

What does God through Christ want us to be?

What sign is seen in the clouds?

How is our relationship with God to grow?

Where is that simple faith that does not require much of Christ's followers?

What is evident in the New Testament regarding our minds?

What torments the saints and the faithful?

How are we to look to Christ?

What is the hope of salvation?

What can we expect during our journey through life?

What does Christ say when we encounter the trials, tribulations, and difficulties of life?

How is the helmet of salvation to be used?

What is the door of A'chor?

What did Paul do when he entered Ephesus by a door of A'chor?

How are we to pass through our door of A'chor?

What should our reaction be toward the helmet of salvation?

How and why are we to strengthen our hope?

Why are we to embrace the true teachings of Scripture?

How are we to become holy and without blame?

Chapter 19

THE SWORD OF THE SPIRIT

And take the helmet of salvation, and the sword of the Spirit, which is the word of God [Eph. 6:17].

What traits did the Apostle Paul admire in the Roman soldiers?

What does *the sword of the Spirit* denote?

What did Paul know about the saints and faithful protecting themselves?

How are we to resist the devil?

What does *take . . . the sword of the Spirit* mean?

What did the Lord Jesus use when He was tempted?

From whence did prophecies come?

What enables us to understand the Word?

What is the relationship between the Word and the Spirit?

What is needed by the saints and faithful regarding the Word of God?

Why did Paul list *the sword of the Spirit* last?

What did Jesus do when He was attacked or confronted?

Why is the Word of God called *the sword of the Spirit*?

How can the Holy Scriptures be divided?

What happened when Luther exposed God's Word in the face of much opposition?

What is the standard for judging a church or denomination?

What has contributed to the decreasing membership in mainline churches?

What criticism has been directed toward Holy Scripture?

What is needed to repel negative attacks and route the adversary?

What penetrating question does William Gurnall ask?

What is required to effectively use *the whole armor of God*?

Chapter 20

STAND THEREFORE—PRAYING ALWAYS

> *Praying always with all prayer and supplication in the Spirit, and watching thereunto with all perseverance and supplication for all saints* [Eph. 6:18].

What did the Roman soldier do after putting on and taking up the whole armor of God?

What are the true believers in Christ to do?

What is the fruit of the Spirit?

What happens when certain conditions occur and continue to exist?

When we abide in Him and His words abide in us, what will follow?

Why are we to keep God's commandments?

What does Paul tell us to do when we have put on the armor and taken up the pieces?

Why does Paul tell us to always pray in the Spirit?

What six significant points are raised by Paul regarding prayer?

Where is our dependence to be placed?

What is the relative importance of prayer in Paul's magnificent letter?

Why are we to be *praying always*?

What is the Apostle's prayer?

How are we to pray?

Chapter 21

HEARING, OBEYING, PERSEVERING

> *Praying always with all prayer and supplication in the Spirit, and watching thereunto with all perseverance and supplication for all saints;*
> *And for me, that utterance may be given unto me, that I may open my mouth boldly, to make known the mystery of the gospel,*
> *For which I am an ambassador in bonds: that therein I may speak boldly, as I ought to speak* [Eph. 6:18–20].

What three things characterized Christ's life?

What commands did Paul provide to Christ's followers?

Why does Paul end his letter this way?

What duty is imposed upon the members of Christ's body?

Why are we to watch by praying?

How are we to *watch thereunto*?

What should we know about praying *with all perseverance*?

Why does God seem to withhold His answers?

What reasons does Scripture give for praying and watching with all perseverance?

What is it to pray?

For what are we to pray regarding all the saints?

Why does Paul say, *and for me*?

For what did Paul ask them to pray in his behalf?

How did Paul present the Gospel?

What do we need to watch for in preachers and teachers?

How does God judge preachers and teachers?

What did the Apostle Paul become after he knew the Lord Jesus?

Chapter 22

AMBASSADORS

> *For which I am an ambassador in bonds: that therein I may speak boldly, as I ought to speak* [Eph. 6:20].

What has God done and what is He doing for *the called out*?

For what does Paul pray?

Why did Paul want this for the saints and the faithful?

What is it that Paul does not talk about?

What did the Master command His disciples to do?

What were the disciples to teach?

What did the disciples learn to do when they were downcast, disheartened, and distressed?

What happened after Jesus departed?

What does God do with His ambassadors?

What are we to do when God's ambassadors speak?

What are the duties of God's ambassadors?

What examples does Paul provide that we should follow as Christ's disciples?

What are the characteristics and traits of Christ?

What are our responsibilities as Christ's disciples?

How does Paul's letter to the Ephesians begin and end?

Bibliography

Volume Eight

Barth, Markus. *Ephesians 4-6*. Garden City, NY: Doubleday & Company, Inc., 1974.

Calvin, John. *Calvin's New Testament Commentaries*. Grand Rapids, MI: William. B. Eerdmans Publishing Company, 1959, 1960, 1961, 1963, 1965, 1972, 1973.

Calvin, John. *Calvin's Sermons on The Epistle to the Ephesians*. Carlisle, PA: The Banner of Truth Trust, 1973.

Calvin, John. *Institutes of the Christian Religion*. Philadelphia, PA: The Westminster Press.

Chambers, Oswald. *My Utmost for His Highest*. New York, NY: Dodd, Mead & Company.

Gurnall, William, *The Christian in Complete Armour; The Banner of Truth Trust*, 3 Murrayfield Road, Edinburgh EH126EL, P. O. Box 621, Carlisle, Pennsylvania 17013, USA, Reprinted 1987 in Great Britain at the University Printing House, Oxford

Holy Bible. The King James Study Bible. Nashville, TN: Thomas Nelson, Inc., 1988.

Lloyd-Jones, Martyn. *The Christian Warfare*. Grand Rapids, MI: Baker Book House, 1981.

Paxson, Ruth. *The Wealth, Walk and Warfare of the Christian*. London and Edinburgh: Oliphants, Ltd., 1941.

Presbyterian Hymnal. Louisville, KY: Westminster/John Knox Press, 1990.

Vine, W. E. *Vine's Expository Dictionary of New Testament Words*. McLean, VA: MacDonald Publishing Company.

Weber, Otto. *Foundations of Dogmatics. Volumes 1 & 2*. Grand Rapids, MI: William B. Eerdmans Publishing Company, 1981, 1983

Scripture Index

GENESIS

15:1	134
17:1	70

LEVITICUS

19:2	32, 71, 105, 172–173

DEUTERONOMY

33:25	72

JOSHUA

1:5	12, 140
24:15	121

1 SAMUEL

17:39–40	125
17:45	125
17:48	125

2 KINGS

6:16	74

NEHEMIAH

6:10	66
6:11	66, 67
8:10	12, 66, 66–67, 102

PSALMS

34:7	59
51:6	83
57:7	125
84:11	74
91:1	59
97:10	76

ECCLESIASTES

9:10	35, 40

ISAIAH

11:1	107
11:4–5	107

DANIEL

11:32	66, 67

HOSEA

2:15	139

MATTHEW

4:19	44
6:9	155
7:29	94
11:30	68
12:13	74
18:3	35

Matthew–continued

20:16	113
22:37	136
22:37–39	101
25:41	109
26:41	46
27:1	4
28:16–20	169
28:19	170
28:20	170

MARK

2:9	74
9:24	4, 5, 9, 15, 130
10:35	13
10:35–38	13
10:40	13
10:43–45	13
12:30	76

LUKE

1:6	102
3:16–17	23
10:25	148
10:26	148
10:41–42	30
12:35	83
12:48	107
17:10	103
18:1	138, 155, 157
21:34	30, 45
21:36	30
24:32	57
24:44–45	94

JOHN

1:1	146–147
1:18	95
1:46–48	25
1:47	26
1:47–50	184
1:48	27
1:50	31
3:30	9
6:26	2, 64
6:27	64–65
6:28	67
6:29	64
6:35	65–66
6:40	66
6:66	3
8:30	84
8:31–32	84
9:25	9
10:29	59
10:34	148
10:35	94
11:45–50	3
11:51–52	3
13:4–5	98
14:6	9
14:15	70
14:16–17	60
14:23	22
14:26	17
15:5	151
15:7	151, 152
15:16	121
15:26	17
16:7	17
16:9	18
16:10	18
16:11	19
16:12–14	19, 182
16:13	22
16:32	74
17:9	120
17:9–10	113
17:14	114, 120
17:14–17	114
17:17	84, 115, 120
20:14–17	192
20:16–18	56

ACTS

1:4	57
1:5	20
1:8	20, 57
2:4	20
2:39	28
4:17–20	170
4:29	171
4:29–31	170–171
4:31	171
6:4	161
9:1	43
9:6	43
10:37–38	73
14:22	76
17:18	168–169
17:31	5
18:9–10	74
20:26–27	173
20:27	84
20:27–28	164
20:28	67
20:32	67
22:6–10	188
22:8–10	41
22:10	43, 44
24:16	102

ROMANS

1:5	107
3:22	106
5:1–2	9, 126
5:1–5	180
6:17	102–103
7:15	110
7:19	54
8:13	61
8:26	156
8:28	126
8:38–39	59
10:8	151
10:17–18	151–152
12:1	118
12:2	120
12:12	161
12:18	127
13:12	80
13:14	80
15:4–6	172
15:5	172
15:13	141

1 CORINTHIANS

1:21–24	89
2:5–8	94
2:10	94
2:12	94, 145
2:13–14	145–146
2:16	136
3:5–7	34
3:9	34
3:11	103
4:1–4	39
4:6–7	38–39
6:19–20	22
9:16	166
9:26–27	61
10:12	37, 47, 81
12:8–11	36
12:20	29
12:22–25	29
12:25–26	162
12:31	36
14:4–6	20
14:18–19	20
15:8–10	39
16:8–9	140
16:13	61

2 CORINTHIANS

1:19	124
1:20–21	106
4:8–10	137
5:21	101
6:14–15	45
6:17	45
11:14	124
12:7–10	53
12:9	54, 58, 114, 134
12:10	54
13:5	6

GALATIANS

1:8	92
1:9	92
2:20	6
3:27	80
5:16	47
5:22–23	150–151
6:9	30, 137

EPHESIANS

1:2–3	48
1:4	105, 129
1:10	4
1:13–14	74
1:17–19	157
1:18–19	59, 131
2:4–5	59
2:8	129
2:18	156
2:19	22
2:20	147
2:22	22, 167–168
3:3–5	164
3:8–9	166
3:16–17	133
3:16–19	157
3:17	132
3:19	133
3:20	163
4:1	118, 162
4:4–6	93
4:13	165
4:13–15	117
4:14	165, 168
4:15	165, 168
4:17	119
4:20–24	12–13
4:22	43
4:23	136
4:24	6, 43, 80, 119, 123
4:31–32	88
4:32	123
5:1	168
5:8	115
5:18	23, 156
5:26	115
6:10	49, 51, 55, 57, 58, 64, 66, 70, 71, 77, 79, 123, 128, 135, 154, 194, 196
6:10–11	119
6:10–12	1, 32, 178, 186
6:11	44, 135, 153
6:11–12	123
6:13	48, 61, 190
6:13–14	79, 113, 118, 206
6:13–18	198
6:14	83, 87, 96, 105, 115, 119, 149, 200, 202, 204
6:14–15	122, 128
6:15	49, 121, 208
6:16	128, 132, 210
6:16–17	128
6:17	49, 135, 143, 144, 146, 149, 153, 212, 214
6:18	150, 153, 162, 216
6:18–20	159, 218
6:19	171
6:19–20	164
6:20	172, 220
6:20–24	167
6:23	174
6:24	174

PHILIPPIANS

1:27	78
1:29	76
2:5	136
2:5–8	40
2:12	61
2:12–13	102
3:6	100
3:9	100, 101
3:9–10	8
3:10–14	61–62
3:13–14	8
3:20	47, 115
4:4	10
4:6	127, 156
4:6–7	31

COLOSSIANS

1:29	60
2:5	38
2:7	38
3:2	117
3:12–13	127
4:2	161

1 THESSALONIANS

1:5	60
5:8	138
5:17–19	17
5:19	21
5:23	126

2 THESSALONIANS

1:5	4
3:1	164

1 TIMOTHY

6:10–12	46
6:11–12	61

2 TIMOTHY

1:7	31
1:12	30
2:1	61
2:14–18	90
3:12	76
3:16	94, 145
3:16–17	67
4:6–8	78

TITUS

2:14	109

HEBREWS

2:10	58
4:14–16	72, 108
4:16	134
6:11–12	140
8:10	136
10:22	5
11:1	133
11:6	132
11:39–40	116
12:2	129

JAMES

1:22–24	44
2:18	44
2:21–24	130
2:26	44, 130
4:4	76
4:7	60, 144
5:10–11	161

1 PETER

1:3	139
1:5	59
1:7–8	8
1:13	85, 136
1:13–16	85
2:11	47
2:11–12	45
2:21–23	45
4:12–13	76
5:8	52, 76–77
5:8–9	61
5:10	138–139

2 PETER

1:1	68
1:3	81
1:3–4	68
1:5–7	68
1:5–8	98
1:8	69, 70
1:19–21	94, 145
2:1–3	84
3:9	137

1 JOHN

1:5–7	117–118
1:6	47
1:6–10	110
1:9	47
2:1–2	111
2:4	76
2:19	15
2:27	111
2:29	111, 112
3:1–3	141
3:2	47
3:19–22	108
3:22	109
4:1	92
4:4	47
5:13	5, 10

3 JOHN

1:9	37

JUDE

20–21	156

REVELATION

3:8	114
3:14–17	5–6
3:17	37
3:19	6
3:21–22	37
3:22	37
19:13	147
22:14–16	117

www.ingramcontent.com/pod-product-compliance
Lightning Source LLC
Chambersburg PA
CBHW062013220426
43662CB00010B/1316